D1035900

Musical Savants
Exceptional Skill in the Mentally Retarded

Musical Savants
Exceptional Skill in the Mentally Retarded

Leon K. Miller
University of Illinois

with an appendix written by Nancy Newman, M.A.

LEA LAWRENCE ERLBAUM ASSOCIATES, PUBLISHERS
1989   Hillsdale, New Jersey   Hove and London

Lawrence Erlbaum Associates, Inc., Publishers
365 Broadway
Hillsdale, New Jersey 07642

Library of Congress Cataloging-in-Publication Data

Miller, Leon K., 1941–
  Musical savants : exceptional skill in the mentally retarded /
Leon K. Miller.
    p.   cm.
  Includes bibliographies and indexes.
  ISBN 0-8058-0034-4
  1. Musical ability. 2. Idiot savants. 3. Mentally handicapped.
I. Title.
  [DNLM: 1. Mental Retardation. 2. Music. WM 300 M648m]
ML3838.M64 1989
153—dc19
DNLM/DLC
for Library of Congress   88-38597
                                                                   CIP
                                                                   MN

Printed in the United States of America
10 9 8 7 6 5 4 3 2

Contents

Acknowledgments

This project would not have come to fruition without the help of many people. Gersh Berkson first alerted me to the opportunity provided by the discovery of Eddie and was a source of moral support and intellectual stimulation throughout the study. Mitch Rabinowitz helped me clarify my thinking about memory and distributed processing models. Harry Steckman and Nancy Newman gave invaluable advice and information on musical matters. Thanks also to my wife Jocelyn, who wielded a critical but understanding editorial pen. Pam Martin exhibited the patience of a saint in typing innumerable drafts.

The staff of Eddie's school went considerably beyond the call of duty in facilitating my work there. My thanks especially to Eddie's teachers, Marie Morgan and Charlotte Robinson.

This research was supported in part by the Illinois Institute of Developmental Disabilities and the Graduate College of the University of Illinois at Chicago.

This book is dedicated to Eddie and all the other participants who shared their love of music with me.

Introduction

My first encounter with Eddie was unexpected and dramatic. At that time, Eddie attended a day program for the multiply handicapped. All the children at the center are legally blind; none has more than rudimentary language, and most are physically handicapped. Not surprisingly, all exhibit massive delays in social, emotional, and cognitive development. The school curriculum is devoted for the most part to teaching rudimentary skills such as self-feeding and dressing. The environment itself occasionally borders on the chaotic. Stereotyped behaviors such as body rocking or repeated shouts and hand-claps are common among the children, and in the limited space serving as the classroom, these sounds and actions collide. Social interactions among the children are limited; instead, each child is under the care of one of the teachers. Moreover, the interactions are often very one-sided, the teachers vigorously and enthusiastically working to elicit responses from children whose interest, if present, is restricted by severely limited communication skills.

Against this background, progress in any area of development is slow, measured more often in terms of months and years than days. Similarly, age-appropriate behavior is rarely encountered. Consequently, I was skeptical when a teacher remarked that one of the new young arrivals to the school played the piano surprisingly well. Curious, I asked to be introduced to the newcomer and shown an example of his playing.

Upon seeing 5-year-old Eddie, I became even more skeptical. He was (and is) a very fragile child, bony thin and small for his age. His motor delay was apparent in his hesitant, splay-footed walking. He seemed to lack the fine

1

muscle control needed for something as demanding as a piano. However, when the teacher mentioned the word "piano," Eddie's face was transformed by a smile of excitement, and he purposefully turned to the room containing the piano. He certainly needed no prompting to exhibit his talent. As we reached the piano, his hands found the keys and he started to play some melodious chords, his head tilted back, staring through his thick glasses at the ceiling with an intent expression on his face.

Eddie's first recital for me was very brief. Asked to play the Christmas carol "Silent Night," he gave a fairly good rendition. The melody was well articulated, the tempo appropriate, and there was a nice rolling broken chord figure in the bass. Eddie's hands, which had difficulty holding a pencil, were clearly at home on the keyboard. Even so, he had evidently learned to compensate for a weak fourth and fifth finger in each hand. Often he used the third and fourth or fourth and fifth fingers doubled in order to strike a single key more firmly. When he finished playing, his teacher and I clapped enthusiastically, and Eddie smiled in appreciation. There certainly seemed to be something special here, and I promised to come back soon.

For a 5-year-old, Eddie's recital was indeed impressive. Such a performance was clearly beyond the range of any other child in the school and of most 5-year-olds. Whether it was truly "precocious" was another matter. Tom Hulse gives a convincing portrayal of a young Mozart playing and improvising a piece in the movie *Amadeus*. He is not a pianist, however, and the piece shown represented his complete repertoire, acquired with intense, but very limited practice. Similar precociousness in this 5-year-old might be the result of intensive practice in a very limited domain—perhaps several Christmas carols or familiar songs. This would be consistent with the view that apparent examples of precocious performance among the retarded are the consequence of persistent or obsessive practice in a context of general stimulus deprivation (Lindsley, 1965).

On my next visit, I came prepared to test the range of Eddie's musical sensitivity in a bit more detail. Piano lessons for the beginning student usually introduce the instrument with key signatures that contain few sharps or flats (roughly speaking, the black keys of the piano). Similarly, much popular music is written in relatively few of the key signatures from among those available. Accurately transposing tunes to any key during performance can be quite difficult. Typically, technical facility across all major and minor keys is achieved only with considerable instruction and practice. How well could Eddie follow a simple melody through a series of transpositions on the keyboard? Would he be constrained to a few common keys or would the particular key of the piece be irrelevant?

Once again, Eddie showed no hesitation at all in going to the piano room, this time with me leading the way. I hoped that even though he appeared to have very little language, he would respond to any musical samples I might provide him. He turned out to be a sociable participant in this respect, willing to listen to something played and then try it on his own. The resulting informal experiment was very revealing. I played the simple melody line of "Twinkle Twinkle Little Star" without harmonic accompaniment, first in the key of C, then G (relatively frequently encountered key signatures), then in Ab, F#, and back to C. To make the series a bit more challenging, I presented each example in a different pitch range from the immediately preceding one, either an octave higher or lower. The staff of the center assured me that the melody was familiar to Eddie. As luck would have it, I misplayed the first example, with the first phrase ending a half step up from the intended note. Eddie dutifully followed my example, however, playing my rendition of the melody with the error. I played the remaining examples correctly, and in each case, Eddie's playing reflected the transposition to a new key with no hesitation. He seemed to be equally at ease with any key signature, at least where simple familiar melodies were concerned. The final trial was probably the most instructive of the series, however. Upon hearing "Twinkle Twinkle" again presented in the key of C, Eddie's response changed in several respects. First, he was no longer content to play the simple melody, instead adding several left-hand chords. Second, he transformed the piece to a minor key with several unexpected modulations in the harmonic structure, using minor thirds rather than the major thirds of the original. He had already demonstrated that he could copy me if he wished, so these could not be considered errors. It seemed unlikely he was retrieving from memory some minor mode version of "Twinkle Twinkle" that he had heard previously in some other context. Rather, Eddie was generating a new version of the piece.

The results of this little experiment answered several questions. It was clear that Eddie's talent was not limited to a few well-practiced patterns of movement on the keyboard. His sensitivity to the tonal structure of a melody line was indeed impressive, and he could follow that melody wherever it appeared in the pitch range represented by a piano keyboard. Moreover, his playing was improvisatory; he had at least an elementary ability to take a melodic line and produce renditions that were consistent with the conventions of musical composition. This was truly precocious musical performance for a 5-year-old. Normatively, 5-year-olds have, at best, a slim grasp of the particular interval relationships in even the simple melodies that they hear (Bartlett & Dowling, 1980). Their spontaneous songs often wander from one tonal center to another with little sense of an overall tonal structure (Hargreaves, 1986). Moreover, Eddie's sensitivity to these aspects of music was easily translated to performance. In other words, not only did Eddie apparently have a much better understanding of the structure of the music than one would expect from a normal 5-year old, but this understanding was manifested in a very natural way in his playing. The piano seemed an extension of Eddie's body, and his fingers effortlessly explored its range of sounds as soon as he came in contact with its keyboard. Other children at the center were attracted to the piano too, but their "playing" was a monotonous repetition of randomly chosen notes. In contrast, Eddie's playing seemed as natural for him as speaking is for much younger children. In fact, when Eddie chose to play "Twinkle Twinkle" back to me in a minor key, he seemed to be saying, "Have you ever thought about it this way?" Was Eddie using music as a substitute for language? Interestingly, Eddie's talent had appeared with minimal direct tuition on the part of the environment, as no formal music lessons had been attempted.

These brief observations also raised many questions. On first thought, Eddie seemed an example of an "idiots savant" syndrome. However, this label didn't really clarify matters very much because each component of the designation "idiots savant" invites controversy. The term "idiot" is both pejorative and archaic. Classically, it was used to designate a certain range of mental functioning (Tredgold, 1952). Whether such a particular range of mental functioning is a necessary "core" characteristic of savant behavior is not clear, however. Thus, such precision in the use of the word "idiot" was not originally intended. Rather, this part of the definition points to a general picture of mental retardation or developmental delay as part of the syndrome. In any case, what exactly did the indication of retardation in the definition imply? Are there lower limits of functioning below which any precocious behavior is not possible? Are patterns of deficit associated with savant behavior? Perhaps it was even inappropriate to use the term "mentally retarded" in describing Eddie. To be sure, Eddie showed some prominent signs of mental retardation, particularly a severe delay in language development. However, judgment of mental retardation is only as good as existing measurement tools. Because traditional measures of intelligence do not include items to measure a "musical sense," Eddie's apparent strengths were not even addressed in IQ estimates. Perhaps IQ tests really were not "fair" to Eddie. Most of us would probably consider it quite unfair if the situation were reversed and our intelligence was measured only in terms of our musical knowledge. This raised another question. How are "musical" and "nonmusical" intelligence related (or are they related at all)?

The meaning of the word "savant" in the term "idiots savant" is no more clear cut. Formally, its dictionary definition includes such descriptions as "a learned person; an eminent scholar" (Webster's New World Dictionary, Second Edition), suggesting a level of understanding and expertise rarely encountered. On the other hand, descriptions of the savant skill provided by the literature describing "idiots savants" often suggest quite a different picture. For example, Grossman's definition (1977) in the Manual on Terminology and Classification in Mental Retardation suggests savant skills, although remarkable, have little to do with expertise: "A person of low intelligence who possesses an unusually high skill in some mental task like mental arithmetic, remembering dates or numbers, or in performing other rote tasks at a remarkably high level" (Grossman, 1977, p. 143). Related views appear in summary descriptions of savants:

> The skills displayed by the savant should probably be reduced to two overlapping categories of sensory/motor and rote memory, which along with concentration seem to represent his abilities best. (Hill, 1978, p. 293)

However, dissenting voices are also heard. Describing retarded twin calendar calculators (who can provide the correct weekday for any calendar date), Sacks (1985) wrote

> The twins, I believe, have not just a strange "faculty," but a sensibility, a harmonic sensibility, perhaps allied to that of music.

This wide variability in characterizing savant behavior stems in part from a lack of detailed examination of the precocious behavior in these cases. Yet fundamental to the issue of defining "idiot" and "savant" is the nature of the skill itself. What was it, exactly, that Eddie knew about music? What were the facets of his musical intelligence? Strangely enough, although "idiots savants" have been mentioned in the literature for over 100 years, there are very few detailed systematic investigations of the savant skill reported. Without such close examination, of course, it is difficult to estimate the level of the skill's development. However, musical savant skills appear to be a particularly fruitful area to explore. First, Western music has a highly structured and well-codified set of rules established for its composition and performance. Musical behavior lends itself to ready analysis in terms of its conformance to that structure. Second, musical skill is a common yet highly varied characteristic of the general population. Consequently, it is possible to describe a given instance of musical ability normatively; that is, in comparison with various levels of performance by other musicians. This is not so easy with some other savant skills. For example, the Genius of Earlswood Asylum (Tredgold, 1972) had a phenomenal mechanical aptitude, exemplified by the intricate scale models he made from original plans. Although people also vary considerably in such mechanical/constructional aptitude, standard norms for its comparison are not so readily found as for music. Thus, we can conclude that the Genius of Earlswood was certainly phenomenal in a general sense, but the singularity of the case makes it difficult to evaluate his skills more specifically. Thirdly, music is an important activity of human beings. We may not all be musical producers, but excepting those with gross sensory impairment, we are all musical consumers. Moreover, understanding music requires a high level of rich cognitive and emotional processing (Sloboda, 1985). It seems highly likely that examination of musical cognition would reflect some fundamental properties of human information processing.

My informal experiment with Eddie also increased my curiosity about the functional significance of savant behavior for him. It was clear that he was enjoying what he was doing and that music was very rewarding to him. What was it about music and his performance that made it such an enjoyable experience? Was there any essential difference in the function served by music and that served by the occasional stereotyped motor behaviors he exhibited? Was the prognosis for Eddie's development any more favorable given the presence of talent in at least one area? It seems obvious that having some skill in one area would be preferable to having no apparent talents, yet one of the consultants to the center had expressed concern that this "excessive" concern with music was preventing Eddie from advancing in other areas of development. This attitude is by no means unique. Sacks (1985) described several calendar savants who were prevented from exercising their skill by their caretakers, presumably to "normalize" their behavior in other respects. Were these concerns warranted? Part of the answer to this question requires an examination of both the apparent role of the savant skill for the individual and its effects on other opportunities for growth.

The following chapters present the results of research directed to some of these questions. The first chapter examines the background of the present case and its historical context. It provides a descriptive review of the recorded cases of other musical savants where the subject was also diagnosed as developmentally delayed. The primary aim of the chapter is to assemble existing data regarding the nature of the skills exhibited and the associated developmental deficits. The historical record is further examined for common patterns of factors that occur across cases.

The middle chapters describe a series of experiments that attempt to define the nature of Eddie's talent. The general goal here was to provide as complete a picture as possible of the skill observed and how it compares with both normative and precocious musical development in the nonretarded. The following chapter examines how the presence of this interest in music affected other aspects of Eddie's life. The final chapter considers some of the more general issues raised by savant behavior, particularly, the functions served by savant behavior, theories regarding its etiology and its role in general development.

1 | Musical Savants of the Past

Was there anything in Eddie's background to suggest that he would develop a strong interest in music? Perhaps a close look at his personal history would reveal some special factors at work. Hospital records of Eddie's birth indicate that, although he was born slightly premature (estimated gestation of 36 weeks compared to full term of 40 weeks) and weighed somewhat less than normal (5 lb. 14 oz.), there were no difficulties in delivery. His Apgar scores were 9 and 10 on a 10-point scale, indicating that he appeared healthy and was breathing well moments after birth. Eddie and his mother were discharged from the hospital two days later. A return to the hospital at one month of age for conjunctivitis, an eye disorder, resulted in a thorough examination, including an electrocardiogram. Eddie was diagnosed as suffering from patent ductus arteriosus, a congenital heart disease. Bilateral cataracts were also noted, and interviews with Eddie's mother revealed for the first time that she had been ill with rubella during the first trimester of her pregnancy. Digoxin was prescribed for Eddie's heart problems, with exploratory surgery planned as soon as his general health improved, as he had lost weight during the first month of life. A series of illnesses prevented surgery until 10 months of age. At that time, Eddie's weight, height, and head circumference were all lower than the fifth percentile for his chronological age. Physical examination revealed no response to a loud noise, so Eddie was diagnosed as being both blind and deaf. These handicaps are commonly associated with rubella in utero, however, and probably were not formally assessed at the time. The operation for patent ductus arteriosus was described in hospital records as proceeding without complications.

During the next two years, Eddie visited the hospital frequently; records suggest that he was developing quite slowly and suffered continuing physical complications. At 2 years of age, Eddie's weight was still quite low (17 lbs. compared to a norm of 25–30 lbs.) and another electrocardiogram indicated possible ventricular septal defect. Eight months later, he was admitted for pneumonia, his weight still at 17 pounds. Interestingly, a comment written by one of the attending physicians at this time questions the diagnosis of deafness, describing Eddie as being able to hear and repeat words, yet no further information is given. There are no medical records for the next two years. At about age 4, Eddie began attending a preschool program for multiply handicapped children. An eye examination soon thereafter indicated that his cataracts were operable and a bilateral lensectomy was performed at age $4\frac{1}{2}$ years. Eyeglasses were prescribed and Eddie's vision soon became good enough to discern colors and large figures.

Not surprisingly, there is much less formal documentation of Eddie's social and psychological development before he attended preschool. The results of the Bayley Infant Development Scale given at age $3\frac{1}{2}$ years were interpreted as inconclusive. Although attracted by brightly colored toys, Eddie did not attempt to reach for objects and was generally unresponsive. Consequently, few items of the scale were attempted. He was reported as having no speech, although responding to the word "no." Eddie was able to sit up, could walk with assistance, but could not feed himself, according to the report at that time. An auditory screening at age 4 mentions extremely restricted receptive and expressive language with possible unilateral hearing loss. The latter was confirmed one year later with a more formal behavioral audiological examination indicating no response to tones presented to the left ear. I first saw Eddie at age 5, and his speech to me was almost exclusively echolalic, or a virtual repetition of what he heard, except for a few conversational cliches (e.g., "How are you? I'm fine. Good-bye."). The staff at the center described Eddie as being somewhat more talkative than the other children at the center, but that his tendency to repeat what he heard also characterized his interactions with them.

The remaining data regarding Eddie's early development were obtained through repeated interviews with his mother. Eddie was described as a sickly child from birth. He was very finicky about eating and often had difficulty retaining food. It was apparent to Eddie's mother that he was quite unlike her other children. When his heart problem was diagnosed, the hospital staff told her that Eddie's chances for survival were not very good. A person of deep religious conviction, she was determined to keep him alive, and worked hard to improve his eating. (Among his disorders were physical problems in chewing and swallowing.) Even today as a 9-year-old, Eddie eats best when his mother serves him. Eddie's mother also reported she tried hard during the first two years to get Eddie to react to her. As a baby, he was very quiet and would whine rather than cry. Later, he vocalized little. Consequently, she recalled singing and "baby talking" to him more than to her three previous children.

Eddie was also relatively unresponsive to his physical environment, according to his mother, although he seemed to listen intently to the radio and phonograph when they were played. In contrast to the medical note at age 10 months, Eddie's mother reported that he was easily disturbed by loud noises. (Even today, when the sound in a room becomes too intense or confusing, Eddie begins to shake and covers his ears.) Brightly colored objects also attracted his attention, and one activity he enjoyed was repeatedly twirling spinning tops and bottle caps on the floor. He also enjoyed toys such as rattles, music boxes, and so forth that made any kind of sound, as long as it was not too loud. Much of the time during his infancy was spent in his crib, although having three older siblings in the house, Eddie was probably rarely far from the center of family activity. His oldest sister often helped in caring for him.

Eddie's mother evidenced some inconsistency in her recollection of when Eddie first showed an interest in playing music. On one occasion, she reported this as being before his first birthday, while in another interview, she said it was at about 2 years of age. In any case, Eddie was given a toy piano and it quickly became his favorite toy. The piano was soon broken, however. Eddie was also exposed to a musical instrument at church, where he was given the chance to pick out melodies on the piano in one of the meeting rooms where his mother attended services. It is not clear how prolonged this musical exposure was, but it was casual and untutored. At the time Eddie was first seen by me, no formal music lessons had been attempted and there was no piano in the home. None of the other members of the family plays an instrument, and there is no history of a special musical talent in the family.

Eddie's history does give some clues regarding the origin of his musical interest and talents. As with any single case, it is difficult to distinguish those factors that are central to his development from those that are incidental. His medical records indicate a series of problems early in his life—rubella by his mother during pregnancy, congenital heart disease, and a general failure to thrive. However, Eddie's mother evidently provided special intensive care during his early years, and was determined to offer her own remediation for his various difficulties. Either the central nervous system anomalies associated with his medical problems or the special care provided by his mother may be factors in Eddie's sensitivity to music. Eddie's early sensitivity to sounds may also have been an important sign of his developing musical talent, but it is difficult to distinguish, retrospectively, these sensitivities from either a low irritability threshold or a baby's normal interest in sounds. Some of Eddie's early behaviors, his delight in twirling tops and bottle caps, for example, are often found in childhood autism (American Psychiatric Association, 1980), and he apparently was not very responsive as a baby. Savant skills have occasionally been associated with autism (Rimland, 1978). As a 5-year-old however,

Eddie's obvious pleasure in social interaction certainly did not indicate a primary diagnosis of autism, because a lack of responsiveness to other people is a central feature of this syndrome (American Psychiatric Association, 1980). In many respects, Eddie's exposure to music was unexceptional, although there was undoubtedly music for him to listen to. (His family's small apartment features a modern stereo system with an extensive record collection.) However, his early reaction to musical instruments was exceptional. Eddie evidently delighted in making as well as listening to sounds, and his early productions were noticed by his family as being very musical in nature. In summary, Eddie's history suggests many potential elements contributing to his developing sensitivity to music, but lacking comparison data, it is impossible to evaluate their importance. Perhaps descriptions of other musical savants can provide clues regarding the particular factors responsible for Eddie's precociousness. These histories may also provide a general framework for considering the type and range of skill found in musical savants.

Estimates of musical savant occurrence among the developmentally disabled vary widely. For some clinical groups, for example autistic children, the estimated incidence is as high as 10% (Rimland, 1978). In an extensive survey of public residential facilities for the mentally retarded, Hill (1977) found the phenomenon to be extremely rare (.06%). As noted earlier, the lack of agreement concerning the definition of "idiots savant" syndrome makes any estimate of incidence difficult to evaluate. Moreover, the very paradox suggested by the label of the syndrome seems to lead to confusion and contradiction in case descriptions. A good example of this problem occurs in the extensive descriptions of one of the earliest known cases of savant syndrome, Thomas Wiggins, also known as "Blind Tom."

Textbooks on mental retardation often mention Blind Tom as an example of the idiots savant syndrome (e.g., Barr, 1973; Sellin, 1979), yet the pertinent literature indicates considerable disagreement in descriptions of both his special skills and disabilities. Thomas Wiggins, born a slave on a Southern plantation in 1849, had exceptional interest in music very early in life. He was blind from birth, but exceptionally sensitive to the sounds of nature, imitating animal and bird calls very accurately. Before the age of 4, he was picking out melodies on the piano in his owner's mansion (Southall, 1983). Early music lessons were apparently provided by the plantation owner's wife, an accomplished musician. By the age of 8, Tom was giving concerts locally and at age 10 was concertizing throughout the South. An active performing career continued through the remainder of the 19th century for Tom, and included tours of Europe as well as much of the United States. These performances usually contained pieces from the classical piano repertoire, Tom's own compositions in various musical "styles," and demonstrations of particular skills, especially his ability to reproduce original compositions by others upon a single hearing. He possessed absolute pitch, and was able to reproduce even complex dissonant chords without error.

Southall (1979, 1983) has provided a comprehensive analysis of popular reactions to Blind Tom's music during his lifetime. Generally, these reactions suggest a level of talent equivalent to that of other concert pianists of the period, comparing him favorably to Louis Gottshalk, among others. Southall (1979) concludes that the occasional dismissals of Tom's playing as "mere empty imitation" were likely to have been politically motivated. More formal documentation of Tom's particular skills was provided by testimonials from music teachers of the day. For example, Tom's ability to reproduce dissonant chords was examined specifically by Charles Halle and Ignatz Moschele when Tom was 17 years old. (Unfortunately, the extent of Tom's memory for dissonant material was not tested thoroughly, for example with a succession of dissonant chords. As we shall see [Chapter 4], such a test may very well have suggested some important constraints upon Tom's immediate memory capacity.) Similarly, his ability to reproduce original material played by others was tested on a variety of occasions. His reproductions of the material were very impressive to those in attendance. However, the original material itself has been described as "trite little pieces of a popular type" (Tutein, 1918); in other words, pieces written in styles with which Tom was likely quite familiar. Even so, there is some disagreement regarding his accuracy. On one occasion, his rendition is described as "perfect as to form, though not correctly as to actual notes" (Southall, 1983, p. 20). A more detailed description is provided by Tutein (1918), who was Tom's teacher for several years:

> I must also dispel the idea that Tom could repeat anything after having heard it once. The lessons were two hours in length, and it was often necessary for me to play over the compositions fifty times before he would acquire them. He could, however, remember an astonishing number of measures. I would "feed" him eight or ten measures at a time and then he would play them over several times and we would go on with others. After he had a fair impression of the piece, I would play it as an entirety and he would listen intently. (p. 91)

This account suggests that to the untrained ear, perhaps, Tom's reproductions were perceived as literal, while in fact, they may have reflected a more general sensitivity to the many melodic and harmonic conventions of the day. In many respects, of course, this makes Blind Tom's musical skills all the more impressive, for it indicates remarkable command of the principles or rules of composition prevailing in his musical environment rather than a literal or rote memory of what he heard. This conceptual understanding is also evident in Blind Tom's musical compositions, which incorporate many of the melodic and stylistic conventions of the nineteenth century classical tradition, albeit in highly personal and original ways (Southall, 1983). Tutein's description suggests another facet to Blind Tom's remarkable musical talent—his long-term memory for material. His active repertoire was estimated to include over 3000 pieces. On several occasions, he is reported as flawlessly recalling original material heard as much as 14 years previously (Southall, 1983).

Blind Tom's frequent billing as an "untutored musical genius" was misleading at best; he was given music lessons throughout much of his life, often by internationally known musicians of the time (Southall, 1983). Most likely, the exaggerated claim of a largely untutored talent was made to enhance the appeal of concerts for the curiosity seeker. Were contemporary descriptions of Tom as an imbecile and a low-grade idiot similarly a fabrication to increase his singularity? Descriptions of Tom's nonmusical side certainly indicate a degree of deviation from normal development. Reports of his behavior on and off stage described several mannerisms—rapid flicking of the fingers, grimaces, and bodily twirling and rocking—which often are present in cases of mental retardation with associated sensory deficit (Berkson, 1983). Possibly these mannerisms were actively encouraged by Tom's guardians to exploit the theatrical aspects of his concerts. However, some described Tom's offstage behavior as even more eccentric. (Barfield, 1868).

Descriptions of Tom's language are conflicting; his earliest speech was described as echolalic. Rather then responding to the intent of speech directed toward him, Tom would repeat what was said (Barfield, 1868). Moreover, he seemed more interested in the sounds provided by his physical environment than by language. Later, Tom was occasionally described as speaking to himself in an unintelligible jargon (Southall, 1983). Tutein described conversations with Tom as a young adult during piano lessons as being minimal and monosyllabic. When not engaged in music during these lessons, personal stereotypies (e.g., head rolling, body twirling) surfaced with some regularity (Tutein, 1918). The testimony during the trials over Tom's guardianship was also highly conflicting. According to his mother at one of these trials, as a child Tom did not "have the knowledge of other children." At the same hearing, Tom's teacher for nine years described him as being "deficient in all senses, except that of music and that which brings the consciousness of dinner time," yet added that Tom had a prodigious memory (Southall, 1983, p. 255). In contrast, Southall mentions several conversations, one with a stranger on a train and one with the judge during the hearing (Southall, 1983), which indicate that Tom had at least a minimal conversational competency in language. A considerably higher level of competency is suggested by the statement that he was writing poetry at age 17 (Southall, 1979). Court judgments of Tom as not being mentally competent (judgments of non compos mentis in 1870 and 1886) did not necessarily reflect his level of overall functioning accurately, since Tom's guardians were quite interested in maintaining control over his lucrative concert career.

Despite these conflicting reports, several characteristics do emerge from descriptions of Blind Tom. First, although there may be some controversy regarding his exact level of mental functioning, it is clear that there was a great discrepancy between Tom's musical performance and other areas of his life.

This contrast was not seen in the functioning of touring musical performers of the day (Trotter, 1878). Second, Tom was strongly interested in music very early in his development; he had an especially sensitive receptivity to the nonverbal sounds of the environment and an ability to reproduce them. Finally, descriptions of Tom's playing suggest that his ability extended considerably beyond imitation of what he heard, although his ability to imitate was certainly remarkable in itself. Both the intensity of Tom's emotional reactions to music (Southall, 1983) and his improvisational sophistication suggest a talent considerably more complex than mere mechanical or literal repetition of what he heard.

Explanations of Blind Tom's talents at the time indicate that critics were quite unsettled by his combination of talent and childlike behavior. One solution was to minimize his talent, and as Southall (1983) documents, this approach was often taken by editorials of the day:

> He is not a genius at all—he is simply a great curiosity. His playing is extraordinary, not because it is very good, but because it is the playing of a blind, foolish, uneducated boy. He is not a great pianist nor can he ever be one because he lacks the intelligence; he has a great perception of the sense of charm of a melody, but of course no comprehension of a musical composition. (p. 83)

Alternatively, perhaps the apparent "imbecility" of Blind Tom was a clever ruse, and an explanation suggesting an element of P. T. Barnum manipulation was at work. Stephen Heller, for example, was skeptical: "He seems a master acrobat . . . Do you believe those gambols, all that idiot and demoniac business to be natural? Ever since Barnum, I have had an extreme distrust of these American marvels" (Southall, 1983, p. 65). In either case, such an extreme skill discrepancy was seen as not possible, unless perhaps some mystical transfer of skill was involved:

> (We) leave our readers to determine whether the Chinese transmigration theory is correct—whether the soul of some unfortunate defunct musician, misbehaving on Earth, has been banished into the awkward and angular body of Blind Tom. (Barfield, 1868, p. 7)

Thus, although articles describing Blind Tom's performance skills are numerous and filled with superlatives, the specifics of the inaccuracies or preferences in his playing are usually lacking. Similarly, it is quite certain Tom was retarded, but descriptions of the nature and degree of retardation are highly conflicting.

Lack of clarity and conflicting reports characterize the majority of musical savants described in the literature. Table 1.1 summarizes some of the information available regarding musical savant cases for which there is more than passing mention in the literature. Additional cases mentioned by Rife and Snyder (1931), LaFontaine (1968), Duckett (1976), and Hermelin, O'Conner,

TABLE 1.1
Summary of Musical Savant Case Histories

Case	Sex	Instrument	Age*	Special Musical Skills/Interests	Music in Family?	CNS/Sensory Deficits	Language/Cognitive Deficits
Blind Tom (Southall, 1979, 1983)	M	piano	2	Absolute pitch, musical memory, classical music	Unknown	Cataracts	Echolalia, jargonophasia
XY Minogue (1923)	M	piano	3 (songs)	Absolute pitch (prob.), jazz	Yes, father, paternal grandmother	Meningitis at 3	Reasoning, judgment
Owens & Grim (1941)	F	piano	?	?	Yes, sisters	—	"Speech limited and repetitive"
L. Sheerer et al. (1945)	M	piano	3	Absolute pitch	Yes, paternal grandparents	—	Language delay, abstract reasoning, pronominal reversal
S. Anastasi & Levee (1960)	M	piano	Before lang.	Absolute pitch, strong dislike of modern "dissonant" music	Unknown	Encephalitis	Echolalia, abstract language skills
Harriet F. (Viscott, 1970)	F	piano	1	Absolute pitch, musical memory, blues, jazz	Yes, mother	—	Delayed onset, reasoning, analogies
J.L. (Charness et al., 1988)	M	piano	3	Absolute pitch, popular music	Yes, maternal grandmother, aunts	Blind, hemiplegic	Delayed onset, echolalia
L.L. (Monty, 1981)	M	piano, voice	3	Absolute pitch, memory for tunes, classical music	Unknown	Blind, cerebral palsy	Delayed onset, echolalia
N.P. (Sloboda et al., 1984)	M	piano	Before 5	Absolute pitch, popular music, moderate improvisation technique	Unknown	—	"Autistic syndrome," echolalia
Joseph (O'Connell, 1974)	M	piano	Before 2	Absolute pitch	Unknown	—	"Autistic syndrome," echolalia
Judy (Burlingham, 1968)	F	piano	6	Absolute pitch	Unknown	Congenital cataracts	jargonophasia
Eddie (Miller, 1987a,b)	M	piano	Before 3	Absolute pitch, blues, salsa, classical music	Unknown	Congenital cataracts, heart disease (rubella)	Echolalia, jargonophasia
C.A. (Comer, 1985)	M	accordian, piano	8?	Absolute pitch, waltzes, polkas	Unknown	Congenital cataracts (rubella)	Echolalia, delayed onset

*First manifestation of exceptional interest or talent.

and Lee (1987), have been omitted because each contains insufficient information to permit comparison of either skill level or characteristics associated with skill presence. In the remaining instances, formal evaluations of aspects of musical performance are available for only two other cases (Charness, Clifton, & McDonald, 1988; Sloboda, Hermelin, & O'Conner, 1985); the results of these investigations are discussed in more detail in Chapters 4 and 5. For the remainder, the descriptions tend to concentrate upon the salient personality characteristics and developmental history in each case.

The brief descriptions of savant's musical performance contained in these reports are at variance with popular conceptions of savant skill, particularly the notion that savant musical performance is like that of a tape recorder (the performance faithfully reproducing sounds without interpretation or even comprehension of what is being reproduced). Certainly, there is occasionally an automatic quality ascribed to savant playing—O'Connell (1974) remarks that while playing, his 8-year-old savant often "did not concentrate on what he was doing." More common are contrasting descriptions suggesting that savants have strong emotional reactions to the music they listen to and play. Savants often have preferences for certain types of music. Both Viscott (1970) and Minogue (1923) report some interest in improvisatory styles in their subjects. L. L., as a young child, was particularly fond of playing country and western music. Anastasi and Levee (1960) report a strong dislike of modern "dissonant" music on the part of their subject. Strong varied emotional reactions to music have also been attributed to savants during performance. Scheerer, Rothmann, and Goldstein (1945) describe L. as frequently weeping over music. According to Anastasi and Levee (1960), "It is only when S. is playing the piano that his face takes on a look of strength, concentration, interest, and emotion." Viscott (1970) described Harriett G. thusly: "She nodded her head and began to play with all the feeling and movement of a concert performer. For that moment in time, she was another person" (p. 499). These descriptions seem inconsistent with the notion that savant skills are automatic or stereotypic.

Charness, Clifton, and McDonald (1988), in reviewing most of the cases in Table 1.1, noted that there is a remarkable diversity in their etiology, no single pattern emerging across cases. There do appear to be some common characteristics among these musical savants, however. Ten of the 13 are male; of an additional 11 cases described very briefly by Lafontaine (1968) and Hermelin, O'Conner, and Lee (1987), 9 are male. This suggests the appearance of musical savant skills is sex-linked, although clearly not restricted to males. Each well-documented case reports that the piano is the instrument through which the skill is displayed. There is evidence that each savant has perfect pitch, or the ability to name the note of any tone heard without either seeing it played or the benefit of a reference note. In some cases, as with Blind Tom, this ability was demonstrated often in his career, being incorporated with his concert programs in a variety of ways. In most cases, however, the ability is mentioned in passing or is suggested by other aspects of the savant's behavior. For example, Owens and Grimm (1941) noted their subject's ability to play a piece in the same key in which it was hummed. It is highly likely that this ability requires at least a very sensitive pitch sense (Chapter 3).

Review of these cases yields quite consistent evidence that each individual had an early sensitivity to or interest in music; Anastasi and Levee (1960) reported that their subject hummed melodies before he could talk. The parents of Harriett G. (Viscott, 1970) reported that she hummed an operatic aria extremely accurately at less than one year of age. The case described by Scheerer, Rothmann, & Goldstein (1945) began to show "a remarkable interest in music, rhythm, and counting" during his third year of life, according to his parents. J. L. (Charness, et al. 1988) first began to show interest in the piano about the age of 3. An apparent exception to this rule is the case of L. L. He was originally described as showing the first evidence of extraordinary talent at the age of 16, awakening his foster parents in the middle of the night by playing a rendition of Tchaikovsky's first piano concerto (Monty, 1981). However, recent interviews with L. L.'s family reveal a far earlier appearance of musical interests, similar to the history of other savants. At the age of 3, L. L. was discovered strumming or "playing" the bedsprings under his bed while he hummed a tune. L. L. was given toy instruments early in his childhood, and a regular piano was installed in the household when he was 8 (M. Larsen, personal communication, 1987). Is there a strong hereditary factor in the appearance of musical talent in these cases? Arguments for such a factor are often made if similar musical skills are seen in other members of the family (Rife & Snyder, 1931). It is difficult to discern the presence of a familial factor in the case histories of Table 1.1, however. Nothing is known regarding L. L.'s natural parents. For the remaining cases, other members of the family are mentioned in the case histories only casually. Consequently, it appears that the issue has not been explored in much detail. In only one case, Harriett G., was a close family member a professional musician. For the remainder, sometimes passing mention is made of another relative who played an instrument, or, more often, there is no mention of musical relatives. These latter cases have been designated "unknown" in the appropriate column in the table. Thus, although there may be some specific hereditary contribution to the appearance of musical skill in the savant, the data are not very conclusive on this point.

Nor is there strong evidence for a particularly intense musical environment early in the life of these savants. That is, parents or other relatives did not appear especially interested in providing a rich musical environment or education for these children in a manner similar to that often found for highly achieving normal children (Bloom, 1982; Bloom & Sosniak, 1981). Here again, Harriett G. may be an exception in that most of her first year was spent in a crib next to her mother's piano while her mother gave voice lessons. However, neither was the developing talent of these savants ignored. Virtually every savant received some degree of musical training, although the kind and extent of training is rarely discussed in the case reports. Perhaps the most extensively trained of the group was Blind Tom, who, as mentioned earlier, was given lessons with a variety of teachers, including some of the most prominent of the day. O'Connell's autistic savant (1974) was given daily 3-hour lessons for several months at the age of 8. However, these lessons were devoted exclusively to learning to read music. At that point, the savant Joseph's ability to "play by ear" was firmly established. Moreover, these daily lessons only lasted several months; thereafter, the training was reduced to several 1-hour sessions per week. L. L. received informal lessons from his foster mother after age 8. These lessons were quite restrictive with respect to repertoire. Evidently, L. L.'s penchant for country and western music did not meet with his foster mother's approval, and she actively discouraged his attempts to play pieces from this genre (M. Larsen, personal communication, 1987). L., S., and J. L. all received music lessons on and off throughout their childhood, but the lessons themselves seem to have been unexceptional with respect to either intensity or extensiveness. There appeared to be no especially strong environmental pressure to "cultivate" the talent in these cases.

The cases described by Burlingham (1968) and Comer (1985) are instances where more careful tutoring was apparently necessary for musical talent to flourish. Burlingham (1968) described strong music interests in a "backward and withdrawn" child with congenital cataracts. In many respects, the information provided in the report suggests a musical savant. The child, Judy, as an infant and young child exhibited little active exploration of her physical and social environment, and showed an "oversensitivity" to sounds and strange noises. Early language consisted of jargon, without communicative effect, or phrases taken verbatim from television. Therapy, beginning at age 5, revealed a particular interest in music, first as a listener and later as a participant. When formal piano lessons were begun at 7 years of age, Judy's piano teacher reported her to have absolute pitch and to learn simple pieces with harmonic accompaniment very easily. Judy transposed pieces without effort and had an excellent memory for the names and composers of pieces. No further information is given about Judy's playing, nor is there any description of her subsequent musical development, other than mention of her playing at a school concert some time later. For this reason, it may be questionable to consider Judy a well-documented example of a musical savant. In any case, the Burlingham (1968) description of Judy at age 8 certainly indicates a marked discrepancy between Judy's musical persona and her behavior in other settings:

> We were left, then, with a double impression. On the one hand there was this nursery school child now 7 years and 11 months, withdrawn, backward, unable to manipulate buttons or toys . . . scoring a mental age of 3 years, 10 months . . . On the other hand, the same little girl was also alert, interested, her body

flexible, her hands graceful, her fingers strong and purposeful, the whole personality animated by what her teacher called "high musical intelligence." (p. 381)

This case may be of special interest for its description of the earlier stages of emerging musical talent. Before entering therapy at age 5, Judy is described as being easily frightened of all sounds. In the first months of therapy the teacher/therapist played tunes for Judy very softly on the harmonica. Subsequently, she was introduced to a series of instruments, and Judy's role changed from listener to performer. One of the instruments was a piano. After an initial hesitation, Judy learned to pick out tunes with one finger and apparently chose this as her primary instrument. More formal lessons followed within a year, with Judy taking an increasingly active role in the process. The description is admittedly sketchy, but several things seem clear. Judy's talent did not emerge full blown; it developed in a series of steps or stages. Second, she benefited considerably from well-matched musical input. Musical activities were structured to be engaging but not overwhelming, and the demands placed on Judy were gradually increased. She appeared to have been given a range of musical choices, but like the other musical savants, settled on the piano as her instrument. Within this environment, Judy's musical growth was rapid indeed, but she does seem to differ from the other cases in that she was more obviously "led" to cultivate an interest in expressing herself musically.

C. A. (Comer, 1985) was introduced to formal music making at an even later age. C. A. was admitted to a large traditional residential institution at the age of 6 with a diagnosis of severe mental retardation.[1] He spoke little and his responses were usually echolalic. He was also quite aggressive, frequently striking out in response to attempts to guide or restrain him. For the next 5 years he resided in the ward functioning at the level of a toddler, being fed, dressed and toileted by the staff. C. A.'s blindness and aggressiveness isolated him from the rest of the younger residents, and his primary recreation was to sit and listen to the radio. He did show evidence of a special sensitivity to sound during these years, however. While in the dining room, if someone tapped a sound on a spoon or table leg, C. A. would tap objects until he found the correct match for what he had heard. He would also strike different objects on the ward, listening to the sounds they emitted. This interest attracted him to the accordion sometimes brought to the ward by one of the supervisors. The supervisor, a self-taught amateur musician, took on the task of trying to teach C. A. the piano accordion. His description of these early lessons indicate many hours were needed to acquaint C. A. with the keys and fingering needed to produce different sounds. The lessons were almost completely nonverbal, consisting of a simple "listen and play" routine. Small pieces were introduced by playing them over many times until he had mastered

---

[1]The information that follows was provided by Dr. Fischel Goodin and Zigmas Brazauskas, Director and Ward Superintendent, respectively, of the institution.

the tune. At times C. A. seemed to get "stuck" on a certain phrase or section of a piece, repeating it over and over, rather than connecting it to a newly presented succeeding phrase. After the first few songs, however, progress was rapid and soon additional private lessons were being given at the supervisor's home on weekends. These lessons sometimes reached "marathon" proportions, (usually on C. A.'s insistence) lasting the whole day. By the age of 14, C. A. appeared in his first public concert, an amateur contest where he won third prize. C. A. has made many public appearances since then, often with his teacher. He currently resides in a private group home, and continues to take lessons, now primarily on the piano. Thus C. A. like Judy, benefited immensely from a musical mentor who was able to adopt a style of teaching and interaction well suited to his limitations. It is also clear that C. A. was highly motivated to learn to make music. His not doing so earlier seems to have been a matter of opportunity; like the other savants, a particular sensitivity to sounds characterizes early descriptions of him. It may also be significant that C. A.'s accordion lessons, like Judy's piano lessons, were almost conversational in nature, the teacher and student alternating in the music making until a piece had been mastered. Within this framework C. A., like Judy, took increasing initiative as the skill developed, engaging in musical dialogues that would last for hours. The waltzes and polkas he learned during those first years remain his favorite music.

This is not to say that music was not a central part of the personal lives of the remaining savants. Their strong affective response to music has already been mentioned. They also spent a considerable amount of time performing or practicing music. Once a piano was installed in his home, Eddie would play almost as much as his family would permit. J. L. practiced (and improved) considerably from the time of his earliest lessons, playing 6 to 8 hours a day. S. became agitated and aggressive if there was any interference with his time on the piano. L. L.'s time on the piano was often curtailed by his foster mother. In summary, once the interest in music has been awakened, savants' motivation to develop music seems to be primarily internal rather than external in origin. Subsequently, of course, performing music provides many kinds of rewards, both private and social.

Although the etiology of the cases presented in Table 1.1 is diverse, and in some cases unknown, there is evidence of associated physical or sensory deficit in the vast majority of savant cases. Many of the cases report severely limiting visual defects; of the remainder, only cases reported by Scheerer, et al. (1945) and Sloboda, Hermelin, and O'Conner (1985) suggest no physical or sensory pathology early in childhood. The case reported by Owens and Grimm (1941) is rather obtuse on this point, noting that her "low ability was obvious before she was one year old," but providing no additional detail.

Particular kinds of language impairment also seem to characterize the majority of savants, the most prominent feature being early, and sometimes persistent, echolalia. As noted earlier, Blind Tom's early speech consisted for the most part of imitations of the various sounds of his environment, including the speech of others. Echolalia is also present to a lesser degree in L. L. as an adult (M. Larsen, personal communication, 1987), and is reported in N. P., J. L., and S. The speech of O'Connell's 8-year old, while apparently not primarily echolalic, was severely disturbed, "a stream of meaningless numbers, words, and phrases," probably a variety of jargonophasia occasionally seen in autistic children (Schwartz & Johnson, 1981).

To what extent are the musical skills exhibited by these savants accompanied by other special talents or by a particular pattern of deficits? Is the musical talent remarkable because it appears against a background of general intellectual impairment? Alternatively, is music but one manifestation of a particular group or subset of cognitive skills? The general level of cognitive functioning among members of the sample is difficult to estimate. In many cases, formal test results are simply not reported. In others, difficulties in adapting standardized tests to the special circumstances (e.g., sensory deficit) make more than a very general statement quite difficult. There are, however, a few instances where more extensive evaluation has been possible.

Formal intellectual assessments are provided in the case descriptions by Anastasi and Levee (1960) and Scheerer, et al. (1945), and to a lesser extent by Viscott (1970). Additional information is available for the case described by Sloboda, et al. (1985). In each case, there is marked variability in the performance upon various subtests administered. Summary intelligence quotient or mental age equivalents indicate, not surprisingly, that all documented savants experienced considerable impairment. The Stanford Binet of S. (Anastasi & Levee, 1960) is 67, that of N. P. (Sloboda et al. 1985) 59, and L. (Scheerer et al. 1945) from 48 to 91 on separate occasions (a score of 100 indicates average intellectual functioning). Probably the lowest functioning of the group is J. L. (Charness, et al. 1988), who, as a young adult, was estimated to be functioning roughly at the 2-year level developmentally on the Vineland Scale of Social Maturity.

In each case, there is marked variability in performance on various test subscales. For example, on tasks permitting a range in performance from 0–19 points, S. (Anastasi & Levee, 1960) had a score of 12 points on a task measuring general knowledge such as that acquired in school, yet a score of 0 points on a task tapping social cognition. L. (Scheerer, et al. 1945) at age 7, showed certain word association and number memory skills at the 9- and 10-year level while failing tasks involving form comparisons at the 5-year level. Such variability makes it difficult to interpret any general intellectual level assignment such as mental age or IQ. An example of this problem is provided by N. P. (B. Hermelin, personal communication, 1987), who has a verbal IQ of 62 and a performance IQ of 60, suggesting no marked differences in his level of functioning in these two broad areas. Within each group of tests, however, there is marked variability—the verbal scale scores range from 0 (vocabulary) to 9 (short-term auditory memory), and the performance scales range from

0 (matching written symbols) to 7 (reproducing designs and completing puzzles).

Although there is heterogeneity across tests within each case, there is some degree of consistency across cases regarding the pattern of strengths and weaknesses. For each savant, short-term memory tasks yield the highest level of performance, particularly tasks such as the digit span subtest of the WAIS, which taps auditory memory. For L. and N. P., digit span performance exceeds any other subtest; for S. digit span is exceeded only by a subtest tapping knowledge of facts such as those learned in school. J. L., apparently the lowest functioning of all reported cases, could nevertheless complete (only) the digit span subtest of the Stanford-Binet, where he received a score in the normal range. Eddie similarly has difficulty comprehending almost all intelligence test tasks, but he can reproduce digit strings at a level appropriate for his (chronological) age. No other task yields such a consistent picture across cases—N. P.'s relatively good performance on tasks requiring spatial skills can be contrasted with S.'s abysmal performance in these areas. S. and L. show a relatively strong vocabulary, whereas N. P. performs poorly on vocabulary questions.

High performance on digit span tasks has also been reported for calculating savants (Spitz & LaFontaine, 1973), whose digit span performance was in the normal range against a background of often severe intellectual impairment. There may, in fact, be some overlap in the two types of savant skills. Of the cases mentioned in Table 1.1, two (S. and Harriett G.) are described as calendar calculators. While the presence of relatively high digit span performance for both calendar calculators and musical savants suggests some shared characteristics, it is apparent that the two savant skills are not coincident. Not all musical savants show evidence of calendar calculating skills. We will discuss possible points of similarity later (Chapter 7). Other forms of prodigious memory and calculating skills have been reported in musical savants as well. Exceptional place/event memory (Anastasi & Levee, 1960; Minogue, 1923), knowledge of musical history (Viscott, 1970), and hyperlexia (Anastasi & Levee, 1960) have been noted. However, descriptions of these special skills are usually only cursory, and hence difficult to evaluate.

Is there a particular type of deficit common to musical savants? One, a type of language pathology represented by echolalia, has already been mentioned. A certain kind of deficit is attributed to their cases by Scheerer, et al. (1945), and to a lesser extent by Anastasi and Levee (1960) and Viscott (1970), who maintain a special problem for savants is any situation requiring abstract thought or an "abstract orientation." According to Scheerer, et al. (1945), the absence of abstract thought is manifested in a variety of ways, and much of their monograph is devoted to detailing the concrete nature of their subject's cognition. L.'s word usage was described as being restricted to concrete, situational, ego-centered attributes. For example, as an adolescent, L. defined "orange" as "that I squeeze with," and his response to the questions "why do we have books" was "because I read books" (Scheerer, et al, 1945, p. 9). When L. did use unusual or abstract words, he defined them very inappropriately. For example, he defined "rheumatism" as "a big doorknob," (1945, p. 10). But there were many additional manifestations of this deficit in abstract thought. L. was able to recall several pages of text after a single reading (the hyperlexia mentioned earlier), but could not answer simple questions concerning the gist of the material. Verbal analogies were also a source of difficulty. To the question "cats scratch, bees _____?" his answer "fly" reflected an associative response to the word heard last, rather than a response relating the meanings of all the terms in the problem in a systematic manner.

These constraints on L.'s thought were not limited to verbal material, according to Scheerer and his associates. For example, difficulties in inference were revealed by the Stanford-Binet. Given a picture of a man holding an umbrella incorrectly during a rain shower, L.'s response was to describe the picture with no acknowledgement of its incongruity. L. also performed poorly on a variety of visual mazes, figural analysis, and completion tasks, particularly when these involved strategy and planning. Faced with an ambiguous figure (the Ruben vase/profiles), L. perceived the alternative interpretation of the figure only after some training with an enhanced variation of the original. L. generally seemed incapable of simultaneously considering two aspects or components of any visual array. In fact, problems of organization, inference, and comparison were more difficult for L. if the material was presented visually. Finally, a lack of reflection characterized much of L.'s interaction with the world. Reports from his mother indicated that, unlike most children, L. rarely asked "why" as a young child. Magic tricks and slight-of-hand did not arouse his curiosity. As a young adult, L. was often unable to explain himself and found it very difficult to make choices.

A similar, though not so detailed picture emerges from the case descriptions of Anastasi and Levee (1960) and Viscott (1970). According to Viscott (1970), Harriett G. as an adult failed to understand problems involving abstract reasoning, inclusion relations, or analogies. Like S., she had a very difficult time extracting items of information from text that she could read adequately. According to Viscott:

> When asked how two things are alike, regardless of how obvious the relationship was, she was unable to answer . . . No amount of pressure would make her say anything except "a nickel is a nickel and a dime is a dime. They are not alike at all." (p. 505)

S. (Anastasi & Levee, 1960), like L., was able to give flawless verbatim reports of text without being able to answer questions involving inferences from what he had read. Not surprisingly, S. failed tasks involving analogies and "symbolic" interpretations (e.g., proverbs).

For Scheerer, et al. (1945), the absence of abstract reasoning skills is fundamental to the cognitive profile of the musical savant in several respects. First, the deficiency pervades all aspects of the individual's cognitive interactions with the environment. In this respect, the absence of abstract reasoning is responsible for failures across many content areas, including music. They conclude "our findings revealed with empirical stringency a unitary disturbance, an impaired abstraction, which accounts for the consistent character of his symptoms in diversified fields" (p. 37). Second, a "core deficit" in abstract reasoning means that the special musical skills exhibited by the musical savant are of a particular pathological variety. That is, without the inferential and analogic abilities found in abstract reasoning, the grasp of music will be devoid of more general conceptual understanding. Once again, in their words "the term idiot savant therefore appears to be a misnomer. Inasmuch as it implies normal performance in a special ability coupled with amentia, it is misleading . . . idiot savants are talented aments who possess an 'amented' talent (pp. 39–40)." As a consequence, the skill, like that of the mathematical or calendar calculator, remains severely truncated, with little possibility for more sophisticated levels of achievement.

The characterization of Scheerer, et al. (1945) is attractive in several respects. It provides a comprehensive framework for conceptualizing the many aspects of savant behavior. Moreover, it does so by using concepts that have proved useful in describing thought disorder in other populations (e.g., Werner, 1948), thereby rescuing the savant syndrome from its status as a unique or at least highly peculiar phenomenon. This makes it possible to consider implications of savant behavior for normative cognitive development. On the other hand, the very strengths of the Scheerer, et al. (1945) model of savant cognition may contribute to some of its more apparent weaknesses. Especially problematic is the generality of their abstract/concrete dimension. It is often difficult to see exactly how particular problems in performing such tasks as the Bender-gestalt figure drawings and part-whole perception discussed by Scheerer, et al. (1945) represent failures in abstract thought. Similar tasks were performed evidently at a reasonable level of proficiency by Harriett G. (Viscott, 1970), although as noted earlier, Harriett G. and S. were quite similar in their pattern of responding to other subtests. Consequently, either the task domain affected by the absence of abstract thought is less extensive than originally supposed by Scheerer, or the complete absence of abstract thought is not necessarily characteristic of a savant's cognitive profile. The latter alternative is the view taken by Viscott (1970). Especially important for Viscott is Harriett G.'s knowledge of various musical styles and her ability to improvise pieces in those styles. Such a talent involves memory considerably beyond the storage of mere sequences of notes and suggests a sophisticated appreciation of some of the more subtle characteristics of a composition, according to Viscott. (Recall that demonstration of a similar skill constituted an important part of Blind

Tom's concerts.) It is not clear from the Scheerer, et al (1945) report whether improvisatory skill was present in L. If it was not, there must be considerable variability in the level of musical sophistication shown by musical savants.

The confusion surrounding the issue of what constitutes an "abstract attitude" in any domain is particularly evident in discussions of the nature of savant musical intelligence. Scheerer et al. suggest L. retained musical selections "by grasping them as whole patterns . . . his learning is configurational as regards to rhythm, melody, and speech sound sequences" (p. 36). This by itself should not preclude some "abstract attitude" in music, but elsewhere Scheerer and his colleagues conclude "The lack of abstract function prevents L. from reaching beyond his concrete grasp of auditory-motor Gestalten" (p. 36). In other words, abstract levels of functioning in music are not possible because they are absent in other areas of cognition. What is lacking is a set of criteria for determining abstract aspects in music independent of performance in those other areas. We will return to the problem of establishing such a set of criteria in the final chapter.

A further problem with the abstract/concrete distinction as applied to savants is its status as an explanatory as well as a descriptive construct. As just noted, Scheerer et al. suggest that the absence of an abstract "faculty" prevents more sophisticated development on the part of the musical savant. However, by their own admission, it does little to account for the original appearance or development of musical sensitivity in these savants. Notions such as 'compensation' and 'channeling' are mentioned in passing. Perhaps the savant concentrates his (limited) capacity on a few areas in order to gain a sense of satisfaction otherwise denied him. We will return to some of these suggestions regarding the development of savant behavior in a subsequent chapter. In any case, as Sarason and Gladwin (1958) note, many of the characteristics of savant behavior occur before abstraction is commonly seen in normal cognitive development. Thus, there may be little value to the term "abstract orientation" as either an explanation or a description of savant musical skills.

Discussion

Which of the many factors noted in Table 1.1 mark the musical savant as a particular syndrome? None of the characteristics occurs only in musical savants. Echolalia is found among children diagnosed as autistic, among those mentally retarded but not otherwise showing aspects of the autistic syndrome, and among those with severe visual impairment (Fay, 1966, 1973). Absolute pitch is found in amateur (e.g., Carroll & Greenberg, 1961) as well as professional (Schonberg, 1987) musicians. An early interest in music is, of course, found in musical prodigies (Revesz, 1925/1970). However, some sensitivity to at least the general characteristics of a melody is present very early in normal development (Trehub, 1987). As already noted, a "concrete" as opposed to "abstract" conceptualization is by no means limited to musical savants (e.g., Werner, 1948). A particular hereditary disposition toward music or an intensive exposure to music at an early age can also be ruled out as a primary or core causative agent in the musical savant. Although there is some evidence for each, neither characterizes all, or even the majority of the cases examined.

It is even somewhat difficult to determine whether certain characteristics are simply more frequent in the savant than in comparable samples. Part of the problem is that the case descriptions often do not contain precise descriptions of the behaviors of interest. Descriptions of echolalia, for example, range from simple mention of the speech characteristic to descriptions with examples. Given the range in frequency and type of echolalia found in more carefully described samples of nonsavant children (Fay, 1966), any comparisons involving this characteristic must necessarily be very tentative. Further, it is not clear what the appropriate comparison might be for a given sample of savants. Their disability and their talent are multifaceted and comparisons limited to one facet (e.g., mental retardation, sensory deficit) must also be treated cautiously.

With these qualifications in mind, it appears that, although no characteristic is unique to savants, several are particularly prominent. First among these is absolute pitch. Mention of absolute pitch is made in almost every case, although absolute pitch in the general population is very rare (Bachem, 1955). Many famous classical composers apparently had absolute pitch (Schonberg, 1981), but actual incidence rates are difficult to determine. Language disabilities, particularly of an echolalic variety, also appear to be particularly prominent in savants. A relatively high incidence of echolalia is also reported in some other groups. Rimland (1971) reports a high percentage of echolalia in a large sample of autistic children who had at least some language. The incidence of echolalia among the blind, as reported by Fraiberg (1977), is considerably lower. Finally Fay (1966) reports frequent echolalia in a group of language disordered children, most of which disappeared by the time the children were four years old. Of these three rates of incidence, only that reported by Rimland (94%) approaches that of the savant sample. This is not surprising, in that links between autism and savant skill have been previously suggested (Rimland, 1978). Scheerer and his colleagues (1945) postulate a common linking factor in savant and autistic subjects, the absence of an abstract attitude, as discussed earlier. A formal diagnosis of autism based upon the criteria originally outlined by Kanner (1943) seems appropriate for only two of the cases mentioned in Table 1.1, however, that described by O'Connell (1974) and by Sloboda, et al. (1985). For the rest of the savants, the descriptions certainly suggest some measure of pathology; however, in each case it appears a degree of connectedness in interpersonal behavior was maintained. That is, these savants were not described as oblivious or nonreactive to their social environment. Rather, their response to music was particularly intense, and environmental events which either nourished or interfered with musical expression, elicited especially strong reactions. Interestingly, six of Kanner's original (1943) sample of autistics also indicated a very early intense interest in music, but only one of these was a playing amateur musician as an adult (Kanner, 1971). Thus, there are some common elements in savant and autistic syndromes, particularly with respect to language disability, but the two syndromes are by no means coincident.

The cognitive profiles provided by the few extensive formal assessments suggest a relatively intact immediate memory span against a background of strengths and weaknesses across various other cognitive skills. It is important to remember that savants' memory skills as assessed by conventional tests merely reach average levels, and stand out only in comparison to their below-average functioning in all other areas. Thus, some prodigious general memory ability seems an unlikely candidate as a primary factor responsible for their superior musical memory. However, the consistency of normative levels of performance for musical, as well as other savants, indicates memory span performance may offer an important clue to the structure of savant intellect.

A variety of other factors is also implicated in the savant histories, among them a special desire to *perform* music as well as listen to it, and a particularly intense emotional response to music early in life. Though possibly central to the development of a savant skill, this desire is even more difficult to document in any consistent or quantitative manner. The central role of musical performance in the savant's life does suggest, however, that analysis of performance may offer an important source of information regarding savant skill. Though this conclusion seems obvious, it is noteworthy that only recently have investigators begun to describe in some detail the actual musical performance of musical savants (Charness, et al. 1988; Miller, 1987a, 1987b; Sloboda, et al. 1985).

Finally, it appears likely that no single factor is responsible for or can "explain" the appearance of savant skill. Both the conditions of its appearance and its manifestations appear to be too complex to suggest a single-factor explanation. Indeed, most main effect models of development are currently seen as untenable (Sameroff, 1975). Rather, the appearance of savant skill probably reflects the operation of several factors working in some particular pattern (or patterns) of development. Discussion of what these factors and patterns might be is reserved for the final chapter.

2 | Evaluating Savant Skill

What, exactly, was the nature of Eddie's musical talent? Clearly, he was more than a mere tape recorder. His modulation of "Twinkle Twinkle" from a major to minor key after a few repetitions had suggested something more than simple literal recall in the very first session. (For that matter, even his apparently good literal recall of music was no simple matter.) His understanding of music seemed more literate than literal. His spontaneous playing was never random or cacophonous, yet it was also not routinely predictable. What kinds of rules was he using in these miniature compositions of his? The general goal of the experiments to be described here was to examine these questions empirically.

Several factors had to be considered in designing each phase of our research project. Eddie seemed able to adopt a "listen and play" format of interacting with his environment quite naturally. Consequently, it was very easy to get samples of his performance. He is not a reluctant player. (A significant exception to this will be described later.) This listen and play format has a certain degree of face validity because it explores the situation most usually associated with savant skill: the ability to perform music with little training. Another clear advantage of using this procedure was that its naturalness made it unnecessary to engage in any extensive training before experimental sessions were begun. Unfortunately, this was about the only reliable interaction possible, particularly at first. Verbal requests or statements directed to Eddie were usually met by silence or echolalia, which meant that experimental procedures which require verbal judgments were not feasible.

One such procedure is the same–different perceptual judgment task. Given two musical selections, chords, melodies, or the like, a subject has the task of deciding whether the two are the same or different—a straightforward judgment and one that is the basis of many frequently used tests of musical ability (e.g., Bentley, 1966; Seashore, 1938). One of the most attractive features of this procedure is that it doesn't require the subject to do very much, overtly, at any rate. Knowing how to play a musical instrument is unnecessary for standard musical same–different tasks. All that is required is that one understand the meaning of "same" and "different" and apply them reliably. Some varieties of the technique have been used with children as young as 3 (Trehub, Cohen, Thorpe, & Morrongiello, 1986). In fact, the decision about what such terms as "same" and "different" actually mean to a young child may not be so straightforward after all, and many experiments with preschoolers have floundered on the problems caused by the exact meaning of the words used by adults (Donaldson, 1978).

For Eddie, the problem posed by these two terms seemed (and still seems) insurmountable. At first, when asked to discriminate even widely discrepant stimuli, either auditorially or tactually, his response was to answer "same or different." Later, there was improvement in his ability to give a differentiated response, and to wait until both exemplars were heard before he answered, but the procedure was never reliable enough to permit us to use it confidently. There was one important exception to the verbal restrictions on task construction; after some time, Eddie began to like to identify the elements of music, notes, chords, and melodies, and this was used in several instances. For the most part, however, procedures had to be primarily nonverbal.

It also proved impossible to adopt a variety of psychophysiological techniques for monitoring internal or covert processing of musical material. Such techniques as monitoring changes in orienting behavior (Demany & Armand, 1984) or autonomic activity (McGuigan, 1979) have been used profitably in studying perceptual processing in nonverbal subjects. Several factors mitigated against using such techniques with Eddie. Most often, these procedures require recording directly from body or scalp surfaces during stimulus presentation. Perhaps by virtue of his many painful experiences during his hospitalizations, Eddie was extremely reluctant to allow anything to be attached to his body; even earphones were not easily tolerated. Second, most psychophysical procedures require a relatively quiescent subject so that motor artifacts can be distinguished from components associated with stimulus processing. This was difficult for Eddie. When hearing music, he would begin to clap his hands, move in time with the music, and, if a piano was in the vicinity, seek it out. The kind of physical quietude required for reasonably unambiguous psychophysiological work was impractical.

These restrictions on methodology have important implications for the kind of conclusions we are able to draw regarding Eddie's musical talent. The primary principle here is the converging operation (Garner, Hake, & Erikson,

1956). In order to specify the nature of the cognitive and perceptual process-ing in a given situation more exactly it is important to be able to measure a phenomenon in more than one way. This allows one to eliminate alternative processes or factors responsible for a given result. The different operations converge upon or indicate a more circumscribed set of processes from among the many candidates proposed at the beginning of the experiment. The classical experiments concerned with the phenomenon of perceptual defense remain a good example of the principle of converging operations at work. Perceptual defense refers to a certain kind of selectivity people have in reporting what they see or hear. When shown briefly flashed obscene or emotional words, for example, people often say they are unable to identify what was presented, although other "neutral" control words are reported accurately. Are subjects truly not registering the words, are they somehow repressing the memory of the words, or are they simply reluctant to report what they saw? Expansion of the design to include other, nonverbal measures of reaction represented an attempt to determine, among other things, whether a response bias of some kind was involved. By finding that subjects reliably reacted emotionally to the obscene words they failed to report, investigators were able to draw some additional conclusions about the location of perceptual defense in the chain of events from the original presentation of the word to the observer's report of what he saw. Without such multiple measures, it is difficult to draw specific conclusions about the factors responsible for a given result.

Similar difficulties in interpretation became apparent when we began to examine aspects of Eddie's behavior during the course of a session. First, there were the times Eddie did not play what he heard. What was the basis of these "failures"? Even calling them failures prejudges the issue to some extent, for it assumes a breakdown or error somewhere between the reception and pro-cessing of the material heard and his translation of it to performance. It is also possible that a "failure" might occur because Eddie was interested in something else when a particular piece was heard, or perhaps he just preferred to play a piece differently from the way it was heard. In fact, in an effort to examine constituent aspects of musical structure, it was often necessary to create stimulus fragments that were not very musical. Possibly, Eddie found these less deserving of his attention.

Failures might also occur for a relatively peripheral motor reason. Anyone who has tried to play a familiar piano piece when tired knows the experience of having the fingers failing to do as they are told. It is important to be able to distinguish such errors from those that occur when one is reading a piece of music for the first time, or errors resulting from deficiencies in a technical facility, for the errors implicate different aspects of the music making system. Occasionally, Eddie's performance problems were obvious. In an early session, I played a simple tune by Bach, "The Musette," to which Eddie listened in-tently. When seated at the piano, however, he stopped after playing only the first few bars and was reluctant to continue, even with coaxing. A second look at the piece revealed the problem. The bass contained a repeating alternating note figure spanning an octave. Eddie's hand span at the time was just a fifth, and the problems posed by the octave figure were evidently very frustrating to him. (In later sessions, he attempted to solve the "octave problem" by playing the lower note in an octave with his elbow!) Subsequently, we tried to insure that pieces were within his hand span. Other manifestations of motor limitations were not so easy to accommodate. As noted earlier, a certain weakness was evident in his fourth and fifth fingers and evaluations in his file indicated delayed motor development. Interestingly, various motor problems were present in several of the savants described in the next two chapters. J. L. (Charness et al., 1988) has use of only his left hand. L. L. has a more mild form of (right) hemiplegia. Although his playing is bimanual, he has little control of his little finger, particularly on his right hand. C. A.'s motor limitation is more a matter of habit than disability. His original instrument was the accordion and his piano playing currently retains fingering habits more appropriate to the accordion than the piano. Bass chords, for example, are played only by the middle three fingers on his left hand. (Attempts to get C. A. to adopt a more conventional left-hand technique have been largely unsuccessful, according to his teachers). The presence of evident musical precocity in these savants against this background of motor limitation is all the more amazing. It indicates that their motivation and "inner ear" for music is strong enough to surmount the inevitable frustrations their disability must cause when they play music. It also suggests a development of musical sensitivity from the inside out rather than from the outside in. That is, it is much easier to imagine some inner melodies which sought, and found, a means of external expression in these savants than it is to imagine that somehow some extensively repeated or practiced motor patterns became internalized to form some basic "musical sense." Practice was and is undoubtedly important. However, these motor impairments rule out some kind of extreme motor dexterity or facility as providing the primary impetus for the emergence of savant skills. The extent to which motor factors imposed limitations on Eddie's performance in specific cases was sometimes difficult to determine, but these performance limitations should be taken into account in interpreting results.

In many respects, interpreting success seems an easier matter than interpreting failure. After all, if the performance was successful, it is obvious the material was attended to, encoded and translated to performance via appropriate motor commands. Everything was working well. But what, exactly, was working so well? Does success indicate exceptionality of a particular nature? By itself, of course it does not. What is usually more instructive is a pattern of success and (relative) failure across different tasks and conditions. In this regard, most of the older descriptions of savant performance are not very informative. Descriptions of savants as being able to reproduce whatever they hear provide little in the way of discriminative information, and may have contributed to the "tape recorder" or rote memory conceptions of savant skill.

In any case, it should be apparent that situations which yield reliable errors as well as successes are the most informative. Consequently, stimulus materials were designed in a fashion that would elicit some degree of error. As will become evident, this objective was not always achieved.

The most important consequence of these methodologic and motoric constraints on research design is that the results probably underestimate the various competencies and sensitivities of the savant group. This follows from the fact that the criterion task almost always required physical reproduction of what was heard. Recall tasks such as this are among the most demanding types of memory assessment. Moreover, the recall required finding and executing the appropriate motor programs for reproducing a musical segment. Attributing the errors which occurred to some basic limitation in competence is risky at best; the savants probably knew more than they told us in their reproductions.

A second problem encountered in evaluating savants is finding an appropriate comparison group. It was clear to all who heard Eddie in those first few months that his playing was extraordinary. None of us had encountered someone like this before. There are, of course, documented descriptions of child prodigies, most notably Revesz (1925/1970). In such cases, the standard of performance is that of an adult professional performer. Adopting such a comparison standard is certainly reasonable since it is implied in the definition of precociousness. Upon further consideration, however, this solution is not so simple. First, the variability among adult performers is considerable. Some have an excellent sight reading ability, others a good ear; some are composers, others interpreters, and so forth. There is an adult standard for musical skill only in a very general sense; there are, in fact, many such standards. Which ones should be used in evaluating precocious talent?

Ideally, some of the more obvious developmental and cognitive differences should be taken into account in making comparisons. As mentioned earlier, Eddie's performance interval span was about a fifth; that of adult performers is usually twice that. How might that affect the encoding and recall of what was heard? Another obvious difference is the role of varied musical experience. Any comparison between a precocious and a mature musician confounds age and musical experience. There is mounting evidence that these two factors make distinctive contributions to musical understanding (Serafine, 1987). For savants, there is the additional problem that the subject's musical history may be quite idiosyncratic. Our work with Eddie has attempted to expose him to Western musical traditions, broadly conceived (cf., Appendix A). It is unlikely such breadth characterizes the musical experience of the other savants. Different still is the musical heritage of a normal adult musician, which is certainly longer, probably more varied, and most likely involves completion of a particular training curriculum. Intellectual differences also cannot be ignored, because they affect some fundamental aspects of the testing situation, such as attention, preference and means of communication. Because a mature or adult level of skill is the normative standard for comparison, it is unreasonable to dismiss cognitive factors as secondary or incidental to the assessment of musical talent. Most standardized tests of musical ability do show some moderate correlation with standard measures of cognitive achievement (e.g., Seashore, 1938). Distinguishing how these different factors contribute to any differences found between precocious and adult musicians is obviously a very difficult task. Given these considerations, it is not surprising that discussions of savant skills have typically lacked formal comparison subjects. For musical monosavants, the single exception is the research of Sloboda, et al. (1985), who used an adult pianist as a comparison for their adult musical savant.

The procedure adopted in the present experiments was to provide selected comparisons with a relatively small number of subjects. The number and nature of the comparison subjects differ somewhat across studies, but almost all had considerable experience with the piano. This was dictated by the basic performance nature of the experimental tasks. Beyond this, the additional restrictions are mentioned for each study. The ideal comparison subject would be one who is like the savant in all respects except general intellectual level— a "normal" prodigy. The literature does provide the opportunity for at least indirect comparisons of this kind. In any case, the choice of comparison subjects was guided by the goal of providing at least a rough idea of where the savant "fits in" in terms of musical skill and sensitivity.

Comparison subjects were of three types. The first consisted of people who, like Eddie, had shown considerable piano playing talent although they were developmentally disabled. Two of these, L. L. and C. A., had achieved some measure of national recognition for their talent. Three additional subjects, C.N., N.Y., and D.W. were identified through a survey of musical talent among the developmentally disabled in metropolitan Chicago. The second group consisted of adult pianists (M.B., P.M., G.J., H.H., and B.A.) who had played or studied piano for at least 8 years. These participants were recruited through acquaintances and announcements at university music departments. The third comparison group consisted of 4 children (K.L., V.K., B.K., and K.J.) who were approximately Eddie's age (actually all were a bit older) and had been referred by piano teachers as being musically quite gifted or having an "exceptional ear" for music.

Subjects in these groups provided the bulk of the data for the study, although no one participated in as many different experimental tasks as Eddie. Given their role in the investigation, it would be useful to know something more about their personal histories. (As it turned out, in several cases, these histories revealed some remarkable facts). A general developmental history was completed for each subject through personal and/or parental interviews and examination of institutional records, when available. A brief description of these participants follows.

Savant Group:
L.L., C.A., D.W., N.Y., and C.N.

Several in this group have already been described at some length in Chapter 1. To summarize briefly: L.L. is a congenitally blind young man in his late 20s. Born prematurely and with a variety of congenital anomalies of unknown etiology, including cerebral palsy, his early prognosis was very unfavorable. He was placed in foster care shortly after birth. His foster parents (later to become his adoptive parents) were dedicated to providing an optimal environment for his special needs. A very slow rate of development characterized his early life, although through the devoted efforts of his parents, there was considerable progress. As an adult, his communicative language skills remain minimal. There are some persisting effects of his cerebral palsy, particularly on his right side. L.L. expressed an early interest in musical sounds and was introduced to the piano sometime before the age of 8. That remains his favorite instrument, although he has recently been introduced to string and wind instruments as well. His repertoire is varied and includes classical, popular, and religious pieces.

Like L.L., C.A.'s early development was not very encouraging. His mother contracted rubella during pregnancy and he was blind at birth. Very little is known about his early years. His family was quite poor and lived in a rural section of Manitoba. At age 6, with a diagnosis of severe mental retardation, he was admitted to a residential institution. His music training and eventual blossoming as a keyboard player came after his institutionalization, facilitated in large part by the efforts of one of the institution's superintendents. As a young man, C.A. lives in a private group home and takes music lessons at a nearby University. His language remains minimal and mostly echolalic or jargon filled.

D.W., N.Y., and C.N. are all adults who attend a sheltered workshop for the blind. Each lives at home with his/her parents. D.W. is a small gregarious woman in her late 30s. Born prematurely, retrolental fibroplasia resulted in total blindness since birth. She also has multiple bony exostoses (as do 5 of her 7 siblings) and a history of epileptic seizures. Her mother reports several seizures have occurred while D.W. was playing the piano. The result of a neurological exam at age 22 revealed a normal waking EEG, and a bilateral Babinski reflex with greater Babinski response on the right. A diagnosis of nonspecific brain injury was given. Hearing is normal in both ears.

Cognitively, D.W. presents a complex picture. A Wechsler Adult Intelligence Scale (WAIS) administered at age 18 yielded a verbal IQ of 83; retesting 6 years later indicated a score of 93. In the earlier test, particularly high scale scores for information and digit span were noted, while problems calling for orientation, size, and shape perception (haptically) yielded poor performance.

An Illinois Test of Psycholinguistic Abilities given at age 20 revealed auditory reception, memory, and grammatical and auditory closure scores above average, whereas verbal expression was far below average.

As a younger adult, D.W. tended to be excitable and prone to temper tantrums. Some of this evidently was in response to attempts at permanent institutionalization and some difficulties with an older brother. Current reports of her participation in group activities in the center describe her as being much better able to handle frustrations. She converses readily with the staff and clients at the center and kept up a steady patter during our experimental sessions together. D.W. had a few piano lessons during her childhood, but she is primarily self-taught. No one else in her family plays a musical instrument. She prefers to play and listen to more traditional popular music.

There is only meager information about C.N., now in his late 20s. He was born prematurely, and weighed 2 lb. 10 oz. at birth. RH incompatibility was also present. Retrolental fibroplasia associated with oxygen use resulted in total blindness. Audiograms show hearing is normal in both ears. C.N. attended classes for the educable mentally handicapped in the public school system as a child. Records from these early years were not available. As a young adult, he attends an adult living skills program. A general reticence characterizes his interactions with others, though he enjoys playing music for other members in the program. His language tends to be echolalic and he has a severe stuttering problem, making communication quite difficult. He is reported to be able to read Braille, but to have a difficult time understanding what he reads. C.N. comes from a large family with 5 siblings. No one else in his family plays a musical instrument. He is self-taught as a musician, and has been playing the piano since the age of 5. His favorite kinds of music are pop, blues, and jazz, and he plays piano in an amateur blues band.

Like C.N. and D.W., N.Y. was a victim of retrolental fibroplasia associated with prematurity. She has no other physical handicaps and hearing is normal in both ears. N.Y. attended EMH classes in grade school and graduated from a special high-school program for the multiply handicapped. A WAIS administered at that time yielded IQ scores of 63 verbal, 59 performance (haptic). The examiner described her as doing best on tests involving rote learning and worst where abstract reasoning and spatial orientation were involved. N.Y. was also described as being very nervous during the examination and quite anxious about evaluative situations generally. Although her expressive language is adequate for conversation, she has some difficulty following the thread of conversations, her answers sometimes being inappropriate to the question asked. N.Y. is an only child and has taken piano lessons most of her life. No other member of her family plays a musical instrument.

Adult Comparison Group
M.B., P.M., H.H., G.J., and B.A.

M.B. is a 16-year-old with a remarkable history to match his exceptional musical skills. As a young child, nursery school teachers remarked upon his unusual ability to memorize and repeat nursery school songs upon a single exposure. According to his parents, themes from television were also learned very rapidly. Piano lessons began at age 8. Progress was very rapid, and lessons on a second instrument, the clarinet, soon followed. These lessons included summer music camps where M.B. soon became recognized for his clarinet playing. Upon entry to senior high school, however, he stopped clarinet lessons, electing to concentrate on voice and piano. He continues lessons in both and has an active singing schedule, including membership in a major symphonic choral society.

M.B. has a most unusual developmental history. Fortunately, there is also very detailed information about this history. His parents have been concerned with documenting as well as working with the special needs and talents M.B. has shown throughout his childhood. He is the third of four sons born to upper middle-class parents. Birth and early infancy were quite normal, according to the family pediatrician and his mother. By the age of 2, however, both precociousness and developmental disabilities became evident. Language quickly became severely echolalic, and attempts to converse were met with phonetically very sophisticated but semantically empty repetitions of what was heard. On the other hand, M.B. began to spell words, primarily from watching "Sesame Street," according to his parents, and was accurately rearranging blocks to spell words by the age of 3. Temper tantrums were also evident, particularly during disruption of schedules and in socially novel situations. M.B. was referred to a special preschool in the city where his diagnosis was severe developmental disturbance of an autistic nature, though the staff refrained from a formal diagnosis of autism. At 3, he proved extremely resistent to testing, with echolalia and/or jargon in response to requests and commands, and frequent tantrums.

Performance on the Leiter International Performance Scale, one of the few tasks eliciting directed and sustained interest, was very good (MA of 4.3 when given at age 3.3 years). He was also described as having a fascination with puzzles. M.B. was placed in a special therapeutic preschool for the next several years. This, with an active intervention/remediation program at home on the part of his mother, led to rapid gains in both social and cognitive development. By the age of 5 1/2 formal testing revealed well above-average performance on many standard tasks. On the Illinois Test of Psycholinguistic Abilities performance on auditory memory, visual memory and manual expression were extremely high (age equivalent of 8 1/2), whereas only auditory reception remained below age norms (4 years, 1 month). McCarthy, Caldwell, and

Goodenough Draw a Man Assessments all indicated levels of performance above average. As an elementary school child, M.B. showed a pattern of exceptional strength in some areas with weaknesses in others. Among his best areas were arithmetic and spelling, his weakest being English comprehension. Difficulties with abstracting the gist of written and spoken discourse remain somewhat of a problem well into high school, and tutoring in these areas continues. However, in most areas, M.B.'s coursework is on an honor's level and his teachers also note a particular knack for certain tasks, for example, picking up inflectional and idiomatic aspects of regional speech differences in his drama class.

P.M. is a 32-year-old Suzuki teacher of the piano. As a very young child, she discovered she could easily play the tunes being practiced on the piano by her older sister. In fact, for a time, she though piano lessons unnecessary, and formal training did not begin until age 9. She progressed rapidly in her lessons and studied music in college. It was only at this point, as a consequence of comparing strategies in transcription with her fellow students, that she realized her ability to recognize specific pitches was quite unusual. An anticipated professional performing career has been curtailed by a series of physical ailments.

In other respects, P.M.'s life history, though not so exceptional as M.B.'s is not without some unusual factors. She has Hashimoto's Disease, a genetic thyroid disorder (her mother also has it). As a child, she was a very finicky eater. In school, her performance on abstract reasoning and spatial tasks tended to be very good whereas English was one of her poorer subjects. Even today, P.M. is sensitive regarding her ability to converse concisely and coherently. Other than some brief remedial work for articulation difficulties, however, language problems were not seen as so serious as to require intervention.

G.J. is a 26-year-old college senior majoring in mathematics with a minor in music. He has been taking piano lessons since the age of 6. European born, he describes himself as classically trained, with extensive experience with the Hannon exercises and the classical repertoire. The piano is the only instrument he plays. He considers himself much better at sight reading than aural dictation. He is primarily a solo player. By his own report, his developmental history is unexceptional, with no memory or knowledge of particular difficulties or problems early in his life.

H.H. is 24 years old and in graduate school, having earned a B.A. degree with a joint major in psychology and music. As a preschooler, she was recommended to State music grade school in Poland after teachers in preschool noticed her ability to recall and sing songs. Her musical education at the grade school is described by her as traditional, with the introduction of note reading at the outset. She describes the repertoire of her training as primarily 18th and 19th century, and restricted to the piano. Currently, she plays primarily the classical piano literature for personal pleasure and teaches piano to several children. Her personal developmental history is unexceptional according to her own report and the recollection of her mother.

B.A., like several of the other participants in the project, exhibited a knack for picking out melodies on the piano at a very early age. When she was 2 1/2, she startled her parents (and angered her older brother) by being able to repeat melodies her brother had just played as part of his piano lesson. Her own first lessons soon followed, but were discontinued after only 6 months. Apparently the lessons began with traditional stave reading and B.A. soon lost interest. After 5 years had passed, lessons were attempted again, this time with considerably more success. The lessons, with a variety of teachers, are described as in "the classical tradition," and included a broad sampling of the piano literature. Currently B.A. is in a graduate music program, with the French horn and piano as her instruments. She plays piano in a variety of contexts; chamber ensemble, solo and choral accompanist, and in a civic orchestra. B.A. is an adopted child and little is known of her prenatal or early postnatal history. She reports no particular allergies, nothing unusual in her medical history other than the usual childhood illnesses, and no particular problems in school.

Child Comparison Group
K.L., V.K., B.K., and K.J.

K.L. was seen just a few weeks before her 12th birthday. She has been blind since infancy; like many others the blindness was due to RLF suffered as a consequence of treatment formerly common in cases of extreme prematurity. (She was born at 28 weeks, weighing 1 1/2 lbs.). She was released from the hospital 5 months later with a weight of 5 lb. Physical development since then has been within the normal range, and the only other physical problems noted by K.L.'s parents were several episodes of convulsions associated with moderate fevers (101 degrees or so) at 4 and 5, and again when she had chicken pox at 9. Although she has not shown any marked allergic reactions, K.L. is a notoriously finicky eater. According to her parents, it is easier to note the few things she does like rather than what she doesn't, and often she just seems disinterested in food.

K.L.'s social and cognitive development has been quite normal, according to her parents. She is the younger of two children. She was talking (and sing-ing) at 18 months, and in other respects seemed a bit faster in learning new skills than her older brother. She has progressed through school at a normal rate and currently attends a local grade school. A teacher described her as occasionally having problems with some of the work, but indicated this more often seemed a matter of application than competence.

K.L.'s interest in music was in evidence at an early age. She sang often as a toddler. Some songs her parents could identify, but others she apparently made up on her own. When given a musical toy as a toddler she delighted in playing different melodies on the toy and impressed her parents with her memory for extended tonal sequences. When K.L. was about 4 or so, a piano was purchased and her older brother began taking lessons. She quickly showed a clear talent for the instrument however, often going up to the piano and easily repeating the tunes her brother just had been practicing. Piano lessons for K.L. soon followed and formal music training in some form has continued to this day. According to her piano teacher, the lessons have progressed at a rapid rate through the standard children's literature, and have included the rudiments of harmony, rhythm, and so forth, as well as fingering technique. An attempt to learn Braille music was soon discontinued due to lack of interest on K.L.'s part. Several years ago, K.L. began to study cello, and this is rapidly becoming her favorite instrument. K.L. also reports liking to play the drums and for a time there was a drum set in the house. K.L.'s father plays the guitar a little, but no other member of the family is an active musician.

V.K., B.K., and K.J. are all girls nominated by piano teachers as being exceptional as students. Although not having extended absolute pitch naming skills, each is described as having a particularly good ear for the melodic line and harmony of a piece, learning new material with relative ease. V.K. is 9 and has been taking piano lessons for 3 years from the teacher who also has been working with Eddie. K.J. is also 9 and has been taking lessons for 3 years under the Suzuki method of instruction. B.K. is 10 years old and has been taking lessons for 5 years. Interviews with the parents of the 3 girls indicated nothing exceptional in the developmental history of any. K.J.'s mother is also an amateur musician (cello), and V.K.'s younger sister is also studying piano. The parents of all 3 participants described an early interest in music by their daughters and all three indicate a keen interest in music currently as well.

It is clear these three groups do not represent a matched comparison set in any usual sense. In fact, probably the only common element running through the histories is an early interest or introduction to music, and the piano in particular. Beyond this, there is considerable divergence. Every member of the savant group, not surprisingly, has a developmental history containing a variety of risk factors. All are congenitally blind. (Note that many of the cases viewed in Chapter 1 were also congenitally blind.) However, pathology or exceptional developmental histories are by no means confined to the savant group. M.B., P.M., and among the children, K.L., all have shown some unusual aspects in their personal histories. Whether there may be similar unreported factors in the other cases is, of course, hard to say. Given Eddie's history of physical ailments and language difficulties, each participant's personal history was examined for similar factors. Parents of the children were asked about early language and physical problems including seizures, allergies, food finickiness, and the like. Except for K.L., none was reported, and it seems unlikely they were simply not recalled by the parents (or by the adults) in our interviews.

Discussion of possible contributions of these factors in savant skill will be reserved for the final chapter. For the present, the presence of these differences led to a bit of a quandary. To what extent is it really valid to treat the participants as comprising three distinct groups? Might other designations (e.g., male/female, child/adult, blind/sighted, developmental history/normal/unusual) be more appropriate? To some extent, this is an empirical matter, and heterogeneity of subject characteristics permits such reshuffling or reorganization along various dimensions. As it turns out, an additional characteristic, so called "absolute pitch" emerged as an important source of individual differences in performance.

How might one best accommodate these differences? The strategy chosen was to stick with the original three group differentiation whenever possible, but to devote considerable time to the description of individual variations. This presents the reader with a considerable cognitive load, compounded by the variety of tasks given most subjects. To help keep track of subjects' participation, Appendix B contains a table of the complete experimental series and the participants in each task. The reader may find this useful in understanding the composition of the complete data set.

A final, and probably most intransigent problem should be mentioned. With multiple measures on subjects, it is inevitable that order and experiment are somewhat confounded. How much did the experience provided by the early experiments "muddy the water" for the later research? How much did the additional experience acquired by Eddie during the course of the research (roughly 3 years) change the outcome of the later studies? Usually evaluation of such factors is accomplished through a careful counterbalancing of test order across different subjects, something that was not possible here.

An additional problem was introduced by the variation of session length across subjects. Eddie's willingness to participate in structured activities was limited to about 10 to 15 minutes at the outset; a bit longer than that later. Consequently, for most experiments, Eddie's participation was spread across at least several weeks, and sometimes months of activity. By contrast, for most of the others, participation was limited to a session or two. Whether this unduly favored (or penalized) Eddie is hard to say. The order of giving the various tasks to Eddie was determined by a variety of factors, primarily the availability of experimental materials and equipment rather than theoretical assumptions about the structure of music. It is possible that transfer across studies, as well as some general experience factors contributed to results, particularly in the later tasks. Suggestions as to what these might be are made during the interpretation of individual experiments.

The results of the experiments have been divided into three sections. The first section examines pitch naming skills in savants ("absolute pitch" or "perfect pitch"). The next section examines short-term memory for various elements of music, such as harmonic, melodic, and rhythmic fragments. Here the primary question is whether the savant is at a particular advantage in encoding and remembering these basic building blocks of music. In Chapter 5, we examine performance on longer, more musically structured material.

About six months after the experiments began, private piano lessons were arranged for Eddie. Given Eddie's eagerness to interact via the piano and his evident talent, more formal musical tuition seemed worth pursuing. These lessons became a regular part of Eddie's routine and eventually expanded to include music related activities in a broad sense. The changes in Eddie over the course of these lessons is an important story in itself, and is described by his piano teacher, Nancy Newman, in Appendix A.

3 | Absolute Pitch

Eddie's excellent sense of pitch was evident in our first brief testing session. When he was asked to repeat my playing of "Twinkle, Twinkle Little Star" in various keys, he did so readily and unerringly. He did not have to hunt around for the first note and then proceed with the rest of the melody. Somehow, the memory of the last rendition of the song contained precise information about the notes he had just heard. This translated to specific keys on the piano with little effort on his part. (Although by this time he was wearing glasses, his visual acuity was so poor it is extremely unlikely he was memorizing the notes played by watching my hands. Most often, he would close his eyes or stare at the ceiling when he listened to another person playing. In later sessions, occasionally he was seated away from the piano when he heard a piece, with no effect on his ability to find the right notes in starting a piece).

Eddie's ability to identify the specific pitch of sounds in his environment often expressed itself in unexpected ways. In one of the early sessions, while Eddie was playing a melody I had just presented, another song began to emerge in his playing. I soon realized the second song was being sung by the children in an adjoining room. On another occasion, the beeping sound made by a construction truck backing up outside the building made its way into his playing. Eddie was sensitive to the pitch qualities of many environmental sounds. It is significant that this well-developed pitch sense was present before he had any conventional names for the notes he heard. In fact, soon after I was introduced to Eddie, I observed one of the teachers at the

41

school trying to teach him some note names with little success partly, perhaps, because the teacher was not very sure of the note names either. The process of learning the terms of music has been a long and slow process for Eddie (c.f., Appendix A). It is clear, however, that terms like note names applied to aspects of music which Eddie already knew in a practical sense. Thus, he would react to the sounds around him by translating them into their "piano" names if not their verbal names. Later, when he had learned the names of different notes, he was fond of pointing out the "names" of sounds to me. The sound of a passing police car siren was F and G. The bell in the elevator at the University was identified as A# (the announcement causing some bewilderment to the other riders in the elevator at the time).

Eddie's gift of "perfect" or absolute pitch (AP) is evidently present in other musical savants as well, as we saw in Chapter 1. What is this gift of perfect pitch and what did it indicate? This question is not easily answered. For example, estimates of the frequency of AP vary considerably; from .01% in the general adult population (Bachem, 1955) to almost 100% in very young children (Sergeant & Roche, 1973). Part of the controversy stems from difficulties in definition. What do people with AP do that is so different? A set of contrasting examples is given by Ward and Burns (1982).

> Suppose we present to an individual the following sequence of frequencies: 260, 260, 330, 260, 330, 290 Hz and ask "what was that?" Individuals who are tone deaf—are apt to answer with something no more specific than "a bunch of tones." The median American nonmusician will probably answer "Yankee Doodle" (identification of tune)—The typical performing musician can do all that and may add the sequence of successive intervals was unison, ascending major second, another ascending major second, descending major third, ascending major third, and descending major second (identification of intervals). But only the person with absolute pitch is able to answer "Middle, C, C, D, E, C, E, D" (identification of the musical designation of individual components). (1982, pp. 431–32)

These examples suggest that the determination of AP should be a fairly straightforward matter. Individuals with AP (and only those with AP) can unerringly identify the specific pitches of the melodies they hear, without recourse to trial and error attempts to match what was heard. Unfortunately, the matter is not clear-cut because absolute pitch is considerably less than absolute. For one thing, accurate pitch naming may be restricted to the timbre and range found in the instrument one usually plays. Ward and Burns (1982) offer the term "absolute piano" to note this relative quality of AP. Simple sinusoids or "pure tones" can be quite difficult to identify for those exhibiting absolute pitch for more complex sounds (Lockhead & Byrd, 1981). The ability may also be restricted with respect to pitch range, accuracy failing for either very high or very low pitches (Bachem, 1948). In some cases, this constraint is so restricted that the individual can identify only a single pitch, for example, 440Hz, or the "A" used as a standard for tuning instruments. Finally, some have suggested that apparent AP may actually be a sophisticated use of relative pitch in combination with subtle cues from the environment (Costall, 1985).

With such qualifications as these, it is not surprising that some have suggested AP is in no sense absolute. Rather, the phenomenon is said to represent one end of a general dimension of pitch discrimination ability (cf., Costall, 1985; Neu, 1948). Bachem (1948), in response, has listed several distinctive characteristics of subjects with AP. Among other things, the speed and accuracy of their judgment is an order of magnitude superior to that of those with relative pitch, they have much better memory for specific tones, and their errors suggest a different way of perceiving pitch. These differences suggest that on most tests of pitch identification, people with "extended range" AP (that is, beyond one or two pitches) will show performance widely divergent from those without AP. Thus, given the "Yankee Doodle" task described by Ward and Burns (1982) earlier, the person with AP will be rarely wrong, whereas the person without it rarely right when asked to name the specific pitches involved. It is in this sense, then, that the operational definition of AP is quite clear.

Although there may be some consensus about what people with AP can do, there is much less agreement regarding the specific mechanisms involved. Siegel (1972) reviews evidence for two prevalent explanations of AP: (a) superior discrimination ability and (b) the presence of particular pitch related internal standards, or categories for processing pitch information. On the former view, AP represents another aspect of the general ability to tell whether two pitches are different. Consequently, those who have AP will show more finely tuned discrimination of pitch differences (Neu, 1948). This model of AP is consistent with what we know about the registration of pitch information in the auditory system. Given the tonotopic organization of projection in the primary auditory cortex (Merzenich, Knight, & Roth, 1975), finely tuned frequency analysis is inherent in the auditory system. The idea of some special discriminative capacity for frequency is also consistent with accounts of auditory hypersensitivity in musical savants (Anastasi & Levee, 1960; Sarason & Gladwin, 1958). Behaviors like Eddie's intense reactions to loud or "noisy" environments (holding his ears, shaking his head) could reflect the negative side of a finely tuned discrimination for certain kinds of sounds. On the other hand, it seems highly unlikely Eddie has generally-enhanced sound discrimination skills because he appears to be deaf in his left ear. Thus, at the very least, his heightened sensitivity must be of a highly restricted sort. Among adults, frequency discrimination is at best only moderately correlated with (absolute) pitch identification (Siegel, 1972). Moreover, in studies comparing simple frequency discrimination and AP, musical training has been a confounding factor. Those with more extensive musical training may be more likely to have AP and are better able to discriminate pitches because of some factor related to their extensive musical background rather than their pitch naming skill. We shall return to this notion later, for it is implicated in theories of the development of AP.

The "internal standard" hypothesis maintains that those with AP have somehow managed to construct a set of internal categories or standards that are linked to specific pitches. Thus, although differences in pitch represent differences along a continuous physical dimension, frequency, presentation of a pitch elicits a specific categorical identification within the perceptual system, rather than just a dimensional response (e.g., higher vs. lower) (Siegel, 1972). The categories represented by standard Western musical notes (the keys on the piano) represent one such identifying system, and the one that is in evidence when people exhibit AP. To some extent, of course, this is merely a restatement of the phenomenon, not an explanation of it. People with absolute pitch are able to attach categorical responses in the form of note names to the pitches they hear. Their accuracy in note naming must imply some memory trace of the sensory qualities of specific pitches, or some "internal standard", for each note of the chromatic scale. Is there any sense in which the idea of "internal standards" can be considered in a less circular manner? There is some recent psychophysiological research that bears on this issue. Adult AP and RP (relative pitch) musicians differ in the topography of their cortical evoked potentials when listening to simple tones, suggesting different central representation of the tonal information (Klein, Coles, & Donchin, 1984).

It is clear that one version of the internal standard model is incorrect. That version claims absolute pitch is a result of extensive pitch naming practice, usually in association with musical training (Siegel, 1972), reducing it to a kind of paired associate learning task. There are reports of attempts to learn absolute pitch in this manner, utilizing extensive experience trying to associate names with specific pitches (e.g., Brady, 1970). Such attempts have met with very limited success, for the most part. In any case, this model does not apply to Eddie, for whom note naming came after evidence of absolute pitch. Nor would it seem to apply to other savants, whose limited or restricted language make such verbal association mechanisms unlikely candidates for learning.

In other respects, however, the notion of an internal standard does imply a representational framework for pitch that is somehow more vivid or informative in the person with AP. In the literature, introspective reports by people with AP suggest rich images associated with different pitches, often involving color terms. An early description of these images in a conversation between Scriabin and Rimsky-Korsakov is reported by Myers (1915). Apparently, Rimsky-Korsakov remarked that the piece to which they were listening (in D major) seemed "yellow" to him. Scriabin subsequently informally inquired about other color-key associations and reported a moderate amount of agreement. Scriabin was perhaps the most ardent advocate of a multimodal view of music, suggesting at one point compositions which would present the natural integration of sound, sight and smell, for example (Schonberg, 1987). Some attempts have been made to determine whether there is a common color-pitch equivalence across subjects with absolute pitch. Generally speaking, the results suggest considerable consistency within an individual regarding color-pitch associations, but much less consistency across individuals with absolute pitch. Contrary to Scriabin, there is no standard color-pitch code (Block, 1983). However, the consistency of association within possessors of AP supports the notion of a very stable or well-anchored pitch identification system. Moreover, the analogy of AP perception to that of a visual color sensation may reflect some important similarities in the two dimensions: sound wavelength (pitch) and light wavelength (color). In each case, gradually increasing values along a dimension, wavelength, result in changing perceptions, color in the case of light and pitch in the case of sound. Now imagine an experiment where one is asked to judge the magnitude of the difference between any 2 wavelengths rather than their specific color. In other words, we would be asked to identify whether the wavelength difference between some examples of red and blue is greater than one between green and yellow or yellow and violet. If we can recall the layout of the visible spectrum from our high-school physics text, we might be able to make some reasonable guesses, but likely as not, the specific colors used would be so salient that our judgments would be subject to considerable error. Our judgments would most likely be based on some other feature, brightness, for example. In fact, even the considerably simpler task of deciding whether a given color was near the short or the long end of the visible spectrum may send us back to our textbooks. Now, consider the same experiment in sound; judging whether one interval or difference in frequency between two sounds is greater than another. Here, there is little problem, particularly with just a little experience (Neu, 1948). And in the easier task, deciding whether one frequency is higher or lower than the other, the problem is negligible until the difference becomes very small. Moreover, it seems the names of individual frequencies, or whether a given note corresponded to a C or a G, is of little importance. In the case of vision, specific values along a dimension, the color names, are salient, whereas in audition, the dimension itself (or more accurately, differences along the dimension) is more salient. This points to the importance of relative information in music; we pay attention to the intervals we hear, not specific note names, and the relations among notes represent the structure of a piece (Costall, 1985). Now, consider the person with absolute pitch. Somehow for audition, as for vision, the specific association or impression of the given frequency comes first, while its relation to other frequencies may be secondary. In some cases, the specific identity carries with it associations with certain colors. Like our usual color perception, in those with absolute pitch, there is a primary individual identity or character associated with each chroma (note type), with dimensional information occurring as a secondary characteristic of the sound.

There are many important differences between the dimensions of wavelength in color and pitch, of course. The nature of sound propagation results in complex recurrent frequencies in addition to the fundamental of a given frequency. This results in chroma repetition (octaves) as well as harmonic overtones. There is no "recurring red" as we decrease light wavelength the way there is a "recurring C" as we decrease sound wavelength. This property of sound may play an important role in our basic musical sensitivity (Bernstein, 1976). Nevertheless, considering absolute pitch in this manner suggests some additional possibilities. First, a primacy of identity over dimensional information as a basic quality of perceptual processing suggests extensive training and/or experience is not as important in establishing absolute pitch. It doesn't appear to be necessary for perceiving the categorized qualities of color. For example, Bornstein, Kessen, & Weiskopf (1976), found that even young infants show evidence of special sensitivity to "primary" colors of the spectrum. There is similar evidence for a strong congenital, if not hereditary, component to absolute pitch (Bachem, 1948). Second, if the primary response of the possessor of AP to a tone is its name or chroma rather than (dimensional) height, octave determination would be secondary to the perceptual process. Thus, in some cases at least, one would expect a reversal in the error pattern for those having absolute pitch; chroma designation would be accurate but octave designation inaccurate. Such reversals do at least occasionally occur in those with AP (Bachem, 1955; Klein, Coles, & Donchin, 1984).

Lastly, the ready availability of a consistent internal standard should make it possible to preserve pitch information more accurately in long-term memory. As Siegel (1972, 1974) has suggested, such categories should make it much easier to store and retrieve information about a given event. Again pursuing the analogy with color, the long-term memory of a color associated with a particular thing is enhanced considerably by the color categories we have to classify the quality. Thus, we should be able to recall with little effort whether the sweater we saw yesterday was blue or red and thereby consider it in conjunction with one we are currently examining. Similarly, having encoded the note we heard some time back as an "A", it should be a small matter to decide whether the note now being heard is the same or different; that is, another "A". On the other hand, having only encoded the sweater as "bright" or the note as "high" we may have considerable difficulty deciding whether a subsequent sweater was as bright or a subsequent note was as high. This does not deny the possibility that relational information regarding things and events can be retained in our long-term memory (e.g., Kosslyn, Pinker, Smith, & Schwartz, 1979), only that such information is likely to have a different kind of precision than that involving categories. An important qualification to this claim regarding memory is that the task involves discrimination across category boundaries. As Siegel (1974) points out, if a delayed discrimination required comparison of two frequencies slightly to either side of 440 Hz, (the note "A"), the categorical information provided by the "internal standard" of one having AP may be of little help, since each note will be classified as an example of A.

The idea that AP should be particularly useful in long-term memory has been put to experimental test. Bachem (1954) presented a delayed pitch discrimination task to adults either having or not having AP. The delay between the two tones was either 3 sec, 15 sec, 60 sec, 1 hour, 1 day or 1 week. For subjects without AP, comparison at the brief intervals was very accurate; by 60 seconds, it had started to deteriorate considerably. For those with AP, on the other hand, performance remained at a very high level even one week later. Absolute pitch provided a clear advantage for long-term memory. Information regarding constraints on this long-term memory advantage is provided by Siegel (1972, 1974). In the earlier study, a small consistent advantage was found for subjects with absolute pitch across a range of delay intervals. No particular advantage occurred for the longer intervals. The task was a very difficult one, requiring the subjects to discriminate a pitch difference of a little over 1 Hz. Siegel argued that given a categorical kind of perception some differential accuracy should still be seen in those with AP. Even with such a fine discrimination, if it occurs near the border of two categories, for example, between C and C$^\#$, discrimination may be considerably better than if it occurs for stimuli which are much closer to the standard or prototypic value for C. Differential discrimination at hypothesized category boundaries is frequently taken as strong evidence for categorical perception (Burns & Ward, 1982). No such differential performance was found in any of the subjects, arguing against categorical encoding of the stimuli. Several factors may have prevented categorical effects from occurring, however. As noted earlier, pure tones such as those used by Siegel (1972) may be very difficult to identify. The procedure also may have made categorical identification less likely a part of stimulus processing. Faced with the task of discriminating minute differences across an extensive set of trials, the inadequacy of pitch name information must have been quite apparent. Whether such encoding occurred to any significant degree is thus open to question. A subsequent study by Siegel (1974) lends some support to this interpretation. Adults were given a delayed pitch comparison task involving either 1/10 or 3/4 of a semitone difference between tones. In the latter case, different pitches were very likely to belong to different note categories. As expected, in this condition those with AP excelled, particularly at the longer intervals. Siegel (1974) concluded the mnemonic furnished by verbal coding of pitch categories provided the advantage for those with absolute pitch. Such a mnemonic could work, however, only if the pitch categories were readily available to the subject. Consequently, the results would seem to point to the presence of some set of internalized standard reference points for pitch, although the precise nature of this internal representation remains unclear.

The exploration of Eddie' pitch naming ability was directed by several questions. First, what was its range? Eddie's tendency to name sounds from his environment indicated he had something more than "absolute piano." Would his pitch extend to pure tones, sounds he had probably heard only rarely?

If so, it would indicate he did indeed have a general purpose tool for classifying and relating the sounds of his environment. Second, to what extent would his pitch identification extend to groups of tones? Being able to identify single notes without a reference point, or translate environmental sounds into their chroma equivalents, by itself, may be little more than a parlor trick. However, informal observation of Eddie at the piano suggested his identification was not limited to single pitches. As he learned the names, he applied them to pitch complexes (i.e., chords) as well. As noted in the previous chapter, one of Blind Tom's pitch demonstrations involved the ability to analyze complex dissonant chords into constituent elements. Did Eddie's talent likewise extend beyond single notes? If so, it may assume considerable importance in unraveling the intricacies in a piece of music. Finally, would it be possible to determine something about any internal standards or set of categories Eddie might be using in making his judgments? Would these standards simply be more finely tuned or discriminative than is usually the case? Might they be biased to process pitch information in certain ways?

Tone Identification

This experiment was designed to document Eddie's pitch naming ability for both conventional piano tones and less familiar "pure" tones. The stimuli were generated on a Yamaha DX-21 keyboard. This synthesizer has a range of voice settings, corresponding to different musical instruments, as well as the capacity to generate both sinusoid and sawtooth pure tones. Sounds were produced through either of two amplification systems, an Ampex model AA620 amplifier/speaker or a Sanyo model 685 stereo system. The particular amplification system used varied across trials and subjects. Although no formal assessment of speaker differences was made, informal observation suggested no obvious differences associated with the sound system used. In the first assessment, the "Ivory Ebony Piano" selection of the DX-21 voice memory was used as the instrument voice. This voice is constructed to resemble a standard upright piano, and was readily identified as a piano sound by all subjects. A second set of tones used the simple sinusoid synthesized voicing.

Two groups of subjects were used for comparison purposes. The first group consisted of 7 young adults who had been playing piano for at least 8 years. They ranged in age from 19 to 27. None of these subjects indicated any absolute pitch ability, restricted in range or otherwise. The second comparison group contained 8 pianists referred through acquaintances as suspected of having exceptional pitch naming skill. The members of this group varied widely in age, musical experience, and the presence of handicapping conditions. All of these subjects except R.S. are described in the previous chapter.

The procedure varied somewhat for the different groups. All subjects were first given a set of 24 examples of single notes drawn from C3 to C5, using

the Ivory Ebony voicing. The sequence of notes was random with the constraint that each note of the (chromatic) scale was presented twice and that
no two successive notes were separated by an interval of less than a minor
third. Subjects were asked to name the notes played. At this point, the experimental procedure diverged. For the subjects with avowed relative pitch
(RP) only, 3 additional sets of 24 trials were given. In set two, the tonic triad
in each of the 12 major keys was presented twice for identification. In the
third set of trials, single notes were again presented for identification, but in
each case, the note was preceded by a presentation of middle C. Finally, in
the fourth set, major tonic triads were played, as in set two, but each was
preceded by the C major tonic triad. Subjects were told in sets three and four
that middle C or its tonic triad would be presented before each trial. For the
subjects with avowed AP (including Eddie), a different second set of 24 trials
was given. For these subjects, the set contained single pure sinusoid tones
as stimuli, presented with the same constraints as those used in set one.

The second condition for the RP subjects was prompted by Corso's (1957)
report that additional key related information may aid the listener without
absolute pitch to make more accurate pitch judgments. Stimulus sets three
and four represent assessments of relative pitch ability. Given the middle C
standard presented on each trial, the listener's task essentially is to judge the
interval between the reference tone and the target. Firm knowledge of those
intervals is characteristic of the experienced musician (Burns & Ward, 1982),
and it was assumed that these tasks would be the most easily performed by
the "relative pitch" group.

The results of the experiments are presented in Table 3.1. Two figures are
given for each entry, using a "conservative" (criterion 1) and a "relaxed"
(criterion 2) criterion for accuracy. In the former case, the note or chord named
had to be the one played, whereas in the latter case, estimates off by one
semitone are added to the score. Several results emerged from the analysis.
Subjects with relative pitch performed as expected, doing much better when
a contextual cue was given than when they had to rely on only the pitch
information itself. It is also apparent that the additional information provided
by a tonic triad context (condition 2) did not help. Interestingly, for both
nonreference conditions (Sets 1 and 2) a "C bias" was evident in the responding of the RP subjects, the value C being chosen on incorrect trials more than
twice as often as any other note. This tendency has been noted by others
(Corso, 1957). Most of the subjects with alleged AP could, like Eddie, identify the notes generated in Set 1 with ease. The scores of P. M. and R. S. were
less than optimal, although their pitch naming accuracy surpasses any subjects in the RP group. At the experiment's conclusion, P. M. said the notes
did not generate the clear images they usually did on her own (acoustic) piano.
As a result, her guesses were made with little confidence. R. S. confided after
the experiment he often "had trouble" with the black keys in pitch naming,
and his accuracy, in fact, was for the most part restricted to the white keys

TABLE 3.1
Pitch Identification Experiment, Correct Identification

Relative Pitch					
(N=7)		Set 1	Set 2	Set 3	Set 4
Criterion	1	4.8	2.8	11.6	7.6
	2	7.8	6.0	14.4	10.8
Absolute Pitch					
Eddie Criterion	1	24	19		
	2	24	24		
K.L.	1	24	24		
	2	24	24		
M.B.	1	24	24		
	2	24	24		
P.M.	1	10	7		
	2	16	10		
D.W.	1	24	24		
	2	24	24		
N.Y.	1	24	24		
	2	24	24		
C.N.	1	24	24		
	2	24	24		
B.A.	1	24	24		
	2	24	24		
R.S.	1	9	4		
	2	19	8		

Maximum score=24. Criterion 1, exact match; Criterion 2, within 1/2 step of original. Significantly different from chance (p<.05), Criterion 1, 7 or more correct, Criterion 2, 12 or more correct, binomial test.

within the range tested. Changing to pure tone stimuli also made little difference for most of these subjects. The five trials on which Eddie missed by a semitone were all judged a semitone lower then the original. For P.M., the sinusoids elicited performance barely above chance levels, and for R.S. sinusoid naming did not differ from chance.

Differences in subjects' reporting style accompanied these marked differences in accuracy. Subjects with outstanding pitch naming skills made these judgments quickly and confidently. Those with relative pitch were (understandably) quite tentative, often offering several alternatives before making their choice. P.M. was perhaps the most uncomfortable about the task, and was quite frustrated by her inability to generate the appropriate pitch names under the experimental conditions of Set 1. She predicted beforehand that her performance on the pure tone trials would probably not be very good. R.S. reported trying to shift strategy in the second, pure tone set. Rather than relying "on his intuition", he adopted an anchor, one of the notes he was quite sure about, and then tried to deduce subsequent tones in terms of their distance from this anchor. This has been suggested as a viable strategy in pitch identification (Costall, 1985). In this case, it proved disastrous as the stability of the anchor began to fade and conflicts between R.S.'s judgments based upon interval estimation and those using "intuitive feeling" became evident. Lack of familiarity with pure tones was apparently of little consequence for the remaining subjects. Although the diagnosis of "absolute piano" (Burns & Ward, 1982) rather than absolute pitch may be appropriate for P.M. and R.S., it is clear the remaining absolute pitch subjects have a generalized and secure ability to classify frequency information according to chromatic scale conventions with minimal contextual cues. It is important to note that some of the more obvious factors can be ruled out as necessary to the presence of extended pitch naming. Eddie's language at the time of testing was minimal, as was C.N.'s. Only P.M. reported any effort to sharpen or train her pitch naming skill during her musical career, clearly with less than complete success. Age, level of cognitive maturity, and musical experience also varied widely among members of the extended pitch naming group. The possibility of a hereditary factor remains (Bachem, 1955). No immediate relations of the participants M.B., P.M., R.S. or K.L. have absolute pitch but this determination could not be made in the other cases. Whatever its origin, extended pitch naming skill stands out clearly in these subjects.

Chord Analysis

Blind Tom's musical ability to name pitches present in even the most dissonant, complex chords intrigued Charles Halle, among others, who described a demonstration by Blind Tom:

> Perhaps the most striking feature was the extraordinary quickness with which he named any notes struck by me on the piano, either single or simultaneously, however discordant they must be. (Southall, 1983, p. 56)

Southall also reports the results of a specific test of Blind Tom's note naming ability:

> To test Tom's powers of analyzing chords, Mr. Joule played the following discordant combinations: The chord of B flat in the left hand with the chord of A with the flat fifth and sharp sixth in the right hand; the chord of A, three flats, in the left hand, with that of A, three sharps, in the right. (Southall, 1983, p. 56)

I tried the first combination of notes with Eddie one day. His response was not a perfect match; one note was omitted and another off by a half step, but even so, quite impressive. A similar ability was noted by Revesz (1925/1970) in the child prodigy Erwin Nyiregyhazi (Revesz also demonstrated AP in Nyiregyhazi using a technique similar to that used here.)

Anyone who has tried to disentangle the notes heard in a complex chord can appreciate the difficulty of this task. One of the things that made Blind Tom's performance so impressive is that his ability to reproduce chords extended to dissonant, "nonsensical" chords. One might expect people with extensive musical training and experience to be able to detect some of the harmonic components of a piece of music. Even untrained adults discriminate the major and minor modes in Western music (Hevner, 1936). Beyond that, formal training in the rules of harmony helps in limiting or structuring the possible configurations in the tone complexes one hears (Cuddy, 1971). Randomly generated chords are another matter. They are not susceptible to the resolution by rule possible with traditionally constituted chords. Dissonant material is much more familiar now than it was in Blind Tom's day, of course, with the progressive relaxation of many traditional rules of composition. Still, much of the music in our environment remains firmly in a tradition of harmonic regularity. However, for the person with absolute pitch, such experience may be relatively unimportant. If the primary consequences or products of absolute pitch are the relevant chroma categories (e.g., the note names), the structure of the chord should make little difference. Corliss (1973) describes her experience as consistent with this view. Key information was deduced after specific constituent notes were identified. This direct coding of note values would therefore be relatively unaffected by familiarity, key structure, and so forth. As an aside, one should note that the chords given to Blind Tom were not really random in that each, by itself, represented a fairly conventional grouping. Their dissonance and relative unfamiliarity were produced by their juxtaposition. The matter of defining exactly what one means by dissonance in a musical context remains a thorny issue (Davies, 1978). It is possible that Blind Tom was able to note the frequency range represented by the left and right hand chords in the example mentioned and thus minimize the discordance. If so, the chords were not perceptually dissonant to him at all. In any case, the argument that he had an extraordinary ability to analyze sound complexes remains valid.

Inasmuch as the "categorical" or "internal standard" model of pitch naming does predict there should be relatively little difficulty in resolving unusual note combinations, it also suggests a special kind of problem. As noted earlier, (Bachem, 1948) octave discrimination may be secondary to chroma classification in the possessor of AP. If the primary output of processing is chroma category rather than specific frequency, given an octave interval as part of a chord, a chroma processing strategy might render it as a single value or note, thereby reducing the chromatic redundancy of the original. Or, one might expect octave transposition in the rendition. Knowing that the three chroma values are C, E, and G, for example, does not specify which note is represented by the lowest frequency. Thus, C could be in the normal, lowest frequency of the canonical C major chord or the chord could be an "inverted" instance of the C major triad (EGC or GCE). In all of these cases, the essential chromatic identity of the original is present, but the rendition is not a literal transcription. Attention to chroma, rather than frequency, should make such transpositions more likely.

Recall that an alternative explanation of absolute pitch performance suggests it reflects a superior discrimination ability of some kind. As we have seen, there is only weak evidence for such a factor in the identification of single tones. However, might superior discrimination skills be of value in deciphering tonal complexes? It is hard to say. On the one hand, almost by definition, one might expect such discrimination to allow one to distinguish at least the number of components in a chord, thereby defining the extent of the problem. This link is acknowledged in tests of musical ability that require the listener to determine the number of notes in a chord (e.g., Bentley, 1966). Sensitivity to octave intervals, a potential difficulty in a chroma categorization model, should not be a problem if those with AP have finely tuned frequency discrimination. In fact, evidence from fusion experiments suggests this could be one area where considerable difficulties remain for the usual listener. Fusion refers to the failure to discriminate two frequencies as distinct. Such fusion effects are especially likely to occur for tones separated by an octave (Davies, 1978, pp. 168–71). However, exceptionally acute sensitivity could put one at a different kind of disadvantage. Among the overtones produced by a tone are frequencies representing octave, third and fifth intervals. Under certain conditions, these are discernable to the "average" ear (Bernstein, 1976). These might be even more evident in one with exceptional acuity. If so, they could also bias or enrich the resulting perception in certain ways, rendering it in some respects more complex (and possibly more structured) than the original.

Thus, the two most general types of models of AP make different predictions about what types of bias one might find in chord analysis. One suggests a possible reducing of the original by limiting report to the chroma categories present, whereas the other suggests, if anything, an expansion or embellishment reflecting the acoustic complexity of a chord. Charness et al. (1988) have recently reported results consistent with the prediction of the category model. The savant J.L., given a series of complex 4-note chords to reproduce, was equally facile with dissonant and familiar chords. However, his renditions of chords more often than not omitted the repeated note when an octave interval was present as part of the original chord. Chord inversions were also quite common in the renditions provided by J.L. (Charness, personal communication, 1987). Revesz (1925/1970) reports a different response by Nyiregyhazi in a similar experiment. The young pianist often added notes in his renditions of the more complex chords heard; most often these were octave doubling or tripling of notes in the original. Occasionally, and particularly for dissonant chords, additional half step modulations were present in the rendition.

The next experiment was designed to examine Eddie's ability to decompose chords. Four-note chords were adopted from among those used by Charness, et al. (1988) and included two types; either they were consistent with traditional harmonic rules or they consisted of unconventional combinations from within the same octave range. Several kinds of comparison subjects were tested. Five subjects from the pitch naming experiment (D.W., C.N., and M.B., B.A., and K.L.) who demonstrated superior pitch naming comprised an absolute pitch group. A second group included four additional adult pianists from the pitch naming experiment; two with good relative but no absolute pitch, and two with some pitch naming skill. Finally, three normal children chosen by their teachers as "having a good ear", but not perfect pitch, also participated. The absence of AP in these children was ascertained in pretesting. These children were a bit older than Eddie and had been taking lessons for a little longer than he had when the experiment was conducted. How would these different kinds of subjects respond to the chord decomposition task?

Twenty-four 4-note chords were taken from those constructed by Charness, et al. (1988). Chords were either conventional or unconventional. Among the former were major and minor tonic triads with the tonic repeated on a different octave, and dominant and supertonic seventh chords. Unconventional chords altered nonduplicated notes of conventional chords by a semitone, with the restriction that this would not result in another conventional chord. This procedure equated for pitch span across the two sets of chords. Stimuli were recorded using the Ivory Ebony voice of the Yamaha DX-21 synthesizer and a Sanyo tape deck. Chord duration was 3 seconds and chord type (conventional vs. unconventional) was randomly varied across the 24 trials. Subjects were instructed to listen to the recording of the chord and were asked to give their most accurate rendition of the chord at its conclusion, using the same keyboard and voicing used in producing the original stimuli. For Eddie and the other multiply handicapped subjects, a simple "listen and play" constituted the instructions. Subjects' protocols were recorded using a Commodore 64 computer, a musical instrument-digital interface and a "Dr. T." keyboard sequence software program in conjunction with the Yamaha keyboard. This system is capable of recording to disk up to 8 keyboard events (e.g., notes) simultaneously in real time with a temporal resolution of approximately 20 msec. with the timing parameters chosen. These protocols subsequently furnished the data for formal analysis.

Two measures were taken from subjects' protocols: the number of notes correctly matched for each chord and the time taken to arrive at a chord match. The latter of the two was defined as the average interval (in seconds) between the first note sounded after the chord was heard and the final chord produced by the subject as his match for the trial. This response characteristic reflected the extent to which subjects tried several different note combinations on a given trial before arriving at a choice of a chord match. Summary

TABLE 3.2
Single Chord Reproductions: Recall Accuracy and Latency

	"Extended" AP Group						Others					
							Adults				Children		
Unconventional	Eddie	DW	CN	MB	BA	KL	PM	GJ	HH	RS	VK	BK	KJ
Chords													
Mean*	3.5	3.8	3.8	3.6	3.8	3.3	1.8	1.2	1.9	1.8	1.4	1.2	1.3
Median*	4.	4.	4.	4.	4.	3.5	2.	1.	2.	2.	2.	1.	1.
Latency**	.3	.3	0	0	0	2.6	1.9	5.0	6.7	.5	1.4	.6	1.5
Conventional													
Chords													
Mean	3.9	3.9	3.9	4.0	3.8	3.3	1.7	1.2	2.2	1.4	2.1	1.1	2.1
Median	4.	4.	4.	4.	4.	4.	2.	1.	2.	2.	2.	1.	2.
Latency	.1	.1	0	0	0	3.8	3.2	2.6	5.2	.1	2.0	.6	1.2

*Maximum score = 4
**Seconds

results for each measure are shown in Table 3.2. The average number of correctly recalled notes by subjects with superior pitch naming abilities stands in marked contrast to that of the remaining participants. The task proved to be extremely difficult for those without extended absolute pitch. Assuming subjects produce roughly the same number of notes in the rendition as were in the original, chance performance is roughly one note correct per trial. Only 3 of the 7 comparison subjects consistently exceeded this. An even more dramatic difference is seen in the number of perfect matches (all 4 notes correct) observed in each subject; for the subjects with absolute pitch these were common, whereas for the other subjects, perfect matches were almost nonexistent. These differences in accuracy were accompanied by differences in the speed with which choices were made. On all but a few trials, all but one of the subjects with AP made a single choice, at the first opportunity after the chord was heard. (The mechanics of the recording procedure meant this was a second or two.) For the remaining subjects, this kind of response was rare in everyone but R.S.

Several response patterns were observed in those not making an immediate choice. Most of the children and the adults with no evidence of absolute pitch would tentatively try a few chord combinations and then settle on the one which seemed the best match to what they had heard. For the children, this meant at most one or two chords, with a final choice arrived at relatively quickly. The adults gave many more variations between the given chord and their final choice, hence the longer reaction time. K.L. and P.M. showed distinctive styles of approaching the task. K.L. performed quickly and flawlessly on the pitch naming task, but was much more tentative in reproducing the chords.

Her approach was to sound individual notes of the chord, rather than chord combinations. This note-by-note analysis was usually quite close to the original, but the notes in combination were rarely reproduced except as her final choice. Consequently, like the other AP subjects, she generated fewer alternative chords than the RP subjects. I asked K.L. after the session whether she was trying to find or use the given names of the notes in her chord analysis strategy. She replied that she was not conscious of naming either individual notes or chords (diminished seventh, etc.) only that she was trying to match "the sounds in her head." P.M., whose response latencies generally fell between the "absolute pitch" subjects and the others, reported varying her strategy across trials. At times, the composition of the chord seemed more evident and her choice was (relatively) quickly made. At other times, she tried to deduce the nature of the chord from a series of possibilities. This more involved strategy often proved ineffective, with no matched notes being generated in the final choice. Consequently, for P.M., the speed of making a match was negatively correlated with accuracy ($-.63$, $p < .05$). For the remaining subjects without absolute pitch, accuracy and decision time were not significantly correlated. Finally, R.S., who had also shown some limited pitch naming ability, usually responded with a single choice, in a manner similar to the AP group, but his accuracy resembled the other RP participants. In post-test discussion of the task, R.S. said he decided to "go with his intuition" rather than to try any specific strategy. Recall that a conflict between intuition and strategy had evidently caused considerable conflict for R.S. in the identification of pure tones. Intuition here proved unreliable, however, as R.S. reproduced only 3 of the 24 chords accurately.

Conventional and unconventional chords differed little on the two general measures of performance, accuracy being slightly greater and latencies shorter for the conventional chords. Only for 2 of the children, V.K. and K.J., did the difference in accuracy for the two chord types approach significance ($p < .10$). To a certain extent, this may reflect the nature of the chord set generated by the procedure. Most of the unconventional chords consisted of diminished or augmented sevenths, and while they are less common than chords in the conventional set, they were not noticeably dissonant by contemporary musical standards. Four of the chords in the unconventional set contained half step intervals (e.g., C and B or C and C sharp) and were not major sevenths, and these could be considered dissonant by most criteria. Subjects' renditions of these 4 chords were interesting. The adjacent half step was reproduced accurately by the absolute pitch group on 19 of the 24 occasions. However, among the other subjects a correctly reproduced half step interval was found only once. This was not due to any disinclination to produce dissonant (i.e., half step) intervals on their part. These intervals appeared in their renditions, but they were incorrect. These results indicate that pitch naming ability enables one to decompose even strongly dissonant chords.

Most of the chords (20 of the 24) featured 2 notes repeated one octave apart, the most usual construction being an octave with 2 internal notes specifying the nature of the chord (conventional or unconventional). Were the participants particularly sensitive to these redundancies in the chords they heard? Given the high levels of performance found in the AP group, it was not surprising to find they detected this redundancy almost all of the time. By contrast, the octave interval was replicated only 7 times across the 80 trials by the remaining adult subjects. Among the comparison RP children, the octave interval was only reproduced 3 times, all by the subject K.J. Thus, for the RP subjects, performance for the octaves was, if anything, worse than their general level of accuracy and indicates the redundancy certainly did not make their task any easier.

Finally, subjects' responses were examined for additional harmonic enrichment or embellishment. Did they tend to add or replace notes as suggested by the overtones of the notes actually sounded? Octave embellishments or transpositions were evident in two cases. Subject K.J., the only RP child who detected the presence of octaves, was also the only subject who frequently added octaves in her rendition, adding them on 9 of the 24 trials. Interestingly, K.J. was the only comparison subject whose training had been primarily by the Suzuki method. C.N. presented a consistent example of transposition, playing all of his renditions one octave higher but leaving the given interval relationships of the original intact.

Trials on which the fifth of the repeated (i.e., octave spanning) note appeared in a rendition, but not in the original, were also rare. Eddie added a fifth on 2 of the 10 trials where this might be expected, B.A. and B.M. on one. Neither D.W. or C.N. produced a "missing fifth." Adding the fifth of the note repeated at the octave was also relatively rare among the comparison subjects: (10 of the 40 trials across the adults, very rarely in the children).

In summary, subjects with absolute pitch usually played only 4 notes for each response and these notes preserved the specific pitch values as well as the chroma of the original (except for C.N. who preserved chroma, but not pitch). The comparison subjects tended to underestimate the number of notes heard and showed very little sensitivity to octave information. The omission of octaves by RP subjects and their recognition by the AP subjects is contrary to what was anticipated by the category models of AP, but is consistent with the notion that those with AP have superior discrimination in addition to chroma identification skills. However, this superior discrimination by the AP subjects did not extend to including harmonics of the notes sounded in their renditions.

Perception of Mistuned Intervals

Ward and Burns (1982) suggested it may be possible to find situations in which absolute pitch interferes with or obscures a perceptual judgment. One candidate for such an effect is interval estimation, identifying the number of (half) steps between two notes, independent of the notes' identities. Consider an interval of two pitches where each pitch is slightly mistuned away from its center frequency, for example, a slightly flat C and a slightly sharp E. If these sounds are coded only by their categorical referents, C and E, the interval would be perceived as a major third, even when the frequency difference of the two notes may correspond more closely to an interval of a fourth. On the other hand, a subject with good relative, but no absolute pitch would attend to the frequency difference rather than the chroma, concluding (correctly) that the interval was actually closer to a fourth. In this respect, his perception would be more accurate than that of the possessor of AP. This prediction is probably more compatible with "internal standard" than discriminative skill conceptions of AP. In fact, if AP is manifested primarily by superior discrimination, one would expect AP subjects to be superior even on mistuned intervals. A brief experiment examined whether subjects with absolute pitch might bias their perceptions of intervals when these are mistuned in certain ways. Four examples of mistuned intervals were generated on the synthesizer using the pure tone (sinusoid) wave form. In two of the examples the difference between the two notes of a major third (e.g., C4, E4) was increased by lowering the lower of the two frequencies (e.g., C) by 40 cents and by raising the higher frequency (e.g., E) by 40 cents. (The difference between the center or prototypic frequencies of any 2 adjacent notes on the chromatic scale is 100 cents, so those frequencies remain closer to C and E than to their chromatic neighbors B and F). In the other two examples of mistuned intervals, the lower note was raised and the higher note lowered by 40 cents. These manipulations render the intervals closer to a fourth or a minor third than a major third in terms of the frequency difference between the two notes. However, each frequency remains just within the range of that usually assigned to the originally specified note. Would these intervals be perceived as major thirds or as fourths and minor thirds?

The 4 mistuned intervals were recorded and added to a series of 10 control trials, representing (pure tone) intervals of a major second to a fourth. The various intervals were presented in a random order on the equipment described previously and the responses were recorded for subsequent analysis. Four subjects with AP for both pure and piano tones comprised one group while 4 adult pianists with no demonstrated AP served as the comparison group. The results were relatively straightforward. The 4 AP subjects reproduced each of the mistuned intervals in terms of the frequency difference rather than the closest note centers (16 of the 16 trials). Identifying the interval rather than the notes was also more frequent among the comparison subjects, though they were not so consistent (11 of 16 trials). Comparison subjects were also less accurate on the control trials (26 of 32 correct) than were the AP subjects (32 of 32 correct). The experiment is obviously limited with respect to both stimulus and response sampling. Still, there is not even a hint that AP sub-jects are less accurate than comparison subjects in frequency discrimination.

Discussion

The patterns of performance exhibited by the different AP subjects varied little, yet as a group, they were distinctively different from those with RP. Wide differences in performance between AP and RP subjects have been found previously (e.g., Corso, 1957). However, it is important to remember that the present sample of AP subjects varied considerably in age, musical training, and level of general intellectual functioning. The consistency of their results against this variability in background strongly argues for absolute pitch as a distinctive skill with several important consequences for music perception. Moreover, the results suggest it is important to distinguish between "secure" or generalized absolute pitch and partial or context dependent absolute pitch. P.M. and R.S. had "statistically" significant pitch naming skill, but were in-distinguishable from the RP subjects on the chord analysis task. (Though it is possible they might have performed much better on the home ground of their own instruments). Only the subjects with secure absolute pitch gave quick, accurate and confident judgments across the tasks presented. The speed and confidence with which young Erwin Nyiregyhazi rendered complex chords also impressed Revesz (1925/1970). "Erwin's verdicts were given immediately without reflection and with perfect confidence. One characteristic of the boy's performance was that during these experiments he always smiled in a superior manner, the tasks put before him being so easy to him that he did not take them seriously" (p. 75). The results of the chord recall experiment suggest ab-solute pitch naming skill goes considerably beyond the identification of isolated pitches. Disentangling sound complexes becomes a relatively easy task as well. The coincidence of these skills in the present sample strongly implicates ab-solute pitch mechanisms in chord analysis skills of the sort shown by musical savants.

The results were less discriminating with respect to the various models of absolute pitch mechanisms, particularly the categorical versus acuity models of superior pitch naming (Siegel, 1972). It was hypothesized that the pattern of errors exhibited by the AP subjects might help decide between these alter-native views of AP skill. Thus, omitting duplicated octave notes would in-dicate the relative salience of chroma (name) over pitch information, as sug-gested by category models. In addition, the salience of chroma would lead to bias in the perception of mistuned intervals. On the other hand, chord embellishment was seen as a possible consequence of a special sensitivity to the frequency information provided by the harmonics of the notes actually presented. In fact, neither chord reduction nor embellishment was seen in the AP subjects. They were more sensitive than the comparison subjects to both chromatic and frequency information, and accuracy was generally so high that model differentiation was not possible.

The sound generating system may have been less than ideal for generating embellished responses. Harmonic overtones are probably less marked on electronic than acoustic instruments and more complex sound patterns may be necessary to elicit differential error patterns. Also, the models are not mutually exclusive, of course, and it is likely some mixture of superior pitch discrimination and pitch naming skill is at work when chord analysis is required. It is also possible that different characteristics associated with AP operate as an individual difference factor, chroma categorization being primary for some subjects, tonality and/or frequency analysis being central for others. This is suggested by J.L.'s (Charness et al., 1988) apparent octave omissions and chord rearrangements, and the general transposition of all chords by C.N. in contrast to the high degree of literal accuracy seen in the remaining AP subjects. B.A., in fact, asked early in the task whether it was important to conserve the register of the original. C. N. may similarly have considered the register to be optional information. We will return to some of these questions in the next chapter when we examine a more demanding chord recall task.

Interviews with the more verbal AP and RP subjects attempted to determine whether there was something singular about their perception of notes. The results are suggestive. None of the subjects reported a particularly rich or consistent color association to specific notes or keys, though other associations were common. B.A. tended to see notes and note clusters as they would be on a musical score. M.B. had very strong likes and dislikes regarding different key signatures, and noted that key signature was one of the things he noted upon hearing a piece of music. P.M. associated certain textures—dense, simple, rich,—with different notes when her pitch naming seemed secure. However, for the most part, these various associations were secondary to note determination. No one described a particularly rich image laden complex that necessarily accompanied or facilitated name retrieval. Rather, note identity seemed to come first, associations following, if they occurred at all. No one reported paying special attention to the harmonics of a note, though several said they sometimes confused a note with its fifth, a prominent harmonic. For the RP subjects, of course, note identity was not present, so specific note associations were not likely. Specific key preferences or associations of the sort suggested by M.B. were also not in evidence, although there were general associations to "types" of music, for example, major versus minor mode. In summary, the admittedly sketchy introspective evidence suggests AP subjects may have richer or more varied associations to individual notes, but these occur secondary to chroma identification.

Setting aside for the present the question of mechanism, what is the advantage of having absolute pitch? The studies described earlier (Bachem, 1954, Siegel, 1974) revealed marked advantages in long-term pitch memory for those with AP, but the task, comparing single pitches over long periods of time, seems pretty far removed from the complexities of processing music. However, given the present results, it is easy to see how AP, at least the "extended" type, might confer a strong advantage to one in a variety of musical contexts. Firstly, an extended AP ability is equivalent to having a general purpose classifying system, one less bound by the specific peculiarities of an acoustic environment. This would enable one to extract certain important invariant information across musical contexts. Thus, the C played by a trumpet is recognized as the same fundamental chroma as the C played on the piano. The C of one octave is related to the C of the next, and so on. If, in addition, the musical system of one's environment builds upon these commonalities across instruments and octaves (Bernstein, 1976), absolute pitch confers an important classification tool to those trying to make some sense out of their musical environment.

Secondly, the "internal" musical environment might be considerably enhanced as a consequence of having absolute pitch. We shall return to this issue again in the final chapter, for the present noting only that such things as the strong color associations reported among those with AP suggest a kind of richness to the auditory images of AP possessors. Bachem (1948) for example, speaks of the brilliance and vibrancy of musical sounds to him. Such associations as color, brilliance, or texture, though apparently not central to chroma identification itself, may serve to fix musical events more firmly in a rich associative memory. The importance of such associations in long-term memory has been demonstrated often. Finally, a more specific advantage of absolute pitch might be key determination. Hearing a segment from a piece of music, one might be able to deduce the key in which it was written. Knowing key identity could, in turn, aid memory by restricting the range of pitches one is likely to hear. Given the structure of traditional (diatonic) music, knowing something is in C major, for example, means that, among other things, "black key" notes are much less likely to occur in a piece. Evidence of such key finding appeared early in Eddie's musical training. Some time after he learned the names of individual notes, he was introduced to the names of the major and minor scales. Soon thereafter, he began to play a game with his music teacher and me, sounding different major and minor (tonic) chords and asking us to identify them and then identifying chords that we played. (Of course, lacking AP, we had to cheat a bit and actually look at the chord he was playing). Given AP and the key "names", the abstraction of key information seemed a relatively easy task for Eddie. Studies by Terhardt (Terhardt & Seewann, 1983; Terhardt & Ward, 1982) provide formal documentation of key finding ability in those with absolute pitch. In one study, musicians heard either the original or transposed versions of the opening bars from each of 12 selections from J. S. Bach's *Well-Tempered Clavier, Volume 1*. Those musicians with absolute pitch were very accurate in determining whether the key heard was identical to the original, those without absolute pitch much less so. Key determination was above chance levels for almost all subjects, indicating that some degree of aural key determination is not restricted to those with absolute pitch. It is unclear whether key identification is a primary factor in identifying and remembering notes for those with AP. Corliss (1973) reports that the key of a group of notes is not a primary characteristic of her perception; rather the individual chroma of the notes themselves are salient. In contrast, for the composer Scriabin (Myers, 1915), the color link between a note and the color of tonality (key structure) apparently was immediate and intense. There was no evidence of a "tonality" or "key structure" effect in any of the AP subjects; their performance on conventional and unconventional material was essentially indistinguishable. B.A. remarked after the experiment that the conventional chords seemed easier and were readily identified. However, key identity did not seem to occur as a primary impression; rather the identity of the notes was paramount in her perception. Like the rest of the AP subjects her performance on the conventional and unconventional chords was virtually identical. Still, the link between chroma perception (i.e., notes) and tonality may well be highly variable across possessors of AP.

An additional clue to the special advantage enjoyed by the AP subjects comes from interviews with the other subjects at the conclusion of the task. As noted earlier, these subjects engaged in a "search and compare" strategy, generating chord patterns on the keyboard and then comparing them to their memory of what was heard. The notes generated by this procedure tended to interfere with the memory of those in the original chord, respondents sometimes exclaiming in the middle of a trial "now I've lost it completely!" These subjects reported that generating some possible chords on the piano seemed to be the only way they could locate or identify the chord they had heard, yet in doing so, they were destroying the very memory they were trying to describe.

In many respects, this seems most akin to forgetting new telephone numbers, addresses, and the like on the way to dialing them or writing them down. Such retroactive interference in memory has been extensively researched and documented (Postman & Underwood, 1973), and is most likely implicated in the difficulties encountered by the participants with limited pitch naming skills in the chord duplication study. If the comparison to the problem of remembering telephone numbers is apt, it means that for subjects with absolute pitch, the situation is considerably more complicated than just having ready names for the notes one hears. After all, the names (i.e., the numbers and/or letters) are provided in telephone numbers, yet we still manage to forget them. What seems to be important is that the information we have just encountered, be it numbers or notes, must generate some stable representation in more permanent memory. The struggle for accurate recall was usually lost by those without AP because a stable long-term representation of the chord had not been established. The note names (or name equivalents—it is extremely unlikely the AP subjects were actually using note names in any literal sense) available to AP subjects implicate some representation of music in long-term memory which provides a ready match to auditory signals (i.e., frequency information). Consequently, the interference caused by conflicting approximations was avoided. One subject volunteered her own version of a fading short-term auditory trace in describing what happened. Shortly after hearing the chord, the sound pattern was clear in her head, but as soon as she started playing possible alternatives, it became weaker and eventually merged with what she was playing, according to her report. This would seem to indicate that a long-term memory or memory transfer skill rather than a special acuity is at work in successful chord recall.

There are several puzzles here, however. First, what kind of long-term memory representation is implicated by the presence of absolute pitch? Does it necessarily have anything to do with musical talent, or with music, for that matter? A large majority of professional musicians do not have absolute pitch; in fact, one can imagine it could be a disadvantage in ensemble playing under certain circumstances. Clearly, stable and sophisticated representations of music are possible without absolute pitch. If it is not a necessary component of sophisticated musical sensibility, is it sufficient? This is a bit more difficult to answer because it involves uncovering negative instances, people with absolute pitch and no special musical interests or skills. Such cases have been mentioned (e.g., Corliss, 1973), but they have received little detailed study.

It may be of some help to know more about the origins of absolute pitch mechanisms in development. Unfortunately, here too the picture is not very clear. There is some evidence of a genetic factor, in that absolute pitch skills often appear in certain families (Bachem, 1955). There is also evidence for a developmental factor, in that musicians whose musical training was begun at earlier ages are much more likely to have absolute pitch (Sergeant, 1969). One theory suggests that something like absolute pitch is the norm at very early stages of development, being replaced by relative pitch in most people (Brady, 1970). There is very little strong empirical evidence bearing on the issue. However, if this is the case, it suggests the relation between special pitch sensitivity and growing musical awareness would be a fruitful area for empirical research. We shall return to some of the developmental aspects of absolute pitch in the final chapter.

It is apparent that relating chord analysis to special long-term memory representations introduces many questions involving linkages between the original appearance or registration of music and its final representation or encoding as a stable memory. It is difficult to think of a task that does not involve memory in some fashion and it should come as no surprise that even such a simple task as reproducing a chord implicates memory in an important way. We turn next to some musical analogues of more traditional procedures for studying memory.

4 | Short-Term Memory

Was the superior performance on the chord reproduction task by Eddie and the others simply a demonstration of their excellent memory? On the face of it, it doesn't seem likely. The chords were not meant to exceed the subjects' immediate memory capacity. Estimates of immediate or short-term memory vary somewhat, but it is usually assumed to be about 7 items or so for adults (Miller, 1956). The 4-note chords were well within this limit. A simple, informal demonstration with several of the subjects without absolute pitch indicated that the number of notes involved did not exceed memory capacity. When shown the chords as printed notes on a musical score, they had no difficulty in recalling them after little more than a glance. No, the problem appeared to be auditory analysis and identification; disentangling the sound complexities of the chord as auditorally presented and assigning the appropriate labels to the fundamental frequencies heard. Indeed, the subjects without absolute pitch often could not even "disentangle" the chords successfully, consistently erring in their estimation of the number of notes actually presented. On one level, at least, the problem (and the advantage for those with absolute pitch) seemed to be a perceptual one. Discriminating and identifying certain characteristics of the (auditory) perceptual array certainly qualifies as a task implicating some basic perceptual processes (Gibson, 1969).

This attribution of chord identification success to "perceptual" rather than "memory" factors is too facile, of course. For one thing, there are the reports of the subjects themselves—the "fading away" effect felt when they tried to provide a rendition of the chord presented. That disappearance of the sound

65

image as well as the strong interference experienced when they produced incorrect attempts at a match strongly implicate memory mechanisms. There is also an empirical reason for suspecting important contributions of memory to the performance by the savants. Their quick and accurate recall of material upon a single hearing is commented upon so frequently in case descriptions of savants, it is almost a defining characteristic. It has undoubtedly contributed to the notion that the musical savant is like a human tape recorder, capable of recording and reproducing musical material in a phenomenal, albeit automatic manner. It would seem reasonable to expect that such an exceptional memory would play some role in any (musical) task given a musical savant. In fact, there is evidence these remarkable "automatic" memory skills may extend to other areas as well (Anastasi & Levee, 1960; Viscott, 1970). Finally, some models of absolute pitch posit the availability of long-term memory representations of pitch (e.g., pitch name information) as central to absolute pitch skill (Siegel, 1974). Given that absolute pitch skill was the discriminating factor in chord analysis, these long-term mechanisms are thereby implicated. In other words, it is likely various kinds of memory were involved in the single chord reproduction task.

The experiments to be described in this chapter represent an attempt to study some of these memory processes in a more traditional fashion. The tasks used were essentially adaptations of the standard short-term or immediate memory format using item recall as the primary measure of memory skill. The task has a long history as a memory assessment vehicle (Wechsler, 1974) and as a subject of considerable experimental analysis (e.g., Dempster, 1981). It also has the advantage of a simple format. Items to be remembered are given at a standard rate and the subject is instructed to recall what had been presented at the end of the list. This format lends itself nicely to the listen-and-play procedure necessitated by the limited language skills of Eddie and some of the other savants who participated. The task also has a certain degree of face validity to it in that it resembles the situation in which savants allegedly excel; listening to and then immediately recalling material. As noted earlier (Chapter 1) there is considerable evidence that musical as well as mathematical savants do quite well on one standard form of the short-term or immediate memory task, digit span.

What kind of performance might one expect of savants on musical forms of the immediate memory task? Different conceptions of the nature of savant skill yield different predictions. On the one hand, if savant skill is exemplified by a particular kind of rote memory capacity or large item span for the fundamental elements of music, notes, one would expect savants to excel generally, whenever musical notes are the items to be recalled. Within very broad constraints, one would not expect the savant to be particularly sensitive to the nature or structure of the material heard. Just as a tape recorder is oblivious to what it is recording, the savants' recordings would be content and context independent. If they reflect the operation of a high fidelity copier and the copier is turned on, the accuracy should be limited only by some fundamental capacity constraints of the memory system. Traditional models of immediate memory span tend to assume that differences in recall reflect such hard-wired or fundamental content-free constraints on memory (c.f., Dempster, 1981).

There was much in Eddie's behavior, even in those first sessions, to suggest this model was not very appropriate. He quickly turned my repeated renditions of "Twinkle Twinkle Little Star" into something a bit different (and certainly more "original") than the original. To the extent Eddie and other savants are something other than faithful copiers, they should show considerable sensitivity to the constraints or structure present in the strings of notes they hear. Hence, a primary function of these tasks was to examine sensitivity to various types of musical structure in the savants' short-term memory performance and the fundamental question was how this selective sensitivity might be expressed by systematic patterns in subjects' responses.

Chord Span

The foregoing suggests a relatively straightforward way to discover some of the savants' limitations in remembering complex chords; simply increase the number and complexity of the chords to be repeated on any given trial. Although increasing the number of chords is a self-evident way of increasing task difficulty, complexity is not so clear cut. One could increase the number of notes in a chord, manipulate the relations among notes within the chord, or manipulate the relations among the chords in a given sequence or chordal cadence.

In a further study of J.L.'s capacity for reproducing chords, Charness, et al. (1988) chose the second and third of these ways of making the task more complex for their savant. Chordal sets contained 2, 3, or 4 four-note chords. Within each set, three different types of chordal cadences were constructed. A conventional set contained sequences of 4-note conventional chords constructed as in the earlier set, and consistent with respect to key signature (e.g., the tonic and dominant triads of a given key with octave repetition of the root might constitute a conventional two-chord sequence). Unrelated sets similarly contained conventionally constructed 4-note chords, but within a chord sequence the chords were not closely related with respect to key or cadence pattern. Thus, for example, a 2-chord set might contain a tonic seventh in the key of C followed by a tonic triad in D minor. Finally, unconventional chord sets contained sequences of 4-note chords whose composition followed no conventional rules, either with respect to individual chord content or cadence pattern, although these chords did remain within the same pitch range as the other sets.

J.L.'s performance on these chord sequences was revealing. Capacity limitation became clear as the sequence increased to 4 chords, the longest sequences rarely being reproduced accurately. Moreover, the nature of the chords and their patterning exerted a significant effect upon recall. Conventional chords were recalled quite accurately, whereas unconventional chords elicited very low levels of performance, particularly for the longer chord sequences. Considered in conjunction with J.L.'s performance on single chords, the importance of chord structure was seen to emerge as the memory demands of the situation increased. Surprisingly, key consistency was of little importance, performance for the conventional chords presented within a changing key structure being not significantly different from those presented in a more orthodox fashion. In other words, chords had to be well-structured units, but the overall structure of the cadence itself was not particularly important.

As Charness, et al. (1988) remark, these results clearly indicate important constraints on the chordal reproduction skills of their savant, J.L. His exceptional memory was limited to chords composed according to conventional rules. In order to determine whether similar constraints would appear in the chordal reproduction performance of the absolute pitch subjects described in the previous chapter, they were asked to reproduce sets of chords adapted from those constructed by Charness, et al. (1988) and given in a similar fashion.

Sets of 24 chord sequence trials were assembled from the stimuli constructed by Charness, et al. (1988). Each set contained two examples of 2-, 3-, and 4-chord sequences containing either conventional chord-key consistent sequences, conventional chord-key inconsistent sequences or unconventional chords. Six single chords, 3 conventional and 3 unconventional, completed the 24-trial set. As in the Charness, et al. (1988) procedure, chords were sounded for approximately 1 second, with a 1/2 second inter-stimulus interval. Instructions were to listen to the chordal sequence and play it at its conclusion. Chord sequence length was randomized within each set of 24 trials rather than blocked as in Charness, et al. (1988). Subjects included, in addition to Eddie, the adult subjects previously found to have extended pitch naming abilities, P.M. who had shown significant, but inconsistent pitch naming, and the savant C.A. (Comer, 1985). Eddie was given 4 different 24 trial sets, for a total of 96 trials, while the remaining subjects were given only two 24-trial sets. All stimuli were tape recorded using the (Ivory Ebony) piano voicing on the synthesizer. Responses were made on the same synthesizer and recorded to disk using the previously mentioned procedures.

The procedures used in scoring the single chords were applied to the multiple chord sequences. Respondents occasionally produced a different number of chords than in the original or appeared to change the order in their rendition. When there was not a clear correspondence between the chords given and those played, each chord in the rendition was compared to each in the original. The trial was then scored using the optimal original-rendition matching.

Figures 4.1 to 4.8 show individual performance profiles as set size increased for each of the three types of chord sequences. Figure 4.9 represents the per-

Chord Sequence Accuracy as a Function of Length (L) and Structure (ST)

CR: CONVENTIONAL RELATED

CU: CONVENTIONAL UNRELATED

UN: UNCONVENTIONAL

:Two Chords

:Three Chords

:Four Chords

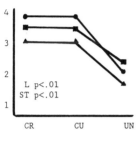

FIGURE 4.1. Eddie

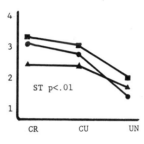

FIGURE 4.2. N.Y.

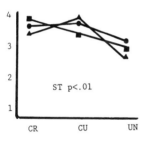

FIGURE 4.3. D.W.

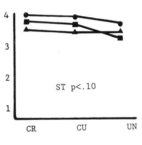

FIGURE 4.4. C.N.

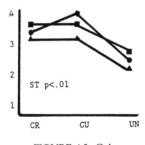

FIGURE 4.5. C.A.

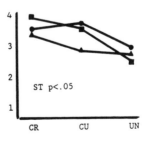

FIGURE 4.6. B.A.

69

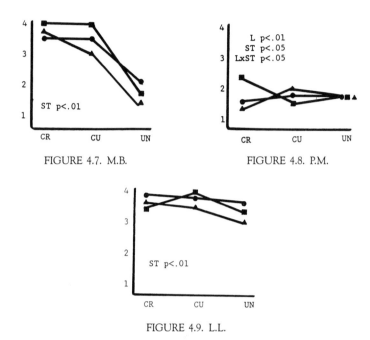

FIGURE 4.7. M.B.   FIGURE 4.8. P.M.

FIGURE 4.9. L.L.

formance of the savant L.L., who was assessed using the same recording equipment, but with chord set size blocked, as in Charness, et al. (1988) rather
than randomized, as with the other subjects. L.L. was also given more trials
than any of the other subjects (60 single chords and 36 of set size 2, 3, and
4). The data for each subject were submitted to a 3×3 analysis of variance
with structure (conventional related, conventional unrelated, and unconventional) and set size as the factors. Because the single chords were not strictly
orthogonal with the other sets, these were considered separately. Differences
associated with set size were further examined with trend analysis, whereas
structural effects were analyzed by means of individual contrasts. These contrasts compared performance on the conventional chords in a consistent key
with the chords drawn from different keys and then with the unconventional
chords.

The results of these analyses revealed remarkable consistency across all of
the adults with extended absolute pitch. In each case, sequence length exerted a minimal influence on accuracy, and stimulus structure emerged as an
important factor in performance. Furthermore, the differences among the
various structured conditions were restricted to comparisons with the unconventional chord settings, which were less accurately repeated than the other
sequences in all subjects. The remaining adult subject attempting the task,
P.M., did so with some hesitation. Her temerity was understandable, given
the additional dimensions of difficulty that were added to the basic chord
decomposing task. Her renditions were marginally better than chance, in that

decomposing task. Her renditions were marginally better than chance, in that she matched between 1 and 1.5 notes per chord. Her general low level of performance suggests the significance levels associated with the various conditions in her case should be treated cautiously. They certainly don't suggest an easily understood pattern of responding to the task. This was reflected in her behavior during the session. Whereas the other adults almost invariably repeated the chords in the order heard (inversions or rearrangements of the chord order were detected on only 5 of the multiple chord trials for the other adult subjects), P.M.'s renditions more often violated chord order than not. This most likely reflected her basic strategy of trying to pick one salient or recognizable chord in the sequence and then working forward and/or back in the sequence from that point. As with the single chords, the interference caused by generating examples led to playing "best guesses" on P.M.'s part. (P.M. was a very game participant in this respect. When I put this task to several of the other adults with relative pitch, they simply replied it was impossible). Generally speaking then, for the adults, the advantage seen in the analysis of chords presented singly extended to chord sequences, with little deterioration of performance for sequences up to four chords. In contrast to the single chords presented in the earlier study, however, chord structure now exhibited a significant effect, unconventional chords eliciting significantly lower levels of performance. It is important to note at this point that the conventional/unconventional difference appeared to extend to the single control or comparison chords presented amongst the various chord sequences. The relatively few trials devoted to single chord presentation prevented their analysis separately for each subject. However, combining the single chord data across subjects, B.A., M.B., D.W., C.N., and Eddie, all of whom participated in the earlier single chord study, formal analysis indicated a significant difference between the two chord types ($\bar{x}$ conventional $= 3.8$, $\bar{x}$ unconventional $= 2.9$, $t = 3.2$, $p < .01$) when they were presented interspersed with the various sequences. L.L., who like the savant J.L. (Charness, et al., 1988) and the subjects in the earlier study received the single chords as a blocked set, showed no difference between the conventional and unconventional single chords. Evidently presenting the single unconventional chords in a mixed trial format made them particularly difficult to disentangle.

Eddie was similar to the other adults in showing sensitivity to the structural differences among the various chords in the chord sequence task. Also, like the adults, the difference was between the conventional and unconventional chords. In contrast to the adults, a marked effect of length was found for Eddie, a significant linear decrease in performance occurring as set size increased from 2 to 4. The only other subject who showed strong evidence of length effects was the 11-year-old K.L. Recall that K.L. also has extended pitch naming skill, and she performed well on the single chord task (Chapter 3), although it took a bit longer for her to make her response. When confronted with the mixed chords task, however, K.L. was overwhelmed, and the series was discontinued after only 12 trials. Her performance on those 12 trials was quite different from that of P.M., who also had considerable difficulty with the chord task. Like P.M., K.L. concentrated on getting one of the chords correct and then going on from there. Unlike P.M., however, K.L. was considerably more successful, getting at least 3 of the 4 notes in one of the chords right on each of the 12 trials. She was unable to recall much beyond the single chord successfully, and consequently, overall her performance was quite low. P.M., in contrast, tended to generate responses correctly reflecting only 1 or 2 notes from each of the chords. Thus, in a sense, K.L.'s performance was length dependent like Eddie's, but even more so. The nonhandicapped young adults M.B. and B.A. showed no effect of list length, but a profound efffect of structure, essentially responding like the adult musical savants. These varying patterns of performance suggest a developmental dimension to the effects of chord sequence length but not chord structure in the chords presented.

Although the performance of Eddie and the other AP subjects was certainly remarkable, errors were now common in some of the conditions. Several different patterns were indicated in the examination of these errors. Recall that in the earlier single chord study, one characteristic that distinguished the AP subjects from the others was their sensitivity to octave information. AP subjects rarely missed notes repeated at an octave interval while non-AP subjects rarely reported them. Table 4.1 presents information about missed and added octave information for all who completed the chord sequence task except P.M., who recalled no octaves correctly. The number of missed and recalled octaves varies across subjects since both Eddie and L.L. had more extended sets than the remaining subjects. Several findings emerged in these data. First, octave omissions were considerably more common that in the earlier single chords. Second, they were much more frequent in the unconventional chords than in the other 2 chord sets. In fact, the decrement in octave reproduction observed across subjects in the unconventional chord condition almost exactly paralleled the general decrease in performance found for the unconventional chords (Figures 4.1 to 4.9). In other words, octave information was not spared in the recall of unconventional material; it apparently suffered the same fate as the nonrepeated notes. This did not mean, however, that the particular chroma represented by the repeated note was lost. Rather, subjects tended to report only one of the two values which occurred in a given chord. Finally, some marked individual differences became apparent. Disregarding P.M., who also failed to recognize repeated notes in the earlier study, subjects varied considerably in this sensitivity to octave information. C.A., and especially N.Y. more often missed octaves than not, whereas L.L. was close to perfect in his octave recall. L.L.'s performance was unique in another respect. He displayed a strong penchant for adding octave information at every opportunity, doubling, tripling and sometimes quadrupling as many notes as he could of each chord on a trial. This persisted in spite of repeated requests

TABLE 4.1
Reproduction of octave intervals, chord sequence task.

	Conventional Chords			Unconventional Chords		
		Octaves			Octaves	
	Recognized	Missed	Added	Recognized	Missed	Added
Savants						
Eddie	98	25	36	21	23	27
C.A.	34	27	2	2	19	0
N.Y.	11	50	3	0	21	0
C.N.	54	7	5	15	6	7
D.W.	51	10	7	11	10	5
L.L.	166	4	*	62	7	*
Comparison Subjects						
M.B.	53	8	5	5	16	0
B.A.	49	12	5	14	7	4

*L.L. added octave information for at least 1 note of each chord on every trial.

to play the chords exactly as heard. C.A. and N.Y., at the other extreme, exhibited a growing awareness of the presence of octaves during the experimental session. For C.A., this occurred at about trial 16; before that point, only 4 of 33 octaves were reported accurately, thereafter 35 of 60 octaves were recalled. N.Y. noticed the presence of octaves at a somewhat later point. Up to trial 35, only 1 of 69 octaves had been reported, from trial 36 to 48, 11 of 24 octaves were recalled successfully. Eddie fell somewhere between the extremes of L.L., C.A., and N.Y., recognizing the large majority of octaves, but adding quite a few as well. No particular pattern was evident in these additions, though there was a tendency for Eddie to double the root of a chord, if it were not already doubled in the original. L.L.'s octave doubling was so frequent no pattern was discernable. Although individual differences were apparent, they were not linked to the savant/comparison distinction. M.B. had considerable difficulty picking up octave information in the unconventional chords, a characteristic he shares with the savants C.A. and N.Y. B.A.'s performance was very similar to the savant C.N. in the pattern of octave omissions and additions.

The other interval examined was the note a perfect fifth above the note value specified by the octave, for example, the note G given the presence of a repeated C already in the chord. As noted earlier, the frequencies associated with such pitches are strongly implied in the harmonic overtones produced when a note is struck. In principle, of course, it is possible to examine the whole family of intervals implied in the series of harmonic overtones (octave, fifth, fourth, etc.). The absence of any strong "fifth" effects in the earlier single chord study indicated that more exhaustive analysis would not be very productive. That was also the reason that analysis was confined to chords with

TABLE 4.2
Reproduction of intervals of a fifth, chord sequence task.

| | Conventional Chords | | Unconventional Chords | | |
| | Fifths | | | Fifths | |
	Recalled	Missed	Recalled	Missed	Added/not added
Savants					
Eddie	99	26	11	5	10/18
C.A.	54	7	3	2	4/12
N.Y.	48	13	3	2	6/10
D.W.	55	6	4	1	1/15
C.N.	58	3	5	0	2/14
L.L.	163	7	18	0	8/45
Comparisons					
M.B.	59	2	5	0	4/12
B.A.	55	6	4	1	2/14

a repeated note rather than all chords having an interval of a fifth. Table 4.2 presents these data, but before examining them a few words of clarification may be in order. For the conventional chords, the fifth was present when another note was repeated in all but one instance. Hence, the question reduces to the number of these pitches correctly recalled. For the unconventional chords, on the other hand, the departure from conventionality was accomplished by moving one of the inner notes of the chord, often the fifth, up or down a half step. In these chords, then, the fifth may be implied by the repeated note, but it is not actually present. Thus, the entries under the unconventional chord section acknowledge this discrepancy. The recalled and missed columns represent those fifths actually present. The added column represents the number of times the fifth was added and not added where it was strongly implied but not actually present in the chord.

How did the subjects fare in recalling these notes? Quite well, it turns out. Collapsing across both conventional and unconventional chords, every subject fared better in recalling the fifth for these chords than in recalling the octave information. For some, like Eddie and L.L., the difference is quite small while for C.A. and N.Y. the difference is substantial. The improved performance for the fifth is especially apparent in the unconventional chords where accuracy (over all subjects) increased from 53% for the octave to 85% for the fifth. It is also apparent that the majority of the unconventional chords with octaves did not contain the fifth as well. Several of the subjects, particularly Eddie, showed a tendency to put the fifth in his rendition anyway; on 35% of these occasions, he supplied the missing fifth. Note that, once again, the adult savants are not distinguished from the adult comparison subjects in any particular fashion.

The earlier discussion of responses to single chords (Chapter 3) attempted to distinguish between two conceptions of the processes at work in absolute pitch. One emphasized chroma categories as a basis of pitch processing, and the other suggested a highly developed sensitivity to frequency information in a more general sense. The results of these patterns of errors on the chord sequences bear on this issue. Recall that a point of divergence in the two models concerned responding to pitch complexes, one model suggesting these might be reduced to the essential chroma in the complex, the other pointing to pitch embellishment as a possible consequence of the additional (harmonic) frequency information available in pitch complexes. The results of the foregoing error analysis suggest the importance of chroma rather than frequency in complex chord discrimination. This is indicated by the relative absence of chord embellishment on the part of all subjects except L.L. Moreover, increasing task difficulty resulted in octave omissions, particularly in some subjects. Even strongly implied notes, such as the missing fifths of unconventional chords, were infrequently included in subjects' responses. Taken together, these results suggest chroma determination rather than frequency discrimination occurs as the core feature in absolute pitch processing.

The analysis of the performance on the intervals of the octave and the fifth provides some insight into what exactly was so difficult about the unconventional chords. Apparently, they did not hang together well as a musical unit. Thus, on the one hand the redundancy represented by the repeated note was often not acknowledged in the subjects' renditions, and on the other hand, the fifth was not reliably present in the original. This contrasts with the

TABLE 4.3
Chord sequence task: Analysis of serial position

	Conventional Chords				Unconventional Chords				I-O*	F-L*
	First	Middle	Last	(N)	First	Middle	Last	(N)		
Savants										
Eddie	2.6	2.7	2.8	(22)	2.6	1.3	2.6	(16)	.05	—
N.Y.	3.3	2.6	2.1	(15)	2.0	1.4	1.7	(8)	—	.05
D.W.	3.9	2.9	3.0	(7)	3.4	2.9	2.2	(8)	—	.01
C.N.	3.8	3.5	2.6	(5)	3.1	3.3	3.7	(8)	—	—
C.A.	3.4	2.8	3.1	(11)	2.5	2.3	2.8	(8)	—	—
L.L.	3.2	3.2	3.5	(18)	3.3	3.2	2.7	(21)	—	—
Comparisons										
M.B.	4.0	3.0	2.6	(9)	2.4	1.7	1.1	(8)	—	.01
B.A.	3.3	2.7	3.0	(9)	2.9	2.5	2.6	(8)	—	(.10)

I-O: Comparison of Inner vs. Outer Chords.
F-L: Comparison of First vs. Last Chords.

conventional chords, where fifth and octave information were very highly correlated. Note too, that the fifth and octave reinforce each other harmonically, because the pitch of the octave is contained in one of the primary overtones of the fifth. One can imagine that in hearing the unconventional chords after presentations of the conventional chords with these interdependencies, subjects may well have noted that some usual element was missing but were not sure how to proceed.

Subjects' errors were also examined to determine their distribution across the various positions in the chord sequence. Typically, subjects in serial short-term memory tasks show differential recall for the various positions in a list, recalling those presented first (a primacy effect) and last (a recency effect) better than those in the middle. These differences are thought to reflect different kinds of interference (or conversely, different kinds of advantages) for various item positions in a sequence (Greene, 1986). Table 4.3 displays position data for all participants in the chord sequence study except P.M. The scores were derived in the following manner. Only 3 and 4 chord sequences in which at least 1 error occurred at one position were considered. For all such chords, the average number of notes recalled correctly was noted for the first, middle and last positions. The results are presented separately for the conventional and unconventional chords. Over subjects and conditions, chords in the outer positions were recalled more accurately than those within and the first chord was recalled more accurately than the last. It is evident, however, that position related effects were much stronger in some subjects than others. These individual differences were formally analyzed by means of T-tests comparing first versus last or outer versus inner chords in a sequence separately for each subject, but combining the conventional and the unconventional chords data. The decision to combine the two types of chords was necessitated by the relatively low number of trials contributing useful data for some of the subjects. These analyses indicated significant primacy effects (superior performance for the earlier chords) in three subjects, N.Y., C.N., and M.B., with a marginal effect in B.A. An examination of the table indicates that these were the only ones showing some degree of consistency across the two types of chords. C.A., for example, appears to show a strong primacy effect for the conventional chords, but this is reversed for the unconventional chords. A similar turnabout occurs with L.L., but in the opposite direction. It's bit difficult to tell what, (if anything) these reversals mean. In any case, all of the adults stand in contrast to Eddie who showed no evidence of primacy effects in either chord set. Eddie did, however, show a significant advantage for the outer as compared to the inner chords of the set, the effect resulting from an especially large difference for the unconventional chords.

In summary, the results of the chord sequence study confirmed in broad outline those of Charness, et al. (1988) with the savant J.L. Like the subject

J.L., participants in the present study were able to handle sequences of complex chords quite well, as long as the chords followed conventional rules in their construction. As chords began to depart from these conventions, however, performance deteriorated to near chance levels in some subjects and conditions. The results failed to replicate the interaction between chord structure and chord length in the savant reported by Charness, et al., however. Rather, the effects of chord sequence length were independent of chord structure, or more often, simply not significant. Several factors may be responsible for this discrepancy. First of all, the scoring procedure used by Charness, et al. differed somewhat from that used here. Charness, et al. scored chord sequences as a unit and consequently did not consider a chord sequence correct unless all chords within it were reproduced accurately. On the other hand, octave deletions were not counted as errors, since they preserved the chroma of the original. Table 4.4 presents the number of correct trials for each of the subjects using these criteria. With this procedure, the effects of list length become more marked; now there is a decrease of at least 40% from set size 2 to 4 across chord type for all subjects except M.B. Perhaps the most comparable subject to Charness, et al.'s J.L. is L.L., who received the same number of chords under the same general conditions. L.L. now shows a strong length as well as structure effect, though the evidence for an interaction between these factors does not seem particularly strong.

Going back over subjects' responses, it is easy to see how the two scoring procedures, one concentrating on correct notes and the other on correct chord sequences, would yield differing views of the subjects' performance. Eddie's performance changed markedly for the 4 chord sequences; chords were sometimes deleted and the order rearranged. For the adults the effects of length were usually more subtle, a few notes being omitted in some of the longer renditions. This difference in performance is reflected in scores that credit

TABLE 4.4
Number of correct responses, chord sequence task,
Charness et al. (1988) scoring procedure.

	Conventional Related			Unrelated			Unconventional		
	2	3	4	2	3	4	2	3	4
Savants									
Eddie	7/8	5/8	2/8	6/8	5/8	2/8	2/8	0/8	0/8
C.A.	3/4	4/4	2/4	4/4	3/4	1/4	0/4	0/4	0/4
N.Y.	3/4	3/4	0/4	2/4	3/4	1/4	0/4	0/4	0/4
C.N.	4/4	3/4	2/4	4/4	3/4	4/4	3/4	1/4	0/4
D.W.	3/4	3/4	2/4	4/4	2/4	3/4	1/4	1/4	0/4
L.L.	11/12	9/12	6/11	8/12	8/12	6/12	7/12	3/12	3/12
Comparisons									
M.B.	2/4	2/4	3/4	2/4	4/4	1/4	0/4	0/4	0/4
B.A.	2/4	3/4	1/4	4/4	2/4	1/4	1/4	0/4	0/4

partially correct answers, and so the length effects remain marked for Eddie while becoming much less so for the other subjects. (Note that even with the Charness, et al. (1988) scoring procedure, the length effect still seems stronger in Eddie than in the other participants.) Whether the partial credit procedure reveals a more accurate picture of some of the individual differences in subjects' performance is probably moot. However, the evidence does fit with our perception that Eddie is becoming more adept at handling longer musical passages as he develops musically (c.f., Appendix A).

Whatever the scoring procedure, it is clear that chordal structure had a profound influence on performance for all subjects. There are several issues to be addressed here. Why were unconventional chords now so difficult to process whereas in the earlier study subjects seemed quite adept at processing unconventional material? Second, why was chord sequence not particularly important? Why were subjects so sensitive to the relations among the notes within the chord while not being sensitive to the relations among chords within a sequence?

We have already suggested one of the factors at work in making the unconventional chords so hard to remember. Not coincidentally, the operations that made the chords unconventional also altered their harmonic integrity. Octaves were still present in a chord, for example, but they did not frame a set of mutually reinforcing internal intervals. Consequently, in addition to the dissonance associated with the frequent half-step intervals in the unconventional chords, strongly implied intervals such as the fifth were not present. The fact that such factors were apparently operating means that chordal decomposition for these subjects is not merely a matter of individual chroma analysis and classification. Some understanding or use of harmonic structure is also implicated in these differences. How is it then that these differences were not apparent in the earlier study (Chapter 3) where the listener also had to disentangle harmonically confusing material? The increased difficulty associated with increasing list length undoubtedly challenged the processing capacity of subjects more than in the earlier study, and the speed or efficiency with which the more regular and well-formed chords could be classified may have played a role in their superior recall. However, latency data from the earlier experiment did not indicate that subjects were processing the conventional chords any faster than the unconventional chords. Note too that for even the single chords in the present study, conventional and unconventional chords now elicited significantly different accuracy. However, this difference was not accompanied by a difference in the speed with which subjects reached their decision on the single conventional and unconventional chords (for subjects Eddie, N.Y., C.N., M.B., and B.A., conventional $\overline{X}$ .15 seconds, unconventional $\overline{X}$ .28, $t = 1.3$), the latencies remaining very short.

It is likely the difference between conventional and unconventional chords in the sequence study was caused by the change in the experimental layout. When subjects were presented single chords, conventional and unconventional chords were equally likely and the subject had the task of attending to a single event and then duplicating it. In the chord sequence experiment, on the other hand, conventional chords were more frequent than unconventional chords by roughly a 2-to-1 ratio, and in addition, subjects did not know in advance how many chords were going to be heard. The presence of influential or salient conditions in mixed designs often can have the effect of inducing a strategy that is more appropriate for some conditions than others. In the present case, this might mean adopting a general strategy geared to optimizing performance on the more readily encoded trials. The behavior of L.L. during the trials indicated he was quite aware of the variety occurring across trials. When the unconventional material was played, L.L. tended to chuckle or smile to himself, acknowledging, it seemed, that these were "trick" trials. Perhaps not coincidentally, his performance on the unconventional chords was by far the best of any subject seen. (One should remember that L.L. did not have the additional problem of trial length to contend with. That is, all trials in a block contained the same number of chords, and this may have made it possible to concentrate more on chord structure itself.)

In any event, although the effects of chord structure were certainly robust, there was not even a hint that subjects were affected by the overall tonal or key consistency of the chord groups. If, as we have argued, the savants appeared to be quite sensitive to tonal integrity within chords, why was it that integrity across chords was of little consequence? One possibility is that the unrelated chord sequences did not represent such radical modulations of musical conventions after all. In fact, the nature of tonality and key relatedness severely restricts the extent to which any series of well-formed chords is completely unrelated. For example, one may begin with a chord in a certain key and then move to a distantly related key (for example, from C to A^b), but then the choice of a third chord necessarily involves some greater degree of tonal relatedness since it will be less than maximally discrepant from at least one of the first two chords. There may be a certain amount of built-in or inevitable tonality in the 3- and 4-chord sequences, assuming the chords themselves are not random note clusters. In fact, the rules about what should follow what in chordal cadences are often relaxed considerably in contemporary music (Bernstein, 1976).

It is also possible that sequences were simply not long enough to allow tonal coherence to emerge as an important factor. Usually the tonality or primary key of a traditional piece is established within the first few measures (Krumhansl & Schmuckler, 1986). However, often even musically sophisticated subjects show some delays in recognizing evolving tonal centers in chord sequences (Krumhansl & Kessler, 1982). Perhaps simply extending the chord sequence a bit would begin to reveal some key relatedness effects. Bharucha and Krumhansl (1983) have reported data consistent with this notion. In their study, listeners were asked to compare 7 chord sequences, which could either represent a conventional cadence in a given key or which were drawn at random from different keys. Recognition memory was strongly affected by the key coherence of the cadence; coherent cadences were compared more successfully than unrelated chords. Comparing chord sequences is quite different from reproducing them and probably favors factors enhancing the chord sequence as a unit. Thus, the nature of the task rather than sequence length may have been responsible for the emergence of key consistency as a factor in their study. The role of key consistency in performance deserves further study.

A less prosaic explanation for the relative unimportance of overall tonal structure is suggested by some recent research by Chase and Ericcson (1981; Ericcson, 1985). These authors have examined exceptional recall for long strings of numbers presented like the chords here, as a short-term memory task in which subjects have to recall the string directly upon its conclusion. Expert recallers tend to package essentially homogenous strings into groups of 3 or 4 numbers, and it is these packets that become important retrieving units in subsequent recall, the relation among packets being at a different level of organization than the relations among the numbers within a unit. For example, subjects' report protocols indicated pauses in recall were more likely to occur at unit boundaries than within a unit (Ericcson, 1985). Possibly we inadvertently provided similar packets to our subjects in the form of 4-note groups, and as long as these groups were well-formed, additional structure was not particularly important. In other words, it may be that the 3 or 4-note group represented by the chords constituted a useful basic unit for storage and that such factors as overall tonality only become important for larger, more structurally complex sequences. This interpretation also suggests another reason for the difference between conventional and unconventional chords. Perhaps the problem with the unconventional chords was that, among other things, since they did not hang together very well musically, they did not present a convenient or familiar unit for organized retrieval.

Melody Span

Probably the closest musical analogy to traditional short-term memory tests (e.g., digit span) is a melody span test, where strings of single notes are given the subject. After hearing a string or "list" of a specified length, the listener simply has to repeat the string as presented. A gradual increase in melody string length provides parametric information about one's "melody span." Variation in list or note string structure provides a means of determining the listener's sensitivity to stimulus structure.

This general format was chosen in the first attempt to assess Eddie's short-term memory. Melodic lines were constructed from notes taken from a single octave (e.g., C4 to C5) on the piano. These melodic lines were constrained or structured in several ways. One constraint involved which notes could in fact appear. From the 12 notes possible in a given octave, 3 constraining diatonic scales were adopted. A conventional major or Ionian scale used notes specified by the interval relationships defining the major scale. A Lydian scale was used for a second set of strings. This scale takes the fourth scale degree of its corresponding major as its tonic, resulting in a set of 7 chroma as in the major scale, but with a different pattern of interval relationships among the various notes. The third set consisted of 7 chroma drawn at random from the 12 notes possible. Note that this constraint limits the number of alternatives possible at any given point to fewer than in the standard digit span task (i.e., any of 7 notes could appear in a given position versus any of 9 digits in a standard digit span task). In this respect, one might expect the musical memory task to be a bit easier. However, this greater ease depends upon being able to perceive the constraint operating in the strings. Would Eddie show evidence of sensitivity to this constraint by limiting his choices to the scale implied by the notes heard?

A second constraint was the probability that a given note in the chosen scale would be presented. In weighted strings, the first, second, third, and fifth degree values were given twice the weighting of the remaining values in determining eligibility for selection at a given string position. For the unweighted strings, all degrees within a defined scale could occur with an equal probability. A final nonmanipulated constraint in all passages was that no two successive notes within a line could be separated by more than 3 scale degrees.

The manipulated constraints, scale type and note weighting, represent sources of structure common in Western musical form. The major or Ionian scale is the most frequent diatonic mode while the use of the Lydian scale is relatively rare. However, these scales use essentially the same general pattern of interval relationships among keys; the difference being the assignment of the position of the tonic within the interval pattern. The "random" scale, on the other hand, was intended to have no such structure and consequently corresponds to no familiar pattern. Similarly, the weighting constraint was based on frequency analyses of the various scale degrees in traditional Western music. According to these analyses, the first, second, third, and fifth degrees of the scale occur twice as often as the remaining (Knopoff & Hutchinson, 1983; Youngblood, 1958). Eddie had been exposed to these constraints by virtue of his musical environment. However, his "training" at this point had not included any formal specification of scale, the concept of the tonic, or the like. Thus, any effects observed would indicate the operation of these constraints in an implicit or unconscious fashion.

Details of the procedure may be found in Miller (1987a). Briefly, major, Lydian, and random strings were of four different lengths: 5, 7, 10, or 15 notes. Two complete sets of stimulus materials were constructed, one in which the octave range of the major scale was C4 to C5 and one ranging from A♭3 to A♭4. Thus, the key signature of the major key grouping in the two sets was

C and A^b, respectively. All stimulus strings were produced on an upright piano at a rate of 60 beats per minute and tape-recorded for later presentation. In any single test session, Eddie was asked to listen to and then play the 16 strings constituting the combination of length (5, 7, 10, 15) and weighting for a given scale type. Each trial began with the direction to listen to the tape-recorder and subsequently play what was heard. All responses were tape-recorded for later analysis.

Each performed note string for the 96 trials constituting the complete set was transcribed from the tape and compared note-by-note with the original. Notes were defined as being matches of those in the original using the following criteria. Any 2-note or larger combination in the rendition which matched a two-note combination in the original (in both register and chroma) was defined as a correct match for those notes, as long as they were placed in the appropriate ordinal position of the rendition. In addition, initial or terminal single notes which matched initial or terminal single notes respectively, in the original, were deemed matches.

The chosen procedure for identifying match responses therefore disregarded absolute position in scoring for other than initial and terminal notes. In addition, consistent responses were defined as non-matches which nevertheless were allowable as defined by the key signature or note group used in stimulus construction (disregarding register). Thus, any white key on the piano was deemed consistent with either the C Ionian (major) or F Lydian scale groups, and any black key was defined as inconsistent. For the "random" note strings, the contrived scale was used to define consistent notes, again independent of particular register. Errors, consequently, were defined as any notes not consistent with the context scale. This procedure is a bit different from the usual one in immediate memory assessment, which requires both item identity and position information to be accurate before the answer is deemed correct. A modified procedure was chosen in the hope it would permit a fine-grained analysis of partially correct responses. Also, on some trials Eddie seemed inclined to embellish the given sequence a bit and so renditions were often slightly longer or shorter than the original, (although overall there was very good agreement between the number of notes heard and played). It seemed reasonable to adopt a measure that would not unduly penalize these modifications. Table 4.5 describes Eddie's performance using these scoring criteria.

These data were formally analyzed in a series of analyses of variance with key constraint, length, weighting, and stimulus set (C versus A^b scale as the major key) as the factors. Details of the analysis may be found in Miller (1987a). Looking first at "match" responses, while the number of matches increased with list length, performance for the longer strings was considerable less accurate than for the shorter strings, and rarely were 7 or more matches found on the longer strings. Even the shorter strings were not completely accurate. Only 6 of the 24 5-note and 2 of the 24 7-note strings were reproduced completely accurately. Thus, by conventional criteria, which requires complete

TABLE 4.5
Mean number of responses as a function of string length, construction
and response type, Eddie.

Construction	Response	Length			
		5	7	10	15
Major					
	Match	4.3	4.5	5.4	5.8
	Consis.	1.5	2.1	3.6	5.4
	Error	.1	0	.4	.1
Lydian					
	Match	3.8	4.0	4.8	5.6
	Consis.	1.3	4.8	4.1	7.4
	Error	0	.1	0	.8
Random					
	Match	3.9	2.5	2.6	4.9
	Consis.	1.6	3.6	6.6	7.0
	Error	1.1	1.8	2.8	2.8

accuracy on at least 50% of the trials at a given length, Eddie's note span was somewhat less than 5 items. Examination of performance for the different key constructions indicated Eddie was sensitive to this source of structure in the note strings. Overall, Ionian mode strings were repeated more accurately than Lydian mode strings, which were, in turn, more accurately reproduced than the random strings. The particular scale, C or A^b, was irrelevant in reproduction of the Ionian and Lydian strings. Eddie seemed equally at home in either key.

Eddie's pattern of "consistent" and "error" responses attests in an even more dramatic fashion to his sensitivity to the constraints used in the construction of strings. Recall that these categories represented notes which were admissible (or not) by the scale used in string construction. For the Ionian and Lydian modes, inadmissible notes were negligible. Errors for the random strings were considerably higher, but still indicated some sensitivity to the constraints suggested by the notes heard. Consider a model in which Eddie was able to encode or store a certain portion of the notes accurately, resulting in some match responses, but had to resort to unconstrained or random guessing for the remainder. Given that the scale restrictions reduce the number of alternatives from 12 to 7, one might expect consistency/error ratios in Eddie's nonmatching responses to be about 1.4/1 on the basis of chance alone. In fact, this ratio occurs in a single condition, random scale strings of 5 notes. For all other string lengths and constraint conditions, the ratio is considerably greater. Eddie evidently needed relatively little information to restrict his choice in a fashion consistent with the underlying scale. This distribution of consistent and error responses also argues against the alternative interpretation that Eddie might have been memorizing note names and forgetting their position in the note strings; a kind of jumbled tape recording of what was heard. Such an interpretation requires no scalar knowledge and might be suggested by models of short-term memory which claim encoding of item identity and item position (or order) information represent two separate problems for the subjects (Huttenlocher & Burke, 1976). If Eddie were only storing individual notes, however, one would expect his consistency/error ratios to be greatest for the smallest strings, where note names are more likely to be remembered. If anything, the opposite occurs, consistency/error ratios being higher for the longer strings.

Thus, the general picture that emerged was that Eddie's literal "melody span" was about 5 notes long under these conditions. In addition to encoding specific notes, Eddie was encoding structural information about key or scalar constraints in what he heard. For conventional, even relatively unfamiliar scalar arrangements, this knowledge was gained on the basis of a very small sample of notes. For Ionian and Lydian scales, as few as 5 notes resulted in renditions almost entirely consistent with the implied scale. For random strings, seven notes were sufficient to yield structural constraints in his answers.

In contrast to the scalar constraint, the weighting factor had little effect upon Eddie's recall. Only random scale strings yielded differential performance associated with note weighting, the unweighted random strings yielding particularly high error rates. The relatively minor role of note weighting might have been due to several other characteristics of the note strings that emerged in stimulus construction. Although the note differential of 2:1 was in fact maintained in the weighted strings, the interval constraint (no more than a fourth) meant that third, fourth, and fifth degree positions were more often eligible for a given slot in a string. The weighting constraint also did not consider note placement in a melody, for example, by insuring that the string begin or end on the tonic, which is often the case in conventional melodies. This probably made the melody strings less "melodic" in nature, and the note weighting less useful as a source of information.

Another important source of constraint in music is redundancy or repetition in musical segments. The redundancy need not be a literal repetition of notes, though this often occurs. More usually, the repetition involves transformations of pitch range, rhythm, harmonic accompaniment and the like (Bernstein, 1976). Larger scale patterns of repetition with transformation define many classical forms of music such as the sonata.

It is easy to see how such redundancy could be useful in improving performance on a short-term memory test for melody. Just as detecting recurrent regularities in a number string (e.g. 2468 or 13579) helps one's recall in the traditional short-term memory task (Miller, 1956), noting any regularities in a stream of music should make its retention easier. Formal documentation of redundancy detection in short-term memory for melodies has been provided by Deutsch (1980), who investigated recall of 12-note melody strings embodying different kinds of constraint. Some of the strings were based on repetition with transformation of a 3-note unit, whereas others were based on a 4-note unit. Thus, a highly redundant string might contain a 3-note unit (e.g., C, D, E) repeated 4 times with each triplet transposed to a higher pitch range (e.g., CDEDEFEFGFGA). Adult musicians who heard these materials gave virtually flawless recall of them, providing there was nothing in the stimulus presentation that might interfere with detection of the underlying unit. Would Eddie show a similar degree of sensitivity to this kind of constraint?

In an additional experiment, 4 sets of 12-note strings were constructed. Two of these were constrained or grouped strings, one taken from Deutsch (1980), and one taken from a piano exercise text. Each of the constrained strings contained either 3- or 4-note units, repeated after transposition until the 12-note length was filled. Control strings contained the same 12 notes as the constrained strings, but in no particular order. Both constrained and random sequences were given in a manner similar to that described earlier. Eddie's performance for the structured set (about 75% correct overall) was not quite as good as that for Deutsch's (1980) adult musicians under comparable conditions, but it was far superior to the control, randomly ordered, strings. Eight of the 16 grouped strings were recalled with one or no errors, whereas control random strings elicited levels of performance quite similar to the longer strings of the earlier set. The marked difference between grouped and ungrouped strings indicated Eddie perceived and used the grouping information contained in the nonrandom strings.

Using the grouping information entails discovering two facts about the string, its basic unit or phrase and the rule by which the unit is transposed or changed to complete the 12 items in the string. For 8 of the structured trials, Eddie's near-perfect performance indicated that both types of information had been processed successfully. What about the other eight strings? On five of these, the basic unit never appeared in Eddie's rendition in a form which preserved its original contour and interval pattern. On the remaining 3, the unit was present but the transposition principle was incorrectly portrayed. The former was the more serious error; for these strings, performance was no different from the random strings. In a session several months later, I repeated the 5 strings on which Eddie missed the basic pattern as well as 5 control strings (random strings from the earlier session). Three of the 5 grouped strings were now recalled without error, but no improvement was observed for the random strings.

These results indicate that, in addition to being able to extract scale information (as in the earlier experiment, responses inconsistent with the key of the exemplar were very rare), Eddie recognized repeating elements or redundancies in a manner which allowed greatly increased retention of material. Repeated note strings such as those used in these segments are common "building blocks" in traditional music composition. Bernstein (1976) has described them as the prose elements in the language of music, and it is no accident that they are presented with various transpositions as fundamental exercises for the developing musician. Eddie, of course, had had no such exercises and his response to this structure cannot be attributed to direct teaching. Rather, the redundancy, like the scale information, is inherent in his musical environment and he had become quite adept at noticing it. As we shall see (Chapter 5) he also has a good "working knowledge" of these prose elements, using them freely in his own playing.

Charness, et al. (1988) also report exceptional sensitivity to scale and grouping information in the immediate memory of the savant J.L. using an experimental format quite similar to that used with Eddie. Like Eddie, J.L.'s responses rarely strayed outside of the scale implied by the notes of a given string. J.L. also performed at a much higher level when some grouping principle was operative in the construction of the note array, although in J.L.'s case, the melodic grouping had to be accompanied by temporal segmentation before the performance improved significantly. The importance of the temporal interval suggests that J.L., like Eddie, may have had a bit of a problem discerning the grouping unit; however, once it was discerned, the transposition rule was readily applied. Some of the melodic strings heard by J.L. differed from those heard by Eddie in an additional respect—they were composed using a whole tone scale. This scale is based on the same tonic degree as the corresponding major (E major) but proceeds through the 12 steps of the chromatic scale in whole step intervals (E, F#, G#, A#, C, D, E) rather than by the sequence of whole and half steps which characterizes more conventional diatonic scales. Some of the ramifications of this difference will be dealt with later, but for the present, it is important to note that it is a relatively unfamiliar or uncommon scalar convention in traditional music. J.L., nevertheless, seemed quite at home with the constraints suggested by the whole tone strings because his responses rarely varied from the whole tone set on these trials. That is, like Eddie, J.L. seemed capable of extracting scale information of a fairly unfamiliar sort.

The question remains whether the similarities that characterize J.L.'s and Eddie's melody memory extend to other savants. To obtain information relevant to this issue, a set of strings adopted from that designed by Charness, et al. (1988) was assembled and given to most of the pianists who participated in the single chord analysis study.

The 24 strings of the stimulus set included four examples from each of 5 string lengths, 3, 6, 8, 12 and 16 notes. Two of the strings at each length were composed using the E-major scale and two used the E whole tone scale. Within the 6, 8, 12 and 16 note strings, the two exemplars from each scale either contained a basic group of notes with transposition of this unit completing the sequence as in Deutsch (1980), or a random note sequence. For the 6-note sequence, the grouping unit was 3 notes in length; for the remainder it was 4 notes. All stimulus sequences began on the note E4. Stimulus sequences were recorded using the piano voicing of the synthesizer described earlier and played at a rate of 2 notes per second. The procedure for presenting the stimuli was adapted from that of Charness, et al. (1988). The strings with the shortest lengths were presented first, with string length increasing in a regular fashion. Within each set of four strings at a given length, the particular string type (random or grouped, whole tone or major scale) was randomly determined. Subjects were instructed that they were going to hear melody-like strings of varying lengths and that, upon hearing each string, they should try to duplicate it. Corrections were allowed. For those subjects with limited language, simple listen-and-play instructions were used. Responses were made on the synthesizer with the voicing set to that used in the recording and responses were recorded for later analysis using equipment and the procedures outlined earlier (Chapter 3).

As with the records of the subjects' responses to the chord sets, the responses to the note strings contained any momentary depressions of any key on the synthesizer during the trial. In order to distinguish misplays from intended responses, responses were ignored if they were very brief relative to the remainder of the notes played on a trial. The deletion rule used defined all notes less than 1/3 the duration of the modal duration for a trial as misplays. By this criterion, fewer than 10% of all notes played were ignored in the analysis.

Table 4.6 contains the accuracy data for 11 subjects, the 5 handicapped musical savants, L.L., C.A., D.W., N.Y., and C.N., who all had been given the chord sequence test, and 6 comparison subjects—3 with AP (B.A., M.B., K.L.)

TABLE 4.6
Note strings: Percent correct as a function of string length and construction
(random or grouped).

Savant	6 RAN	GPED	8 RAN	GPED	12 RAN	GPED	16 RAN	GPED
D.W.	100	100	81	100	38	100	31	100
N.Y.	92	92	62	94	58	83	13	44
C.N.	100	100	100	100	46	100	59	100
C.A.	100	100	100	100	96	100	59	100
L.L.	100	100	88	100	79	100	63	100

$\bar{x}$ RAN=60 $\bar{x}$ GPED=95

Comparison	6 RAN	GPED	8 RAN	GPED	12 RAN	GPED	16 RAN	GPED
B.A.	100	100	100	100	75	100	68	81
M.B.	100	100	94	81	38	79	47	88
P.M.	42	50	50	63	42	38	9	34
H.H.	100	100	69	69	46	58	28	100
G.J.	92	92	42	42	38	83	31	75
K.L.	58	89	69	63	46	42	28	53

$\bar{x}$ RAN=52 $\bar{x}$ GPED=82

and 3 with RP (G.J., H.H., P.M.). All of these subjects had also participated in the chord analysis task (Chapter 3). Three children participating in the chord analysis also attempted the melodic short-term memory series (subjects V.K., B.K., and K.J.), but no one completed even the 3-item series with high accuracy and beyond 6 notes very few matches were found, so these subjects were not included in the analysis of correct responses. The means represent averages across the two types of scales (E major and E whole tone) examined at each string length. Preliminary analysis of each subject's correct responses under the 2-scale types revealed a significant difference only for the 11-year-old with AP, K.L. ($t(11) = 2.3$, $p < .05$). A comparison of the scores in the two groups indicates that while the savants generally did better than the comparison subjects on the short-term memory task, there is some overlap in the two groups. Recall that the point at which Eddie recalled at least 50% of the unstructured strings correctly was less than 5 items. As a rough comparison, every member of the savant group except N.Y. reproduced at least one of the two unstructured 8-item strings without error and C.A. reproduced 1 of the 12-item strings flawlessly (making a single error on the other one). Of the comparison subjects, only B.A. and M.B. (both with AP) did as well, with correct responses up to 8 items while G.J., K.L., and H.H. recalled unstructured strings of 6 items. Any conclusions based on these comparisons must be very tentative since they are based on so few trials for each participant. Nevertheless, it seems fair to say these musical savants probably have a higher melody memory span than their nonhandicapped fellow pianists. This was confirmed more formally in an analysis of variance of correct responses with group, length and structure (grouped vs. ungrouped) as the factors. The difference in overall performance of the two groups was significant ($F(1,9) = 8.2$, $p < .05$).

Once again, the presence of absolute pitch obviously made a big difference and it is likely no coincidence that the three comparison subjects who did quite well had absolute pitch. In one respect, the advantage conferred by absolute pitch was neutralized by the structure of the strings. Because each string began on E natural, the starting point was constant and subjects could "solve" the task by remembering the sequence of intervals from that point. The presence of the standard E starting point also introduced a bit of a dilemma. Should participants be told of it or allowed to find it out for themselves? Given that this fact could not be communicated to some of the savants with any assurance that it would be understood, the decision was to remain silent and let the participants find it out for themselves. In the end, this turned out to be not too much of a problem in that within the first few trials, the 3 non-AP subjects "caught on" and began their rendition with an E. The problem was deciding where to go from there.

The possibility of the interval solution to the task by the non-AP subjects should be given serious consideration because, in informal testing, the adults G.J., P.M., and H.H. all showed excellent interval discrimination, being able to name any interval played (within the octave span) with few errors. However, it seems unlikely this skill could be used in the short-term memory task with any great effect. Subjects' recognition of intervals tended to be slow and measured; they more often reflected a moment or two (as they did in the chord decomposition task) before they answered. This doesn't indicate a readily available coding system able to handle the fairly rapid sequence of sounds presented in the serial memory task.

We shall return to this point again shortly. For the moment, returning to the data presented in Table 4.6, it is quite clear that for all subjects, savant and comparison, the presence of note grouping had a strong influence upon accuracy. The structure effect was formally confirmed in the whole sample in the analysis of variance ($F(1,9) = 60.8$, $p < .001$). Like Eddie and the savant J.L. (Charness, et al. 1988), the savants had little difficulty with even very long strings as long as they contained regularity. The comparison subjects, too, were assisted by the presence of structure, particularly at the longer string lengths, and, not surprisingly, there is a significant interaction between string length and structure ($F(3,24) = 9.8$, $p < .001$). Structure did not interact with subject group, however. This means that although savants did better overall than the comparison subjects, they were neither more nor less sensitive to the simple structural grouping available.

Recall that when Eddie's performance on structured strings was discussed earlier, a distinction was made between errors on the grouped strings that appear to reflect failure to abstract the basic grouping unit rather than failure to apply the transposition rule for the unit in a consistent manner. In Eddie's case, the former seemed more of a problem than the latter. An examination of the errors made by the comparison subjects indicated a similar pattern. On 13 of the 22 renditions of structured strings where their performance was less than optimal, the basic grouping unit never was produced. Only N.Y. of the savant group made any errors in any of the grouped trials, so the contrast provided by the savant group is severely restricted. Interestingly, N.Y. seemed to have a different kind of problem. On the grouped trials where some error occurred, the problem seemed to be the transposition rule (4 of 5) rather than the basic unit (1 of 5). With this possible exception then, both the pattern of errors and correct responses suggest the savants and the comparisons reacted in much the same way to the kind of information contained in the structured strings.

The analysis of the melody memory task has up to now been based on a restricted view of what constituted a correct response; whether the subject's rendition matched the original in a particular sequence of chroma. This seems the most straightforward translation of the scoring procedure used in traditional short-term memory tasks. Yet, in a musical sense, melody strings convey other important information. In addition to the specific pitches or notes chosen to construct a melody, most models of melody composition make a distinction between the particular intervals that characterize the succession of notes in a melody and the overall contour or pattern of rising and falling pitches. Thus, "Twinkle, Twinkle, Little Star" is represented by the intervals unison, up perfect fifth, unison, up major second, unison, down major second and by the contour no change, up, no change, up, no change, down. Contour is generally held to be the least complex aspect of melodic structure (Davies, 1978). Developmentally, contours of a melody are reproduced successfully at an earlier age than the specific sequence of intervals it contains (Hargreaves, 1986). Given that the AP subjects extracted the actual pitch categories ("names") with considerable accuracy, accurate interval and contour information is assured because it is contained in the pitch code (assuming the pitch order is preserved and octave substitution doesn't occur). Did the other subjects perhaps retain either contour or interval information even if they could not recall the specific pitches?

We argued earlier that it seemed unlikely the non-AP subjects were approaching the task with any explicit interval recognition and storage strategy. Still, given their excellent interval recognition skills, it is quite possible much more information was present in their responses than was revealed by the note matching criterion. Even the children who were dropped from analysis up to this point probably were able to recall contour information and it would be useful to determine the extent this was so. For several reasons, it was difficult to determine the extent of interval or contour information retained when the specific pitches were not recalled. First, subjects responses rarely contained exactly as many notes as in the original, so a straightforward correspondence in terms of the complete segment was not possible. This means that some melody fragment needed to be used in trying to match the rendition to the original. As already noted, the unit taken from the pitch match analysis was 2 consecutive matched notes. This seemed reasonable under the assumption that given a single correct note, the choice of a succeeding correct note on a chance basis should be 1/12 (because only chroma and not register was considered and note repetitions were possible in the original melodies). Applying an analogous criterion to interval units, two successive matching intervals is roughly equivalent to successive matched notes. However, this criterion does not seem reasonable unless contour is also considered. Thus, a major third followed by a rising major second in the original represented by a major third followed by a falling major second in the rendition intuitively seems a poor match because contour information is not preserved. Changes in contour have profound effects upon perception of melody (Deutsch, 1972; Dowling & Fujitani, 1971) and it seems highly unlikely that interval information is retained with no reference to contour. Thus, measures of interval retention are difficult to make independent of contour. The reverse is not true. The pattern of ups and downs in a melody need not refer to interval at all. Here, however, the size of the unit must again consider the problem of accidental or chance matches. By its nature, contour information is less specific than interval information and it is easier to generate partial matches on the basis of chance. Moreover, melodic contour may refer to several levels of analysis in the strings that were used, pointing to local variations (up, down, up) or to general characteristics (the string generally went up).

With these difficulties in mind, interval and contour evaluations were made as follows. First, two successive intervals which matched (with contour intact) intervals of the original were regarded as a match for those intervals. Contour matches were based upon groups of 3 successive contour events (e.g., up-down-up or same-up-up). Next, each string was evaluated as a complete unit. That is, each of the successive interval changes or set of 3 contour changes within the original also had to be in the rendition in order for it to be scored as a correct response. The measures, therefore, determined whether all of the contour or interval information in the original was represented in the rendition, though not necessarily without repetitions or additions.

The results of this analysis can be summarized fairly quickly. Cases in which a response was correct with respect to interval matching but not correct as to actual notes were very rare. Only three such cases could be detected, one each by M.B. and K.L. (AP subjects) and one by P.M. Importantly, neither of the other adult RP subjects (G.J. & H.H.) ever gave an interval consistent response which was not an accurate pitch match. Thus, there was very little evidence for interval encoding as a distinct strategy in the incorrect responses.

Contour preserving answers presented a different picture. These were quite common when the response was not completely correct with respect to the actual notes of the original. Of 29 responses which contained some pitch error in the savant group, 11 were judged correct as to contour. Twenty-five of 55 cases fell into this category in the comparison sample. An examination of the children whose data were not considered previously indicated that they too were sensitive to contour; of 56 trials that failed to match notes, 30 did match contour. Although the difference between the savants and the other 2 groups was significant ($Z = 2.09$, $p < .05$) this finding should not be overinterpreted. As we shall see shortly, members of the savant group usually made fewer nonmatching responses than those in the other groups. In fact, occasionally their (incorrect) response was shorter than the original. Given that the answer was shorter than the original, it was impossible for it to be considered correct with respect to either contour or interval, since all intervals were not represented. For the comparison subjects, adults and children, on the other hand, longer nonmatching responses gave a greater opportunity for matching contours or intervals to turn up in their renditions. The important point to note is that even the children who were rarely correct did not respond randomly. That contour, but not interval information, did appear indicates that the contour was often readily perceived by all; it was the more specific information regarding interval and chroma sequence that was the problem for the comparison subjects, and particularly the children.

Another way in which subjects could be partially correct involves their adherence to the note values of the scale used in constructing any particular note string. Thus, given that all strings were either composed in the E-major

TABLE 4.7
Summary of consistency scores, note strings.

	E Major			E Whole Tone		
	N	%	Z	N	%	Z
Savants						
D.W.	25	.84	2.65**	27	.78	2.98**
N.Y.	30	.73		65	.69	3.17**
C.N.	11	1.00	2.80**	12	1.00	3.85**
C.A.	4	1.00	a	14	.93	3.58*
L.L.	44	1.00	6.00**	59	1.00	7.14**
		x̄=.89			x̄=.85	
Comparison						
B.A.	6	1.00	a	15	1.00	4.10**
M.B.	34	.79	2.63**	15	.67	
P.M.	106	.68	2.08*	115	.61	
H.H.	36	.86	3.50**	63	.71	2.17**
J.G.	54	.87	4.83**	66	.52	
K.L.	95	.78	4.00**	122	.58	
		x̄=.77			x̄=.60	

*=p<.05 **=p<.01
a=insufficient data

or E-whole tone scale, responses could be consistent with the scale though not providing a match for a particular sequence. Both Deutsch (1982) and Charness, et al. (1988) refer to this as understanding the alphabet of the strings. Deutsch noted that her subjects (adult musicians) gave few responses not consistent with the alphabet of the original in their notations and similarly J.L.'s renditions remained within the alphabet of the original. As we saw earlier, Eddie was also very adept at giving key consistent responses when his answer was not an actual match to the string (c.f., Table 4.5). In Eddie's case, this was perhaps even more impressive in that across trials, the key signature varied more than for J.L. or Deutsch's participants.

Table 4.7 provides comparable data regarding key or "alphabet" consistent responses in the present sample. The analysis examined all non-matching responses on each trial and determined whether they were allowed given the implied key signature of the string. Thus, allowed notes for E major are E, $F^\#$, $G^\#$, A, B, $C^\#$ and $D^\#$, and allowed notes for E whole tone scale are E, $F^\#$, $G^\#$, $A^\#$, C, D. Note that three values are shared as a consequence of a common tonic in the two scales, and that the whole tone scale holds only 6 values while the major scale has 7. The difference in the number of permissible notes means that using a scale note "by chance" varies slightly in the two conditions. This difference was taken into account in calculating whether the conformance of the nonmatching responses to the implicit scale was greater than one would expect on the basis of chance or random matching. The table, therefore, contains the percentage of notes that were key consistent, the number of notes analyzed, and the Z values for the test of significance. Data from the three comparison children, V.K., B.K., and K.J. were also analyzed, and their performance was not above chance.

For those subjects represented, there is strong evidence that each was sensitive to key constraints present in the melody strings. Overall, the savants show greater key-consistent responding than the comparison subjects. This appears to be due to the difficulty the comparison subjects had with the whole-tone strings. For the savants, conformity was almost as great for the whole tone scale as it was for the more conventional E major scale. For the comparison subjects, on the other hand, consistency fell significantly for the E whole-tone scale (Z (E major vs. E whole tone) = 5.0, $p < .01$). Only 2 of the 6 comparison subjects showed evidence of significant key-consistent responding for the whole-tone strings while every savant did so.

One way of interpreting these differences between the savants and the comparison subjects is that they indicate a greater sensitivity on the part of the savants to various musical rules implicit in a musical segment. Perhaps because of their better encoding of the specific chroma values present in a piece, savants are better able to discover some of the rules implicit in the intervals contained in a note string. This would be consistent with the finding that the comparison subjects were fairly adept at recovering contour information about a string, even if they did not match the notes very well. Contour information, while important, is equivocal with respect to key structure, and consequently would not help increase key consistency.

There is a danger in attributing too much implicit rule recognition to the savants on the basis of these data, however. One could turn the argument around and claim that the difference between major and whole-tone scales that one finds in the comparison subjects is also a rule sensitive effect. It shows the extent to which the comparison subjects are reflecting the rules usually operative in their musical environment. In this respect, it is analogous to the rule discovery implied in the grouping effect found in the analysis of correct responses. After all, pieces written entirely in a whole tone scale are quite rare in the musical literature, certainly in comparison to pieces written in the major mode. By this reasoning, the performance of the savants has more of a tape recorder quality, since it doesn't reflect these broader differences in context familiarity.

Part of the problem here is deciding what constitutes reasonable evidence that some more abstract principle is implicated in a subject's performance. For example, a mere repetition of several of the note values heard could yield a very high consistency score, yet intuitively this hardly seems to point to the discovery of key structure. More convincing would be a response that showed rule extension or extrapolation; playing notes which were consistent with the key, but not actually played in the original. These could be extensions in another octave, for example, or better yet, implied notes within the same octave. Such generalized, yet constrained response patterns are usually taken as strong evidence of rule usage. (This same argument does not apply as well to the grouping effect discussed earlier, where rule usage was indicated by successful performance on the grouped, as compared to the ungrouped strings. In that case, the generalization of the rule was implicit in the correct rendering of one kind of array rather than the other). Unfortunately, neither the note array construction nor the data set permits clear resolution of the issue. Within the note arrays, every chroma value was usually presented in the longer strings, where most of the errors were generated, so it was not possible to find notes that were appropriate, but never used. Within the data set, there was rarely evidence of subjects straying beyond the pitch range of the original array, so generalization in this sense was not found. L.L. was a bit of an exception in this regard, because once again he played almost every note in his renditions simultaneously in 4 octaves. (These repetitions were not counted in his consistency score.) Thus, the meaning of the greater consistency in the savant group remains ambiguous. We shall return to the issue of discovering key structure in music again in the next chapter.

Finally, the participant's responses were examined for serial position effects of the sort discussed earlier in the analysis of the chord sequence data. Analysis here was confined to the ungrouped strings. For each string of size 6 or more, correct responses were calculated for the first two, middle two and last two positions, and these constituted the first, middle, and last scores for each string. The relatively few data points for each subject prevented an individual analysis. Instead, the 2 groups were compared in an analysis of variance with group, position and string size as the factors. This analysis revealed significant effects associated with string length ($F(3,27)=12.5$, $p < .01$) and position ($F(2,18)=21.5$, $p < .01$). These effects reflected a decrease in accuracy as length increased and higher accuracy for items at the beginning of the sequence. There was also a significant interaction between length and position ($F(6,54)=5.5$, $p < .01$), reflecting an increasing advantage for items early in the sequence as sequences became longer. The results of this analysis clearly pointed to a "primacy" effect for the melody short-term memory task. Items at the beginning of the sequence were recalled more accurately than those at the end. This primacy effect was a bit stronger in the comparison group, performance falling from 92% to 78% from the first to the last items for savants and from 91% to 59% for the comparison subjects. Examination of individual records revealed its presence in each participant in the melody memory task except C.A. There is a confounded factor contributing to the size of the primacy effect in these data. Because the first note of the trial always began on E, as noted earlier, subjects could have enhanced primacy scores due to their recognition of this consistency. However, the differences in accuracy for the first vs. last notes (.92 vs. .67) was no greater than the difference between the second and next to last (.90 vs. .65). Therefore it is unlikely that the primacy effect is enhanced very much by the use of E as the starting note.

In the earlier study of Eddie's melodic memory (Miller, 1987a), a similarly strong primacy effect was not in evidence. Instead, accuracy was about equivalent for the first items and last items across the arrays. Differences in procedure across studies make formal comparisons difficult, but the results of the earlier study suggest Eddie's sensitivity to the various parts of the strings was perhaps different from the other participants. In an additional session, Eddie was given the note strings of length 4 through 12 used in the present study, using the same procedures as those outlined earlier. Eddie committed one error on the 4-item strings and no errors on the 6-item strings, indicating a "note melody span" similar to the other savants. Performance on the 8 and 12 note strings was considerably less than perfect, but did show the expected grouping effects. Moreover, errors on these trials suggested, if anything, a recency rather than a primacy factor at work in his recall. Accuracy for first, middle and last most items in these arrays was 56%, 63%, and 69%, respectively.

In one of the experiments of the earlier study, Eddie was given melody strings consistent with different major keys and accompanied by various kinds of context (Miller, 1987a, Expt. 2). In one set of trials, the strings were preceded and followed by the major triad of the key used in string construction. In a second set, the context key of these framing chords was quite discrepant from the key of the string itself. Thus, for example, the key of the string might be C major while that of the context chords F$^\sharp$. A third control set of strings contained no context. Originally, it was thought that some benefit would derive from a consistent context. Providing a diatonic context improves recognition memory for individual tones in the sophisticated adult listener (Krumhansl, 1979). In addition, Eddie's tendency to give tonic conclusions to his renditions of simple note strings indicated he considered them less musically finished than they might be. By providing these conclusions in the stimulus array itself, the consistent triads were expected to make the note strings more meaningful. By the same token, providing discrepant or misleading key information was expected to disrupt note processing by interfering with the establishment of a consistent context. Eddie's performance on these strings revealed an unexpected pattern of response under the various conditions. Consistent context did not improve performance relative to the control strings but inconsistent context interfered dramatically with string recall. On many strings with discrepant context, performance was little better than chance. Especially noteworthy, in this respect, was the decrease in Eddie's key consistent responding. Often his response pattern showed no evidence of recognizing the alphabet of the note string.

A subset of these trials was also given to the savants L.L. and C.A. and to comparison AP subject M.B. to determine whether such interference effects were characteristic of savant recall for melody information. This subset contained 36 10-note strings, 12 of each kind; context consistent, context discrepant, and control. The procedures for presentation were essentially those

TABLE 4.8
Mean match, consistent and error scores, context experiment

	Context		
	Absent	*Consistent*	*Misleading*
Eddie			
Match	3.3	3.6	1.4
Consis.	6.5	5.3	3.6
Errors	1.1	.2	3.2
C.A.			
Match	9.3	7.9	6.7
Consis.	.6	4.7	4.8
Errors	—	—	.2
L.L.			
Match	7.4	7.5	5.3
Consis.	2.9	3.1	3.3
Errors	—	—	.4
M.B.			
Match	6.9	6.8	4.9
Consis.	4.7	3.4	4.2
Errors	.5	—	2.0

described in Miller (1987a) with condition of context blocked in sets of 4 trials and counterbalanced across the 36 trials in a Latin square design. Like Eddie, C.A., L.L. and M.B. were virtually flawless in their reproduction of the context chords (L.L. and C.A. dropped an occasional terminal chord). Response to the note string portion of the trial was analyzed as previously, and performance on the strings is summarized in Table 4.8. All three comparison subjects did considerably better than Eddie across all sequences. It appears that all were also adversely affected by the misleading context, but not nearly to the degree that Eddie was. Thus, for L.L. significant differences among conditions were found on the match (note pair identical to the original) but not consistent (nonmatches consistent with the key of the original) scores. For C.A., significant differences among conditions were found for both match and consistent responses. More important, errors, or responses not consistent with the key of the note string were very rare in C.A. and L.L. under the misleading condition, but they were quite common in Eddie. M.B. falls between the extremes of Eddie and C.A. or L.L., showing effects of the misleading chords extending to error responses as well as affecting the match response. The low level of errors in the 3 comparison subjects made comparisons across conditions impractical. Instead, individual t-tests on the error scores were conducted to determine whether these were significantly different from zero. Only 1 of the 9 tests, M.B. on the misleading trials, was significant. Note, however, that the ratio of consistent to error responses by M.B. under the misleading condition is considerably above chance, while in Eddie's case it is not.

In the earlier study (Miller, 1987a), prevalence of errors in Eddie's performance on the misleading context trials was thought to reflect Eddie's dependence on the overall structure of a musical segment. Such an interpretation would be consistent with Bamberger's (1982) notion that early stages of musical precociousness are characterized by a holistic or unarticulated approach toward music. The other participants, in contrast, were able to distinguish the key information represented by the context from that by the strings, responding to the changing key structure in the discrepant trials. Perhaps their superior performance reflected a more sophisticated analytic approach to the problem presented by the ambiguous melody strings.

Recall, however, that similar discrepant key information was given in one of the conditions of the chord sequence experiment (the changing key structure condition), and neither Eddie nor the other musical savants had any problem with changing key information. How is this situation different? Earlier, it was argued that key discrepant chord sequences may have been recalled with such ease because each chord was a harmonically well-integrated unit. Thus, as "packets" of information, the chords may have lent themselves to processing strategies in which relations among chords are irrelevant. Such is not the case with random note strings. As successively presented events, harmonic interactions of the sort experienced within chords are much less pronounced. In addition, the key consistency in the note strings was likely much less constraining than the harmonic regularity of the chords. In other words, the nature of the information in the chord sequence task may have provided a better fit to the particular processing strengths of the savant. The structure of the note sequence did not provide such a match and consequently any additional complication introduced into the task was likely to disturb performance. In Eddie's case, the disturbance was quite profound, extending to the key information itself. It is also significant that the interference observed in the misleading context trials was always asymmetrical. Although there was clear interference with note string recall, there was no indication of the note string affecting the recall of the accompanying chords. The favored position of the chords at the beginning and end of the sequences, no doubt, played a large role in protecting them from interference; their harmonic coherence probably helped too. It may be that Eddie was particularly affected by the salience of this coherence when it was at odds with the intervening information. This coherence likely made the context chords quite salient for Eddie relative to the intervening melody. In other words, in addition to (or instead of) a global processing strategy, attentional effects may have been at the root of Eddie's problem with the discrepant sequences.

In summary, the results of the melody span experiments indicate that savants' superior recall of musical information extends to melodic information, although the differences are not so great as those seen in the chord sequence experiment. Savants' memory for melodies also showed the kind of sensitivity to musical structure that one finds in the mature musician. They effectively used information about key structure and grouping or redundancy in note strings to play more accurate or at least more consistent renditions than the comparison sample.

An important factor in savants' success is again associated with absolute pitch, although in contrast to the chord decomposition tasks this factor is now less critical. Thus, N.Y. with absolute pitch, did not fare particularly well on the melody span test, while H.H., without it, still managed to do quite well. The results, therefore, implicate a wider range of musical factors than those represented in absolute pitch, and suggest the processes at work in encoding and storing melodic information have only partial overlap with those concerned with harmony.

Mention of the patterns of performance exhibited by N.Y. and H.H. emphasizes the fact that there was considerable individual variation among subjects within each group on the melody span task. The performance of Eddie was quite distinctive in this respect. He outperformed most of the other children by a wide margin, and even surpassed K.L., who also had absolute pitch and is 3 years older. Eddie appeared to be particularly adept at extracting key and grouping structure in the music he heard. His performance was distinctive in other ways. As in the chord sequence experiment, Eddie showed some evidence of a position or location bias different from the other savants. For the others, items near the beginning of the sequence were recalled most accurately; for Eddie, this tendency was reversed. Finally, Eddie seemed affected more by the overall tonality of the pieces heard. This was suggested by his performance on the note strings with discrepant context, where in contrast to the others, Eddie found it very difficult to separate the tonal information implied in the context from that of the string itself. One obvious explanation for this difference is some factor associated with the ages of the participants. We will discuss possible developmental factors behind these differences at the conclusion of the chapter.

Memory for Temporal Patterns

Musical events take place over time and any attempt at a comprehensive description of musical skill must consider the role of this temporal context. Temporal aspects of music are usually distinguished as to beat, meter, tempo, and rhythm. Beat refers to the underlying pulse of a melody. Meter represents a format for signifying the number of standard beats in a recurring temporal interval (measure) and the relative note duration of a single beat (half note or minim, quarter note or crotchet, etc.) within this framework. This information is clearly fundamental to describing what the underlying temporal structure of a piece might be, although complex temporal patterns are described by conventional meter only with considerable difficulty, if at all (Davies, 1978). Tempo refers to the overall speed or rate at which the basic meter is applied and hence characterizes the temporal dynamics of a piece. Tempo variation also has a profound impact upon the way music is performed and understood by the listener. Many a popular song has undergone a revitalization in a new rendition which drastically changes the tempo of the original.

Knowing both the meter and tempo still leaves much unstated about the actual temporal patterns in a piece of music, however. For one thing, these patterns may be congruent with the meter in only a few cases. Also, important temporal patterns may extend considerably beyond the basic temporal units represented by the metric and measure aspects (Davies, 1978). Rhythm is the term usually used to characterize these more complex, multifaceted aspects of temporal structure. The complexity of these aspects is undoubtedly one reason for some disagreement regarding a definition of rhythm. Nevertheless, there is general agreement that it is the overall pattern in the succession of events that specifies the rhythmic component. Davies (1978) suggested this patterning essentially is imposed by the listener. For Fraisse (1982), too, the ordered characteristic of succession is the core element of rhythm. Dowling & Harwood (1986) noted that rhythmic patterns are extended in time, yet recurrent, and hence capable of eliciting expectancies on the part of the listener.

In any case, while the accurate perception of beat and tempo are interesting problems in themselves (e.g., Wang & Salzberg, 1984), it is the understanding of temporal patterning that is usually taken as the central issue in tests of the temporal component of musical aptitude. The rhythm test designed by Bentley (1966) is typical. In it, a single note is sounded in a characteristic pattern spanning an interval of several measures. A second example is then given, and the subject must decide whether the temporal pattern of the second example is identical to that of the first. The critical feature distinguishing the examples in a pair is their temporal pattern rather than tempo or meter.

The role played by rhythm in music varies considerably from culture to culture. Davies (1978) described Western music in the classical tradition as being fairly simple rhythmically, although Dowling and Harwood (1986) suggested this may be more a matter of metric rather than rhythmic simplicity. In any event, this stands in marked contrast to the sophisticated polyrhythms encountered in certain African and Eastern musical traditions. This variability across cultures suggests that the rhythmic dimension in music is to a certain extent independent of other dimensions such as melodic or harmonic. Thus, although quite simple rhythmically (or metrically), traditional Western music is usually held to be quite complex harmonically (Davies, 1978).

There are other reasons for suspecting that rhythm in music might be, to a certain extent, independent of melody or harmony. Developmentally, rhythmic components of music emerge and mature earlier than tonality (Hargreaves, 1986). A different time course for rhythm in development suggests it may be sensitive to a different set of influences. There is also evidence from the neurological literature that structural damage to the cortex may affect rhythm perception while leaving other skills intact. Luria (1966) described patients with severe defects in the perception and reproduction of temporal patterns associated with damage to left auditory secondary association areas, while other aspects of music were relatively intact. Milner (1962) described the complementary situation; patients whose right temporal lobes have been removed. Here severe decrements were found for the tonal and timbre section of the Seashore tests of musical aptitude, while rhythm was much less affected. Evidence from normal, intact adults also supports different loci for rhythmic and melodic aspects of music. For example, rhythmic material is more accurately heard when presented to the right ear, which projects primarily to the left hemisphere (Robinson & Solomon, 1974), whereas melody information is processed better when presented to the left ear (e.g., Borod & Goodglass, 1980) although the effect seems to be complicated considerably by the nature of the task and the musical experience of the subject (Bever, 1983). Perhaps the strongest evidence for the independent nature of rhythmic skill comes from empirical tests of musical aptitude such as the Bentley (1966) or Seashore (1938) mentioned earlier. Bentley (1966) for example, found performance on his rhythm subtest was not significantly correlated with chord analysis skills, although it was correlated with tonal memory.

With these considerations in mind, how well might musical savants be expected to do on rhythmic aspects of musical aptitude? The case histories provide a clue, albeit of a negative sort. Anecdotal descriptions in the cases discussed in Chapter 1 focus on the extraordinary melodic and harmonic retention of their subjects and occasionally on their ability to improvise in different musical styles. An especially highly developed sense of rhythm is rarely mentioned. In fact, in one case, (O'Connell, 1974) a rhythmic sense was evidently lacking. Minogue (1923) remarks that of the various components of musical performance, her case's rhythm was the most affected by emotional fluctuations and hence the most variable. The reasons for little mention of rhythmic skill in the savant are not at all clear. Perhaps, as "tonality's poor relation" (Davies 1978) in most treatments of music, rhythm is just less likely to draw one's attention. Perhaps the lack of rhythmic sophistication in much music makes any difference in rhythmic aptitude less important or apparent.

There may also be something intrinsic to musical savant skill that does not extend to rhythm. This is suggested by the results of the melody and chord memory span tests. In each case, the presence of absolute pitch was implicated as a critical component in superior performance. For the chord sequences, this meant simply that those who did not have absolute pitch could not perform the task. That absolute pitch was necessary but not sufficient was suggested by the failure of K.L., the 11-year-old with AP, on the chord sequences. On the melody task, the differences were not quite so extreme, although the participants with absolute pitch generally were at an advantage. In both of these tasks, having an efficient system for classifying and storing the tonal information must have been very helpful. In an atonal rhythm task, on the other hand, pitch classification is not involved and so exceptional skill in this area would not be relevant. In this sense then, performance on the rhythm test provides a test of the hypothesis that the exceptional skill of the musical savant is limited to pitch-related rather than temporal aspects of musical structure. If it is so limited, they should do no better on tests of rhythmic accuracy than comparison subjects.

From a different perspective, there are reasons for expecting that savants' musical precociousness may extend to rhythmic elements of music. Although it is true that rhythm is dissociable from tonality, as suggested earlier, it is also the case that rhythm and tonality have much in common. A melody without some rhythmic element is almost unknown in our musical environment. Moreover, the rhythmic component makes an important contribution to a tune's identity. Thus, it is reasonable to suppose the melodic sensitivity of a savant might extend to rhythmic aspects as well. In fact, Sloboda (1985) suggested that rhythmic and harmonic components often reinforce each other in musical practice, for example, where elements of the tonic triad appear more often in stressed note positions.

The elements of rhythm and tonality also have some interesting formal correspondences. The elements of rhythm, note durations, or more exactly successive note onset intervals, are organized according to a set of rules. These rules take the continuous dimension of time and subject it to a series of classifying principles which generate the standard subdivisions (eighth note, quarter note, etc.) describing event succession in a composition. However, this classification system is only loosely analogous to that which generates note values (names) from the continuous dimension of pitch. The temporal classification system doesn't have the anchors of the tonal system, for example, and the temporal value of a quarter note depends on meter and tempo. A quarter note can take on an infinite number of actual temporal values, but a designated chroma (e.g., "C") is much more restricted. Whereas the subdivisions represented by tonality have a long history in music, those associated with temporal regularity are likely more recent and occurred with the development of polyphonic music (Sloboda, 1985). Still, both represent the application of a formal rule structure in the organization of auditory input, and as far as tonality is concerned the savant's performance shows considerable sensitivity to those rules. One might note, in this regard, that the primary musical input for almost all savants is auditory rather than visual (i.e., musical scores). There is some evidence (Sink, 1983) that the rhythmic structure of a piece may be more subservient to its melodic structure in auditory presentation, and the regularities of rhythm may therefore be less salient for the savant. To further complicate matters, the neuropsychological evidence could be interpreted to suggest a special deficit in encoding of rhythm among savants. This follows from the evidence presented above that left hemisphere temporal areas are implicated in rhythm perception. These areas also mediate many language functions. Severe disturbance in language functions among savants have suggested to some that left hemisphere structural damage is associated with the syndrome (e.g., Treffert, 1988). It seems reasonable to expect other left hemisphere functions such as rhythm might be impaired as well.

To summarize, the historical descriptions of savants do not indicate any particular talent with respect to the rhythmic aspects of music. Empirical evidence suggests rhythmic development is sensitive to a different set of influences than tonality, although there is also evidence suggesting tonality and rhythm have much in common, particularly in musical practice. Against this background, it is not entirely clear whether one should expect savant skills to extend to rhythmic structure when it is presented independent of tonality. All things considered, it appears savants should be less likely to excel in rhythm.

The assessment of savant rhythmic memory followed a course similar to that in the chord and melody span tests. A set of rhythmic patterns at a common metric setting (4/4) constituted one part of the sessions. These patterns were either 2 or 4 measures in length and incorporated common rhythmic patterns. A second set consisted of randomly determined successive onsets of a tone. This manipulation was seen as roughly analogous to the unconventional chords of the chord series and the ungrouped strings in the melody experiment. The issue of primary interest was how the savants and the comparison subjects would fare on reproducing these patterns. Would the savants no longer excel when tonality was not a major factor in stimulus construction?

Structured rhythmic patterns were adopted from examples provided in Bentley (1966) and in Hilley and Olson (1985). These patterns could be either 2 or 4 measures in length, and were further grouped into two types, those in which the temporal subdivision within the pattern was always by a factor of 2 (e.g., half note, quarter note, eighth note) and those containing both 2:1 and 3:1 subdivisions. Thus, the latter contained such combinations as triplets or dotted eighth notes as well as the more conventional 2:1 combinations. Random sequences were generated in the following manner. Using the temporal range of the structured series, 6 note-duration values were taken from tables of random numbers. These values thereby represented roughly the same degree of temporal variation as in the structured series, but the values represented no regularly divisible system. These values were then used in assembling sequences whose total duration was equivalent to the 2 measure sequences. A total of 12 sequences constituted the set; 4 each of the 2 measure, 4 measure, and random variety. (Appendix C contains specific descriptions of the sequences used). Stimuli were recorded for later presentation using the "Dr. T." composing and editing software and the synthesizer and computer described earlier. The program provides exact control of note onsets and offsets. Stimuli were recorded using the Ivory Ebony voicing of the synthesizer at a tempo of 96 beats/minute and 4/4 meter. Each sequence was sounded using a single note on the synthesizer.

Four different groups of subjects participated in the rhythm task. Three groups, the savant, adult comparison, and child comparison groups, have been described already. The fourth group was comprised of three adult percussion students. All had been studying percussion for at least 4 years and one had some training on the piano (2 years) as well.

Subjects were given the rhythmic patterns using the same general format as that followed for the other tests. All subjects were asked to try to duplicate the rhythmic pattern as precisely as possible. The comparison subjects were also told the specific note they used need not be the same as the original, only the pattern was important. Whether a 2 measure, 4 measure, or irregular pattern occurred on a trial was random. However, each example was presented twice, giving subjects two opportunities to reproduce it.

Analyzing the results of this experiment proved to be quite complicated. Most of the time, the number of notes in the participants' renditions did not match that in the original. Several conventions were adopted to allow evaluation given this basic nonequivalence. First, each rendition was divided in two and each half was considered as corresponding to the first versus the second half of the sequence heard on that particular trial. Each half was then searched for the sequence which represented the best fit to the original, defined as the minimum difference between the varying onsets in the original and in the rendition, summed over all notes. Thus, following Davies (1978), the basic datum was the interval between the onset of one note and the next rather than note duration. Occasionally, a best fit was obtained by assigning all notes played to one half of the original. (For example, in cases where the attempt at a rendition was terminated before completion.) Such cases, therefore, did not follow the rule of separating the rendition into two halves. These cases were quite rare, representing less than 5% of all trials examined.

The objective of this overall scoring procedure was to find the best match available, using as much of the rendition as was possible. It is evident that this approach to scoring trials differs considerably from that used in the chord and note string experiments. Because accuracy in temporal patterning was of primary interest, however, it did not seem reasonable to adopt the smaller subdivisions used in the scoring of the chord and melodic sequences (i.e., single note or pair matches). Thus, the best fit criterion was applied to all summed differences across all intervals within a trial half, rather than to any individual interval.

Two different summary scores were calculated for each trial. An absolute difference score took the absolute (unsigned) difference between each interval in the original and its corresponding interval in the rendition. Mean difference scores were then computed for the first and second half of each trial. The second summary score examined ordinal rather than absolute differences in the intervals heard and those rendered. For this measure, each original temporal pattern was considered in terms of the number of different types of intervals it contained. Thus, a trial containing eighth, quarter, and half notes would have 3 types of intervals while one having, in addition a dotted quarter, would have 4. Values ranking the intervals from shortest to longest on this basis were then assigned. Renditions were similarly rescored in terms of the number of intervals contained in the original. This meant collapsing or combining several different durations within a single rank level because subjects invariably generated a greater variety of intervals in their rendition than were present in the original. (To some extent, this was probably due to the sensitivity of the recording system, which detected small variations in duration.) Intervals in the rendition were collapsed according to an adjacency principle wherein all values at the shortest end of the interval set would be assigned a 1, those at the next level a 2, and so forth, in a manner that yielded the same number of interval types as the original.

Before examining the actual results, a brief discussion of the rationale for using both an absolute difference and a ranked difference score is in order. If, as Davies (1978) has argued, the essential character of a rhythm is its pattern, the actual duration of individual notes in a rendition is of little importance. Rather, their relation to other note durations or intervals is critical. This means a measure reflecting deviation in the ordinal pattern is more appropriate than one reflecting absolute differences. Indeed, ordering, rather than absolute difference measures are more often used in assessing reproductions of rhythmic patterns (e.g., Heimlich, 1975). Given the history of characterizing savant skill as a literal reflection or copy of material, however, a measure that could assess literalness, in addition to one reflecting pattern fidelity, seemed appropriate. Hence, the decision to examine both absolute and rank difference scores.

Missing data, or intervals for which no potential match could be found in the rendition, turned out to be a bit of a problem for some trials and conditions. Table 4.9 gives the percentage of missing data in each type of trial for each of the 4 types of participants in the study. It is clear that data were frequently not complete for the 4-measure condition, particularly for the children. Upon closer inspection, there were some additional individual differences. K.L., the 11-year-old with absolute pitch was distinguished among the children by having a relatively complete data set (only 7% missing in the 4-measure set). In contrast, among the savants, subject D.W. had a missing data profile more typical of the comparison children (60% missing in the 4-measure set). In other respects, the group means give a fair representation of individual performance.

The reasons for the large amounts of missing data were quite apparent in testing. When faced with the very complex 4-measure sequences, the 4 participants with large amounts of missing data balked at the proposal of duplicating the series. (They were naturally not required to do so). The presence of incomplete protocols means considerable caution must be exercised in interpreting the results of the rhythm reproduction task. In one respect, however, the distribution of incomplete protocols across groups is quite informative.

TABLE 4.9
Rhythm task: Percent of intervals omitted in rendition.

Savants		2 measure	4 measure	Irregular
Eddie		.08	.04.	.10
N.Y.		.03	.01	.03
D.W.		.24	.60	.30
C.N.		.08	.15	.13
C.A.		.00	.09	.00
L.L.		.03	.10	.03
	x̄	.07	.16	.10
Comp. Adults				
M.B.		.05	.05	.05
P.M.		.10	.10	.08
J.G.		.03	.23	.03
	x̄	.06	.13	.05
Comp. Children				
K.L.		.00	.06	.03
B.K.		.13	.55	.15
K.V.		.00	.59	.00
K.J.		.08	.63	.15
	x̄	.05	.46	.08
Percussion Students				
D.J.		.03	.23	.05
W.J.		.00	.13	.07
T.S.		.02	.19	.07
	x̄	.02	.18	.06

Eddie and most of the other savants approached the rhythm examples with interest and appeared quite willing to concentrate on reproducing temporal patterns divorced from any melodic component. Their relatively complete protocols suggest they did not consider the requirement to concentrate on rhythm unreasonable.

Missing data were treated in several ways. If more than half the intervals for any trial could not be estimated, the trial was eliminated from further analyses. For the remaining cases, estimates of missing intervals were made by assigning them a value equal to the average of the 3 most discrepant intervals for that particular half of that trial.

The first analyses considered the performance of the savants, comparison adults, children, and percussion students across the 3 types of trials, 2-measure, 4-measure and irregular (or "random"). Additional factors in the analysis included trial number (1 versus 2) and temporal pattern component (first vs. second half of the pattern). In these analyses and those to follow, K.L. was assigned to the adult rather than the child comparison group. This decision was based on her relatively complete data set, her particular interest in rhythm instruments (c.f. Chapter 2) and her similarity to the other adults in the earlier melody memory task. Results of the analysis using the absolute difference score

TABLE 4.10
Mean scores on the rhythm reproduction task

	Absolute Difference			Rank Difference		
	Two Meas	Four Meas	Irregular	Two Meas	Four Meas	Irregular
Group:						
Savant (N=6)	4.8	8.9	7.0	.48	.91	1.20
Adult (N=4)	4.8	8.8	6.2	.44	.85	1.10
Percussion Students (N=3)	3.4	9.0	5.8	.21	.88	.98
Children (N = 3)	7.6	15.0	8.6	.68	1.23	1.37

revealed significant effects associated with group $(F(3,12)=4.0, p < .05)$ trial type $(F(2,24)=28.3, p < .01)$ trial, $(F(1,12)=9.2, p < .01)$ and pattern component (first vs. second half) $(F(1,12)=6.5, p < .01)$. There was also a significant interaction involving trial and group $(F(3,12)=3.8, p < .05)$ and one involving trial type and pattern component $(F(2,24)=6.3, p < .01)$. The equivalent analysis using the rank rather than the absolute difference score yielded only two significant effects, of trial type $(F(2,24)=69.2, p < .01)$ trial $(F(1,2)=8.3, p < .05)$, and pattern component $(F(1,12)=11.6, p < .01)$ the differences among groups being only marginally significant $(p < .10)$.

Table 4.10 contains the mean scores for each of the 4 groups of participants on each of the trial types, presented separately for the absolute difference and rank difference scores. It is clear that the significant group differences on the absolute difference trials arose because of the divergent performance of the children. Using this measure, the comparison adults and savants are virtually identical, whereas the percussion students showed the best overall performance. Contrasts indicated only the difference between the children and the other groups was reliable. When the rank difference score was considered, differences among the groups were ordered in a similar fashion, although they were not as marked. In both the absolute and rank measures, trial type was an important factor in accuracy for all subjects. Either increasing the length from 2 to 4 measures or decreasing the regularity of the sequence made the task of reproducing a sequence much more difficult, and equally so for each group of participants.

Returning to the other results revealed in the formal analyses, although it is not too surprising that participants did significantly better on their second attempt than on the first, the additional interaction of trial and group in the absolute difference score may be of some interest. Essentially, what is reflected was an improvement in performance from the first to the second attempt for the percussion students, comparison adults, and children, but not the savants. Note, however, that all groups improved equally from the first to the second trial according to the rank difference score. Taken together, these results indicate all groups were adept at improving their rendering of the interval ordering, although the savants were less likely to improve literal matching of the durations they had heard. Generally speaking, subjects were better able to reproduce the first half of the patterns than the second, thus showing a sort of primacy effect. In view of Eddie's tendency to show diminished primacy effects in the chord and melody memory experiments, individual differences in primacy/recency were examined in a bit more detail. The relative accuracy of the first (F) versus last (L) half of the array was determined for each subject using the formula F-L/F+L. Most participants showed a primacy effect in this analysis and Eddie was squarely in the middle of the distribution of scores. In contrast to the previous tasks, therefore, Eddie's sensitivity to item position was not particularly distinctive. The interaction involving trial type and pattern component (first half versus last half) reflected higher literal accuracy for the first half of the pattern for the conventional 4-measure and random, but not the conventional 2-measure trials.

The second set of analyses examined the differences between the 2- and 4-measure patterns in more detail. Recall that these trials varied in pattern complexity as well as length. Two trials at each length contained intervals defined by a 2:1 division rule, while the other two trials contained mixed 3:1 and 2:1 patterns. This distinction (2:1 versus mixed 2:1 and 3:1) was therefore entered as a factor in an analysis of variance which also included group (savant, percussion student, adult, and children), trial number (one versus two) and pattern half (first versus second half).

Differences among groups were evident in both the absolute difference $(F(3,12)=4.8, p < .05)$ and rank differences scores $(F(3,12)=4.1, p < .05)$. In each case, the child comparison group did not do as well as any of the other groups, which were not reliably different. The discussion of the other findings revealed by these analyses will be limited to complexity effects because results regarding the other factors are to a large extent redundant with those in the preceding analysis. Complexity (i.e., 2:1 versus 2:1 and 3:1 trial types) emerged as a significant effect in the analysis of both absolute difference $(F(1,12)=21.2, p < .01)$ and rank $(F(1,12)=41.8, p < .01)$ scores. In addition, complexity showed statistically significant interactions with several of the other factors in the analysis. The importance of these interactions is compromised to some degree by the large amount of missing and estimated data in some of the cells of the design. Not surprisingly, the missing data were more likely to be for the longer, more complex examples attempted after a single hearing. It seemed prudent to adopt a more conservative criterion in evaluating these interactions and the criterion of $p < .01$ was chosen. In the absolute difference analyses, significant interactions (i.e., $p < .01$) were found between complexity and pattern component, and among complexity, length and group. These interactions reflected predictable effects of the various difficulty manipulations. Thus, differences between the simple 2:1 and mixed 2:1 and 3:1 sequences tended to be greater for the 2- than the 4-measure sequences, whose length already made them quite difficult. Indeed, for the comparison children, the general difficulty of the 4-measure sequences prevented the emergence of a strong interactive complexity factor for these trials. Second, whether the first or last half of the pattern was reproduced more accurately depended on the particular stimulus sequence. In particular, the mixed 2-measure sequences tended to show a recency effect (better recall of the second half), whereas the remainder of the trial types showed a primacy effect. A look at the structure of the various sequences suggests a reason. The first measure of the mixed 2-measure sequences tended to be more complex rhythmically than the second measure, and so pattern component and difficulty were confounded to some extent.

The mixed trials proved to be very challenging for all subjects. There is considerable empirical evidence to suggest that rhythms representing simple 2:1 temporal divisions are both more common and more easily mastered than those with 3:1 configurations (Fraisse, 1982). Moreover, when given the latter, listeners often modify them in the direction suggested by a 2:1 system. In a further analysis, the presence of such a strategy was detected in a sample of the mixed trial intervals. This analysis was confined to the savants, the percussion students, and the adult comparison group and to the first half of these mixed trials, where data were more often fairly complete. The average signed deviation for the notes representing a triplet, eighth and quarter notes for the mixed trials was examined for each subject, separately for the first and second attempt at each trial type. These notes were chosen because they represent the 3:1 and 2:1 variation roughly matched for trial and location. Across all subjects, the quarter note interval was reproduced most accurately, the savants slightly underestimating its duration, the comparison subjects overestimating it. The groups varied in their treatment of the eighth and triplets, however, the savants being more accurate on the eighth notes, the comparison subjects on the triplets and the percussion students most accurate overall. For the savants, the errors on the triplets were almost invariably in the direction of overestimation, effectively transforming them into regular eighth notes. The results, therefore, suggest a somewhat greater "regularizing" tendency in the direction of the 2:1 metric on the part of the savants.

Overall, however, it is clear that the rhythm task did not differentiate the savants from the comparison groups to the extent seen in the chord and melody tasks. These results give strong support to the hypothesis that the particular strength of savants involves the tonal aspects of music. When these aspects are missing, they do not excel. It is important to note that neither was their performance especially error prone, their scores equaling those of the adult comparison group more often than not. Moreover, like the comparison pianists and the percussion students, savants showed considerable sensitivity to the structural variations across the various types of sequences, doing much better on those sequences that conformed to the metric structure usually present in music.

These conclusions should be tempered a bit by a reconsideration of the task as a valid measure of rhythmic sensitivity. For example, while the percussion students were the most accurate of all groups, they were not markedly so, and the discriminative validity of the task may be suspect. Moreover, the stimulus sequences represent, at best, a first approximation to a satisfactory rhythm reproduction task. It lacked several important qualities of conventional rhythmic structures. Accent or loudness variation was lacking, and this is typically an important clue in determining the underlying meter of a piece (Dowling & Harwood, 1986). Also, although each pattern was repeated, rhythmic redundancy was not built into the patterns themselves (c.f., Appendix C), thereby preventing the establishment of clear expectancies during the course of the sequence. As noted earlier, some see such expectancies at the core of understanding rhythm. The same criticism can be leveled against traditional tests of rhythm, however (Lehmann, 1968) and the present examples are not exceptional in this respect. The reliability of rhythm assessments has also been a problem (Gordon, 1965). Given the role of rhythm as a fundamental component in music performance, it seems clear that a more sophisticated treatment of rhythmic sensitivity in the savant than that attempted here would be illuminating.

Discussion

The results of the chord, melody, and rhythm tasks suggest some general boundaries for the savant's exceptional immediate memory for music. Savants do extremely well when the task requires retention of harmonic information. On tasks involving tonal material presented sequentially, or "melody like" information, they also do quite well, though their performance does not seem so exceptional. Finally, when the task omits any tonal element, the savant appears to do no better or worse than other musicians.

This conclusion seems to fit well with what we have already discovered about the savant's special sensitivity to pitch categories. The ability to classify pitch information according to the categories of conventional chromatic scales would obviously be an asset in tasks which require the retention of such information. Exceptional memory for individual tones is characteristic of those with absolute pitch (Bachem, 1955; Siegel, 1974) and the savant is typical in this respect. However, explaining how this skill might translate into superior short-term memory for more complex arrays such as chord or melodic sequences requires a closer examination of the nature of short-term memory tasks.

As mentioned earlier, the conventional serial short-term memory task requires the retention of a series of items (e.g., numbers, words, and the like) presented at a relatively fast rate (usually 1 second per item or less) for immediate recall. This task has been subjected to considerable scrutiny in recent years (e.g., Dempster, 1981; Ericcson, 1981). Several characteristics of short-term memory emerge as particularly noteworthy. We can usually recall a very limited amount when we are given a series of pieces of information at a rapid rate (Miller, 1956). Second, there are marked individual and developmental differences in people's ability to retain material presented in this manner (Chase & Ericcson, 1982; Dempster, 1981). There are also differences associated with the nature of the material to be remembered (e.g., Case, Kurland, & Goldberg, 1982; Dempster, 1981). Finally, these differences indicate that while the task is usually identified as a measure of short-term or immediate memory, long-term memory is almost inevitably involved (Chase & Ericcson, 1982). This means a variety of complex cognitive processes associated with long-term memory are likely to be engaged in even relatively simple versions of the short-term memory task.

Dempster (1981) has recently described 10 such processes hypothesized as responsible for differences in performance in short-term memory. Four of these are identified as strategic, and the remaining are considered nonstrategic. The difference between the strategic versus nonstrategic factors hinges upon the optional nature of the former; subjects can bring strategic processes to bear on the task or not, depending upon motivation, availability of the processes, awareness of their applicability and the like. Examples of such processes are verbal rehearsal, grouping, or specific retrieval strategies. Nonstrategic factors tend to be obligatory rather than optional. Moreover, they occur as a consequence of the usual or typical way a person encodes the stimulus material rather than as a conscious application to a particular memory task. Traditionally, large differences in short-term memory performance have been attributed to strategic factors (c.f., Brown, Bransford, Ferrara, & Campione, 1983; Dempster, 1981 for a review). Differences associated with rehearsal have been especially prominent in this approach. Thus, large age differences observed in short-term memory tasks are usually accompanied by large age differences in the presence of rehearsal strategies. Older children and adults are often observed applying various rehearsal strategies, whereas young children (Flavell, Beach, & Chinsky, 1966) and retarded subjects (Brown, Campione, Bray, & Wilcox, 1973) are less likely to do so. Moreover, specific training on rehearsal strategies can improve short-term memory performance (e.g., Brown, et al., 1973).

While the case for strategic factors in short-term memory does seem strong, more recently non-strategic factors have emerged as particularly important in the usual short-term memory situation. As Dempster (1981) noted, evidence for strategic factors such as rehearsal tends to be of a general nature. Large differences in memory span and rehearsal may be found in different groups; however, this does not mean differences in the one factor (rehearsal) are primarily responsible for differences in the second. Furthermore, in the usual short-term memory task material is presented at a rate which severely limits the amount of rehearsal that can take place. This certainly seems to be the case in the musical memory tasks described in this chapter. Thus, while strategic rehearsal is undoubtedly important in many aspects of musical performance (c.f. Sloboda, 1985) it seems less likely a factor in immediate recall of note strings or chords presented only once.

The specific hypothesis that strategic rehearsal is a primary factor in savant performance runs into additional difficulties. First, it becomes an exception to the rule that strategy use is relatively rare in the memory performance of the retarded. Strategy application usually comes about only as a consequence of careful and prolonged training procedures (Butterfield, Wambold, & Belmont, 1973). Second, there is no independent evidence that rehearsal strategies have been acquired by the savants. It is highly unlikely that rehearsal strategy training is common in the savants' musical background. Indeed, several of the participants were largely self-taught. Of course, one could assume savants have developed a series of conscious memory strategies on their own, but if so, they are not able to describe them. (This ineffable characteristic of performance typified the highly verbal B.A., M.B., and K.L. too, none of whom could provide a clear description of any particular strategy.) This stands in contrast to the memory performance of experts in other domains who often have consciously developed complex encoding and rehearsal strategies to improve their memory (Brown & Deffenbacher, 1988). By contrast, nonstrategic factors are more apt to be operative in the usual short-term memory task. Prominent among the nonstrategic factors in memory is item identification or encoding rate (Case, et al., 1982; Chi, 1978; Huttenlocher & Burke, 1976). The core notion is that superior immediate memory derives from a ready means of identifying the items to be memorized. In addition, this identification must engage some general system of representation in long-term memory. Most often, this system is linguistic, but it need not be (Chase & Simon, 1973; Halpern & Bower, 1982). Manipulating the ease of identifying the individual items in a short-term memory task has dramatic effects upon memory span; given a more difficult identification situation for example, adults' memory span for material may be no better than children's (Chi, 1978). Moreover, individual differences in encoding speed show direct correspondence to individual memories spans (Case, et al., 1982).

It is easy to see why memory would be aided by quick and accurate identification. To the extent this identification makes contact with long-term memory, it provides a means for preserving information from the kind of interference that is so problematic in the usual memory experiment. In short, having ready names or categories for things helps keep them from getting confused with each other. In the savant, the presence of these names or categories is indicated by his performance on pitch naming tasks. Every savant (and three of the comparison subjects) named individual notes accurately and without hesitation. This ability meant they could encode the individual items in more complex strings with relative ease. It also meant they were less likely to generate alternative (and thereby mutually interfering) classifications of a given musical event. When these categories were not so useful, as in the rhythm task, performance suffered.

Attributing the primary memory advantage of the savant to nonstrategic factors is consistent with other characteristics of savant performance. The apparent ease with which they performed these memory tasks typifies a process that requires relatively little conscious effort. O'Connell (1974) provides a description of such effortless music making in his 8-year-old savant who, in one session, casually observed "I forgot my lunch today" as he was playing a piece. Furthermore, if nonstrategic factors are responsible for savant performance, it is not necessary to posit an exception to the often replicated finding that the developmentally delayed are seriously deficient in the application and maintenance of conscious strategies in memory tasks (Butterfield, et al., 1973). It is in this sense then, that the characterization of savant skill as automatic (e.g., Treffert, 1988) seems appropriate. It is automatic in that it involves the relatively effortless and "natural" application of a system for encoding musical information.

This is not to say that the memory "trick" in the savant is simply a matter of applying convenient labels of some sort to the music he or she hears. The advantage enjoyed by the savant extends considerably beyond having an efficient classification scheme for individual notes. At almost every point where additional structure or organization was present in the material to be remembered, the savants showed evidence of sensitivity to that structure, often surpassing that shown by the comparison subjects. In fact, as a general rule, the more the stimulus array was composed of "just notes" (e.g., unconventional chords, random tones, irregular intervals) the less remarkable savant performance was.

This means the use of the tape recorder as a model for representing the musical process (and product) in the savant is not appropriate. Rather, their performance bears more resemblance to the selective memory found among those with expert knowledge in a domain. Just as expert chess players excel at remembering chess board configurations when they are well-structured and meaningful (Chase & Simon, 1973), so the savants' memory excels most when the more meaningful or structured aspects of music are present. In each case, it seems most parsimonious to assume that the excellence of immediate memory reflects a complex and well-structured representation of the domain in long-term memory.

The patterns observed in savant performance point to several central characteristics in their representation of music. First, key or scale information is especially salient; rarely did responses stray outside the boundaries of the (implicit) key signature of a piece. This sensitivity extended to unusual or rarely heard scale conventions, indicating it does not reflect a simple familiarity or frequency principle. Rather, it seems to reflect some more general rule or pattern discovery skill, applicable to unfamiliar as well as familiar material. Second, harmonic patterns, particularly those with a high degree of coherence, are easily encoded and retrieved. This is seen most clearly in the comparison of conventional versus unconventional chords in the chord sequence experiment and in the nearly flawless rendering of the context chords in the context experiment. Given that this harmonic structure provides the foundation for much Western music of the last three hundred years (Bernstein, 1976), the organization of musical knowledge in the savant demonstrates a point of resonance or contact with this larger milieu. In other words, this sensitivity is particularly well-suited to the harmonic tradition of Western music. Third, savant musical knowledge includes a sensitivity to the hierarchical structure of musical. This was reflected in their performance on the grouped strings in the melody memory task. Understanding the principle of successive transposition as applied to groups of notes extended their musical memory span just as it does in the mature musician (Deutsch, 1982). Eddie's performance was noteworthy in this respect, surpassing all of the other nonhandicapped children in the sample by a considerable margin.

One situation where structure may not be useful to the savant should be noted. Grouping by temporal interval has often been found to play a large role in short-term memory performance (Dempster, 1981; Huttenlocher & Burke, 1976). In her original investigation of grouping effects in mature musicians, Deutsch (1980) also examined some aspects of the temporal grouping factor, having temporal intervals either correspond to the juncture of successive note groupings or not. The presence of the additional temporal cue did not improve performance significantly when it was congruent; however, it interfered with performance when it was not congruent. A similar variation in temporal/melodic congruence in the savant J.L. (Charness, et al., 1988) seemed to have a slightly different effect in that the congruence of melodic and temporal information materially helped J.L.'s performance. J.L. was also given some strings that contained temporal but not melodic structure (e.g., random strings where the notes are temporally grouped in three or four). This manipulation, by itself, was apparently ineffective. L.L.'s performance on the same task also suggests that temporal structure alone was not helpful. ($\overline{X}$ not temporally grouped = .94, $\overline{X}$ temporally grouped = .78).

I tried a slightly different approach with Eddie, giving him a series of random 9-element strings as in Miller (1987a), but either presented at a steady rate or with temporal gaps describing groups of three. Across 20 trials of each type, I could find no evidence of temporal grouping improving performance. Thus, the temporal manipulation, by itself, seemed to have little effect in all three cases. This is in marked contrast to the usual verbal short-term memory task where temporal grouping effects can be quite profound (Huttenlocher & Burke, 1976). Perhaps the salience of tonal information for the savant makes temporal cues less relevant. Perhaps too, temporal variation doesn't provide much in the way of added coherence to assist packaging melodic information in long-term memory. A more detailed examination of temporal cue use in savant memory would help to clarify these issues.

Although the patterns of performance seen in the various memory tasks make it possible to talk about general characteristics of the musical savant, there was also heterogeneity within the savant sample. L.L. was outstanding on the chord and melodic memory tasks, showing excellent retention of even the unstructured material. This high level of performance did not extend to the rhythm task, where L.L. was actually the least accurate savant (based upon the rank measure). N.Y. did not do particularly well on the chord task but was well above average on the rhythm trials. The most consistent subject is C.N., the only one to stay in the top half of the sample across the structured and unstructured versions of all three tasks. Eddie fell in the middle of the savant group on the structured versions of each task and toward the bottom on the unstructured versions.

Assuming these differences reflect reliable individual variations, what might they mean? The particular musical experience of each savant probably plays a considerable role. L.L., for example, has likely sharpened and developed his ability to pick up new melodic and harmonic information as part of his concert repertoire; the "challenge" sessions have become a featured part of his concerts. However, he does very little ensemble playing. In contrast, N.Y., C.N., and C.A. all did much better than L.L. on the rhythm task, and all have done a considerable amount of ensemble work. It is important to note that specific formal musical training does not seem to play a large role in these differences. N.Y. has had lessons most of her life. C.N. is self-taught, as far as we can determine, yet outperformed N.Y. on every task.

Eddie's distinctiveness was revealed in his pattern of errors rather than in his overall level of performance. On the two tasks where order or position effects were especially prominent (chords and melody), Eddie's performance did not show the typical serial position curve of the others. More precisely, Eddie did not show a strong "primacy" portion of the serial position curve. Although his recall of the most recently presented items was as good as the other savants, his recall of the first appearing items was quite a bit worse.

What made the first items in these sequences relatively hard for Eddie to retain? Although Eddie was unique among the savants in this respect, the absence of first-item retention or primacy effects has been well-documented in young children (Atkinson, Hansen, & Bernback, 1964; Siegel & Allik, 1973) suggesting some developmental factor at work. Recovering the first items in a series is especially difficult for young children when auditory information is involved (Siegel & Allik, 1973). One factor often cited as responsible for primacy effects and their increase with age is rehearsal or some comparable strategy during the task. The evidence for this comes from studies showing that primacy and rehearsal tend to be correlated (Brown, et al., 1973) and that experimentally induced rehearsal can improve performance at the earlier positions in a sequence (Chi, 1977). As noted earlier, neither of these results proves that rehearsal is the operative factor in tasks such as those used here. The assumption that rehearsal is responsible for the appearance of primacy affects in the present sample is also inconsistent with our conclusion that the excellent performance in the savant group did not reflect the sophisticated use of strategy. Rather, it was seen to reflect characteristics of the general (musical) knowledge system operative in stimulus encoding.

A similar argument can be made here. First, accurate performance on serial memory tasks requires retrieving accurate information about item position as well as identity. One must know when something occurred in a sequence as well as what occurred. These types of information may be affected differently by different variables. For example, temporal grouping may aid position more than identity information (Ryan, 1969). Huttenlocher and Burke (1976) suggest that there may be a developmental dimension to the identity/position distinction as well, sensitivity to order being the later developmental achievement. It may depend on the acquisition of number related ordering concepts, for example. Greene (1986) recently outlined how the salience of order information may be responsible for the accurate recall of the most recent items in memory. Borrowing an analogy from Crowder (1976), Greene suggested items in memory might be like telephone poles seen from a passing train; those most recently seen are most distinctive with respect to relative position as well as identity. Retaining order position for the earlier items may have been a bit of a problem for Eddie, thereby contributing to their confusability and the absence of as good recovery of these items as was found in the other savants.

Several other pieces of information are at least consistent with the hypothesis that item ordering was a factor in the position effects exhibited by Eddie. First, it seems clear that the most salient cues for Eddie involved tonality; his responses always showed very close agreement with the tonal structure of what he heard, as long as it was coherent. Although tonality may be very helpful in establishing an item's identity, it is more often neutral with respect to position. Because the chords and melodies used usually did not follow harmonic cadence conventions, these could not be used to infer order information. By itself, order seems not to have been so salient. Second, Eddie was the only savant who occasionally rearranged the order in his renditions of the chord sequences; among the others, this was very rare. Although order rearranging was harder to document in the melody renditions, it seems as though Eddie frequently reversed order within the melody sequences as well. Eddie at times spontaneously reorders material according to his own "inner ear" in his playing of conventional music (c.f., Appendix A), suggesting this is a more mutable characteristic of what he hears. If this is the case, we should see developing attention to order and an increased or more "normal" primacy effect emerge as Eddie grows.

In summary, the immediate or short-term memory exhibited by the savant is comparable to the exceptional memory shown by experts in other domains. Both hinge on an ability to encode the fundamental units of the area quickly and efficiently, and in both, this encoding involves representation in a complex knowledge system. In the musical savant, this knowledge involves, at the very least, sensitivity to harmonic relationships, scale or key constraints, and melodic structure.

This conclusion is obviously constrained by limitations of subject sample and procedure, and it may be useful to consider some of these limitations in a bit more detail. Superior memory involves more than finding a way to encode elements in long-term memory. Some mechanism of retrieval is also required (Ericcson, 1985). Constraints imposed by the listen-and-play methodology prevented the use of experimental procedures often used to examine different retrieval processes (Crowder, 1976). Consequently, it is impossible at this point to say how much of savant superiority lies in the retrieval as opposed to the encoding side of memory. One characteristic of retrieval became apparent as a consequence of watching savants perform some of these tasks. The motor programs associated with note production were closely linked to the reception or encoding process. The savant subjects almost literally itched to get to the keys on hearing a segment. The response of the comparison subjects, on the other hand, tended to be more measured. In part, this rush to play on the part of the savants no doubt reflected a desire to "get the information down" before it was lost, not unlike hurrying for a pen and paper when we get a new telephone number. Perhaps, too, like the external memory aid of pen and paper, it had the function of fixing the information more permanently. Often, however, it seemed as though the encoding actually contained important statements about required motor programs for successful reproduction. Eddie, for example, was often observed in early sessions to engage in a kind of musical shadowing, playing along before a segment ended. (Though this could be construed as rehearsal, it was of a most unusual type, often containing harmonic variations of the original, rather than a reproduction of the actual notes being heard). The formation of an appropriate retrieval strategy at the time of encoding is a crucial component in skilled memory (Ericcson, 1985). Savants clearly have this ability to integrate perception and performance with ease. How they do so remains a mystery.

Concentrating on the ease with which savants encode and store musical information tends to suggest the savants' performance is "mindless" or unconscious. We shall return to this issue later. For the present, several examples reveal some degree of musical self-reflection among the savant participants. For the two participants with some reasonable communication skills, D.W. and N.Y., awareness of their abilities and limitations was often expressed during a session with comments such as "that's easy" or "I'm not so sure." For the others, evidence of such metamemory components (Brown, et al., 1983) as knowledge assessment and task analysis tended to be indirect. Eddie was fond of a game he called "one note" we developed early in our sessions together. I would play the opening bar of a small piece and Eddie would complete it, finishing with the statement "I can play one note." Later, as we worked through some of the more tedious sessions described in this chapter, Eddie developed a way to tell me the task was getting either too difficult or boring by suggesting with the statement "one more left," that this was the next to last trial.

Saying "I don't know" still comes hard to Eddie. It seems nearly impossible for L.L., who exudes confidence in being able to play any song named and faithfully comes up with something, though sometimes certainly not what was in the mind of the one making the request. L.L. readily expresses his musical likes and dislikes, however, and as noted earlier is quick to note musical jokes or incongruities in what he hears. Examples such as these provide only a glimpse of the more general understanding that may be present in the savant. Traditional methods of assessing metacognition (e.g., Flavell & Wellman, 1977) are usually inappropriate for most savants' elementary communication skills. A fuller picture of savant metacognition must await innovative methodology.

Finally, at this point, it is difficult to decide which aspects of the data reflect some general dimensions and which reflect more idiosyncratic factors. Particularly problematic in this regard is Eddie, who differs dramatically from the remainder of the sample in age and musical experience. Eddie's distinctive responding has been emphasized to suggest possible developmental factors at work in savant skill. The limited sample of subjects and behavior means that any conclusions about savant memory development are tentative at best, and the need for additional data is evident.

5 | Musical Idioms

It could be argued that the musical fragments given the participants in the last two chapters were not, in fact, very musical. At best, they have some resemblance to what Bernstein (1976) has termed the prose elements of music, those conventional note configurations that constitute the building blocks of composition. Savants' recognition of these prose elements was evident in their immediate recall, and this awareness is surely a factor in their musical precocity. However, savants' fame comes from their ability to recall intact music, not fragments. Although the materials of Chapters 3 and 4 were often constructed to embody different musical conventions, they would never be confused with a musical composition. They certainly did not become part of the participants' personal repertoire.

The present chapter considers more intact or completed musical compositions, and these often did become part of Eddie's repertoire. Before describing the specific experiments it may be useful to consider some of the more general qualities distinguishing these materials from those examined so far. The various elements of music; harmony, melody and rhythm, were dissociated in the experiments of the last chapter but are integrated in musical composition. One consequence of this integration is that the three components naturally reinforce and complement each other in a variety of ways. For example, the scale degrees represented by a particular note or interval in a melody constrain the accompanying harmony; some chords will fit in or harmonize well with the note or melody fragment in question, others will not (Krumhansl, 1983). Thus, each reinforces the other. Or, chord structure may reflect rhythmic structure by a simple correspondence of the two. Melody and rhythm also interact, the down beat in a measure often being distinguished by melodic conventions as well as accent (Sloboda, 1985).

Rhythmic and tonal patterns are highly consistent within themselves as well as with each other. Polyrhythms in a piece can pose a problem for a pianist, and one that is often solved by resorting to some incorporating mnemonic. Thus playing 2 notes in one hand against 3 in the other can be construed as corresponding to the pattern of stress in "not difficult." Even so, the pattern may seem a bit disjointed to the listener (but evidently not in many societies where complex polyrhythms are the rule rather than the exception (Davies, 1978). Polytonality can be even more challenging for the ear (Bernstein, 1976). Music in our culture contains considerable redundancy, to use the terminology of information theory. One obvious consequence of this redundancy is that its presence can make the task of understanding or "processing" the music easier for the listener (Sloboda, 1985).

Music also has constraints built into its temporal structure. Unlike the note and chord strings of the short-term memory experiments, conventional compositions usually have a fairly well-defined beginning, middle, and end. The beginning and end, for example, may be marked by harmonic and melodic information specifying the basic tonality of the composition. What goes on in between may range from formal compositional constraints such as sonata form to less formal, but no less real conventions like the 12-bar blues form, to the creation of more circumscribed expectancies within the piece itself (Meyer, 1956). The melodic and harmonic conventions underlying these expectancies may be archetypal (Rosner & Meyer, 1982). Once again, a consequence of this kind of structure is to make the task of understanding somewhat easier for the listener. Knowing the underlying form of the composition or being able to establish more "local" expectancies readies the listener for what is to come, a condition that usually facilitates processing (Lindsay & Norman, 1977). When used judiciously, violations of these expectancies create excitement and interest in the listener (Meyer, 1956).

Listening to and playing music is also a personal experience. That is, music is considerably more than the cognitive operation of "figuring out" what the basic structure of a piece might be, or what is likely to come next. Indeed, a strong argument can be made that these cognitive components are secondary, if not peripheral to the musical experience. In any case, one's personal connection to music can take many forms, and extensive discussions of these various kinds of reactions to music can be found in Meyer (1956) and Cooke (1959) among others. For the present, the important point to note is that the emotional, personal impact of an object, person or event has profound effects on its memorability (Winograd & Killinger, 1983). Music frequently has that emotional, personal impact. By contrast, the materials used in the short-term memory tasks were much less likely to elicit much in the way of a personal reaction, (other than the desire to please the experimenter by reproducing them accurately).

Considering everything that was lacking in the musical fragments examined in the earlier chapters, it is surprising the savants performed as well
as they did. That they would be even more impressive with intact music
was almost a foregone conclusion. When reduced to its underlying structure, much of the music in the Western diatonic tradition lies well within
the immediate memory limits indicated by these experiments. Archetypal
melodies in the classical musical corpus are often 8 notes or less in length,
not counting gap-filling or elaborative devices (Rosner & Meyer, 1982). Traditional chordal cadences are usually expressed in groups of not more than
4 chords, also within the savants' processing capacity. However, the results
of the short-term memory studies suggested some particular ways in which
savant musical sensitivities would be expressed in renditions of music. Sensitivity to harmonic structure should be outstanding, melody and rhythm
less so. Moreover, a clear sense of tonal center should be evident. On the
other hand, the particular key signature of a composition should be irrelevant. This follows from Eddie's demonstrated ability, apparently present in
the other savants as well, to extract the implicit scales used in constructing
the note strings of Chapter 4.

There were several puzzling aspects to this picture, however. These involved
the savants' ability to handle even relatively uncommon note combinations
with relative ease. Eddie and the other savants seemed equally at home in
strings constructed from a familiar conventional E-major diatonic scale, and
the much less familiar E-whole tone scale. Moreover, their incorrect responses
rarely strayed from the scale of the original. In conventional western music
of the past 200 years, certain scale types are encountered much more frequently
than others (Norton, 1984). Although scale usage is typically quite restricted,
pieces often include some chromaticism (i.e. notes not conforming to the scale
structure) as part of theme development. Will savants be sensitive to these
variations present in conventional music? Examining savants' responses to
pieces with varying types of scale structure should help determine whether
the general tonal sensitivity demonstrated in short-term memory tasks is found
in music as well.

Although long-term memory mechanisms were clearly implicated in the
analysis of short-term memory performance, the evidence was indirect, involving inferences about the knowledge present in long-term memory. The
materials themselves, however, were not particularly likely to be stored in
long-term memory; they were not "memorable" in that sense. In contrast,
music is memorable, sometimes to our dismay when we find we can't get
a recent hit tune out of our mind. As noted in Chapter 1, savant memory
of this sort is described as often phenomenal. However, it is only by using
more conventionally constructed "intact materials" that such long-term memory can be examined. These, then, were the objectives of the studies which
follow.

Reproduction of Conventional Diatonic Music

The material used for the initial investigation of Eddie's music making was taken from a popular music teaching series, John Thompson (Book 3, 1939). This book contains a series of short (4 to 8 measure) preludes, one in each of the 12 major and minor keys. The pieces vary considerably in stylistic content. Some are entirely arpeggios, others are primarily chordal in nature. Each has been given a name by the composer to reflect a possible association (e.g., "March Wind") a stylistic ("Spanish Dance") or a technical ("Cross-hand") quality of the piece. All of the pieces are written for a small hand span, and therefore all fit Eddie's span at the time, which was about a fifth. The procedure was essentially that used earlier. Each piece was played through, and Eddie was asked to play it at its conclusion. Some of the original compositions contain a repeat of the basic motif with first and second endings. In order to increase format consistency across preludes, the nonrepeating pieces were also played a second time before Eddie attempted a response. Details of the procedure are given in Miller (1987b).

These preludes constituted the first experimental materials tried with Eddie after the initial brief "introductory" sessions. They were played over a span of several months and were completed before Eddie had begun any of the instruction described in Appendix A and before a piano had been found for his home. Thus Eddie's performance on these pieces represents his musical sensibilities at a very early point in his development.

Eddie's renditions of the preludes were recorded on cassette tape and later transcribed to musical staves by a professional pianist. These renditions were than compared to the originals in a manner similar to that followed in the studies described in Chapters 3 and 4. The task of matching original and rendition turned out to be more straightforward for the preludes than it was for the musical segments described earlier. In part, this was because Eddie's renditions followed the originals quite closely in terms of the number of notes

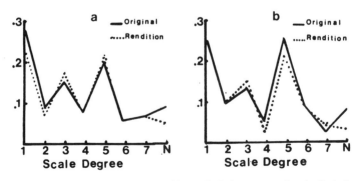

FIGURE 5.1. Note distribution, Eddie (a=Preludes in major key, b=Preludes in minor key).

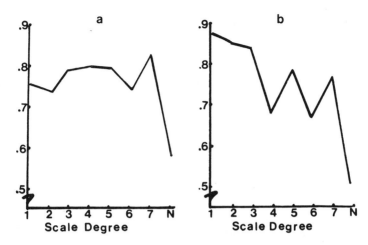

FIGURE 5.2. Matching accuracy, Eddie (a = Preludes in major key, b = Preludes in minor key).

played. Across major and minor preludes the length of Eddie's renditions was always within 5% of the originals.

The overall composition of Eddie's responses also closely resembled what he had just heard. One way of measuring this is to consider the distribution of the various scale degrees in the original preludes. Adopting the convention of designating the tonic as the first scale degree, the supertonic, degree number 2, and so forth, it is possible to describe compositions generally in terms of the relative frequency of the various scale degrees, (cf. Knopoff & Hutchinson, 1983; Youngblood, 1958). Figure 5.1 shows the frequency distributions of the original preludes and Eddie's renditions, separately for major (a) and minor (b) mode preludes. All preludes of each mode are transposed to a common scale for purposes of analysis. As expected, the particular key in which a piece was originally written had no effect on Eddie's error rate, so this method of analysis loses little of the information contained in the literal translations. Because the preludes were composed to exemplify some of the more conventional harmonic and melodic regularities of Western music, not surprisingly the distribution of notes in the original reveals a predominance of tonic triad elements (scale degrees 1, 3, and 5) and relatively few notes outside of the scale used in the prelude's composition (notes designated "N" in the figure). It is evident the general character of Eddie's renditions closely resembled the originals, and assessing the degree of correspondence by means of goodness-of-fit tests indicated the distribution of notes in renditions did not differ significantly from that in the original in either the major or minor mode.

Figure 5.2 shows the matching accuracy for the major (a) and minor (b) preludes. These data indicate the extent to which notes in the rendition actually duplicated those in the original, both in pitch and chroma, using a correspondence pattern that produced the best overall match, measure by measure, to the original. Thus, unlike Figure 5.1, this considers the actual placement or sequence of notes in the renditions. Eddie now shows more divergence from the original, particularly for some scale degree classes. Performance for the regular diatonic scale degrees tends to be quite high. Usually around 80% of the notes in this range are produced accurately, although there are two significant departures from this level of performance (relative to the other degrees) for scale degrees 4 and 6 in the minor mode. Eddie did not do so well on the nondiatonic notes, duplicating these successfully between 50 and 60% of the time, a level significantly below any of the diatonic scale degrees in either scale.

Nondiatonic notes were relatively rare in the original preludes and even rarer in Eddie's renditions (cf. Figure 5.1). However, it is unlikely their rarity in the original was the primary factor responsible for their omission in the renditions because some of the conventional scale degrees were also rare. Nondiatonic notes also tended to appear in unstressed positions in the preludes; for example on the off-beat. This also does not seem to be the factor responsible for their omission since similarly nonstressed diatonic notes were still reproduced accurately. In making an error on a nondiatonic note, Eddie could have resorted to several strategies, substituting its nearest scale degree, substituting another nondiatonic note, or simply omitting it altogether. Examination of the protocols suggested the error was more usually one of omission, about 60% of his errors being of this type. In other words, Eddie seemed to be regularizing the preludes in his renditions somewhat, simply deleting what did not seem to fit into a standard diatonic format.

This regularizing tendency on Eddie's part does not mean that Eddie invariably simplified the renditions. As suggested by the actual frequency distribution of notes played (Figure 5.1) there was fairly close general correspondence with the originals. Often, embellishment or reinforcement of a chord was evident, for example in providing an additional tonic conclusion to a piece. Octave substitution also occurred occasionally. In these cases, a note of identical chroma but different pitch height was substituted for the original (e.g. "high C" for "middle C"). These occurred primarily for the first, and fifth degrees and reflect an appreciation of octave equivalence (Dowling, 1982). Thus, the embellishments or additions tended to reinforce the basic tonality of the composition.

Some of the preludes did challenge Eddie, and in one case, prelude #18, performance was quite a bit below 50%. Eddie seemed to have problems grasping the melodic minor, and he experimented with the scale a bit in his rendition of this piece particularly. In an attempt to facilitate more adequate encoding, preludes were played again after the rendition, and occasionally a third and fourth time. Ideally, analysis of these repeated presentations might provide a picture of how Eddie's accuracy might improve with practice. Sometimes his performance across trials did indicate such improvement. On other pieces, however, Eddie's second and third attempts would turn into embellishments and/or improvisation of the original. Of course, the simple "listen and play" instructions did not demand a literal rendering and Eddie's inclination to explore sounds on the piano made some eventual addition almost inevitable. Even with some improvisation on Eddie's part, second renditions tended to contain more of the detail in the original. Examinations of these later attempts indicated an improvement for both diatonic (78% to 83%) and nondiatonic (51% to 65%) material. Note, however, that even in the more accurate second rendition diatonic notes were still reproduced more accurately than nondiatonic notes.

In summary, Eddie showed considerable facility in reproducing pieces composed in either the major or (probably less familiar) minor mode. His responses tended to resemble the more orthodox forms of these modes, however, omitting those notes less likely to conform to conventional scale structure. His substitutions were almost always key consistent, and also reflected the structural characteristics of the composition as a whole. If a piece contained arpeggios, so would his substitutions. Given this sensitivity and the constraints operating in prelude construction, Eddies' musical short-term memory capacity is now considerably greater than indicated in the memory string experiment. Eddie reproduced several of the preludes (which averaged 40 to 50 notes in length) virtually flawlessly. This performance was possible because he was able to use the various kinds of redundancy the preludes exemplified.

In order to place Eddies' performance in perspective several comparison groups were also given examples selected from the set of preludes. In the first group, the adult savants L.L., C.A., and D.W. were given a set of 12 preludes from the original set of 24. The 12 preludes sampled both major and minor keys and, naturally, a range of key signatures. The procedures for administration were similar to those used with Eddie except that the stimulus materials and renditions were made using the synthesizer and microcomputer system

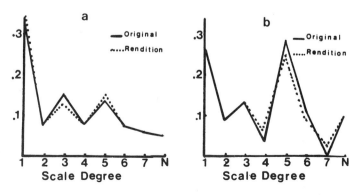

FIGURE 5.3. Note distribution, C.A., L.L. and D.W. (a=Preludes in major key, b=Preludes in minor key).

TABLE 5.1
Overall matching accuracy

Subject	Major Preludes	Minor Preludes	P
Eddie	.78	.76	NS
L.L.	.91	.71	< .01
C.A.	.81	.75	< .05
D.W.	.74	.63	< .01

described in Chapter 3. Subjects' renditions were recorded to disk and converted to staved manuscript representations using available software.

The savants C.A., L.L., and D.W. were all more loquacious than Eddie, musically speaking, in their renditions of the preludes, often offering quite a bit more than what was heard. L.L. continued the octave doubling and tripling that characterized his responses on the chord and melody experiments, his renditions often containing twice as many notes as the original. L.L. also engaged in octave substitution frequently, with the result that only chroma, rather than chroma and register, was adopted as the standard for considering a note to be a match in the original. (Recall that for Eddie such note substitutions were relatively rare.) The relative length of these renditions also meant that there were more alternative "candidates" for matching a given measure in the original. A measure-by-measure match with the original was again followed, with the constraint that if at least 50% of the notes in the original measure were not matched, no credit for that measure was given. The application of a similar constraint in scoring Eddie's protocols leaves the scores virtually unchanged, given that average performance was 75% to 95%. The constraint as used for the comparison subjects may have penalized them slightly for partially correct answers, but this was probably neutralized by their longer renditions.

Figure 5.3 shows the frequency distribution of all notes played for the major and minor preludes for the savants C.A., L.L., and D.W., expressed, as in Figure 5.1, as a percentage of the total. Comparison of the distributions of responses by means of x^2 revealed no significant differences in the relative frequency of the various scale degrees across the three adult savants for the major preludes. Thus, although the three savants varied considerably in rendition length, the overall distribution of their responses was very similar. For the minor preludes an analogous comparison did suggest some differences among adult savants in the patterning of their rendition ($X^2 = 33.5$, $p < .01$). The variation appeared to reflect rather more use of the third and fifth degree by D.W. and the tonic by L.L. The variation across subjects, although statistically significant, is not very marked, and it is apparent that the adult savants, like Eddie, closely approximated the overall character of the originals in their renditions. X^2's comparing these distributions with the originals were not significant.

How did the adult savants compare with Eddie in their actual duplication of the preludes? Table 5.1 gives the actual matching accuracy for major and minor preludes and comparison data from the same subset of preludes as played by Eddie. (Eddie's data were rescored to consider only chroma rather than register and chroma in deciding whether a note was a match.) It is apparent that Eddie's performance falls within the range represented by the older savants. Unlike the other savants, however, Eddie's general accuracy was no different for the subset of major and minor preludes given the older savants. (This was also true in a comparison of Eddie's performance on the complete set of preludes.) C.A., L.L., and D.W. all found the minor preludes significantly more difficult to repeat, the difference being particularly marked for L.L. The relative difficulty of the minor preludes for these subjects was also expressed, perhaps, in the length of their renditions. The minor preludes contained slightly more notes than the major preludes; for C.A., L.L., and D.W. minor prelude renditions were on the average almost twice as long as those of the major preludes, whereas for Eddie the difference was negligible.

Figure 5.4 portrays matching accuracy as a function of scale degree for the 12 preludes. For all adult savants, the diatonic notes (scale degrees 1–7) generally were more readily matched than the nondiatonic notes, although there appear to be some obvious exceptions. These will be discussed shortly. The pattern of performance across subjects and scale degrees was analyzed formally as follows. First, the distribution of correct responses as a function of scale degree was compared across the adults by means of x^2 statistic. This analysis indicated no differences among the adults in patterns of accuracy across the various scale degrees for either set of preludes. That is, although the adult savants did differ from each other in their overall level of accuracy, their relative

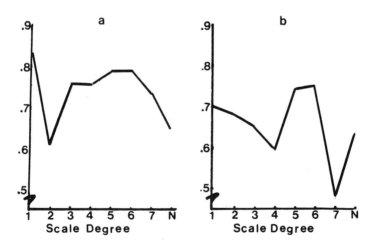

FIGURE 5.4.   Matching accuracy, C.A., L.L. and D.W. (a = Preludes in major key, b = Preludes in minor key).

accuracy across the various scale degrees did not vary in an individually distinctive fashion. A similar analysis comparing Eddie with these savants again revealed no significant individual variability in the pattern of results across all scale degrees, suggesting Eddie's pattern of accuracy for these preludes was quite similar to that of the adults. Finally, the accuracy for diatonic versus nondiatonic notes was compared using the data from all 4 participants. This analysis indicated significantly lower performance for the nondiatonic notes for both the major ($z = 9.5$, $p < .01$) and minor ($z = 5.9$, $p < .01$) preludes. Given that the adult savants appeared to be more willing to include nondiatonic notes in their renditions (roughly 6% of the adults' notes were not diatonic, whereas only about 3% of Eddie's were) one might expect them to react to the presence of nondiatonic information a bit differently. In fact, the adults were more likely than Eddie to reproduce nondiatonic notes accurately ($z = 2.6$, $p < .05$). However, when they missed nondiatonic notes, their response was, like Eddie's, more often to omit the note in context, rather than to substitute its nearest diatonic neighbor.

Thus, the adult savants' response to the prelude task resembled Eddie's in some ways, but not in others. Before discussing these similarities and differences in more detail, several caveats should be kept in mind. First, it is important to remember that the data collection procedures for Eddie and for the adults varied somewhat in this particular experiment. Eddie's piano renditions were transcribed from audio tape, the adults' synthesizer renditions were automatically transcribed via computer. One possibility is that the former technique introduces some systematic bias in the transcribing process. This is difficult to evaluate. An independent transcription of 4 of Eddie's renditions yielded almost identical scores, indicating the transcriptions were reliable. However, ascertaining the reliability of the transcription does not solve the problem if the systematic bias reflects some general musical conventions or practices biasing the ear of the listener. A second problem concerns behavioral sample size. Because the adult sample was given only half the preludes, their scores on the various measures are probably less stable than the scores for Eddie based on the complete set.

These differences in procedure mean that comparisons of Eddie's and the other savants' renditions are necessarily speculative in nature. It appears that Eddie was less affected by the mode of the piece. Eddie performed just as well on the minor as on the major modes, whereas every adult performed significantly better on the major modes. This could reflect an acculturation effect. Given the relative predominance of the major as opposed to the minor mode in Western music, perhaps the performance of the adult sample reflects an experiential bias in that direction. This might indicate the tastes or sensitivities of the younger savant are somewhat less culturally circumscribed than those of the adult.

The diatonic organization of music is itself a cultural effect (Norton, 1984) and all savants presented a response profile clearly consistent with this diatonic tradition. Notes of the tonic triad appeared often, other diatonic notes somewhat less so, and nondiatonic notes less still. The particular key of the piece (excepting the already mentioned major/minor distinction) was irrelevant. What mattered was how the notes fit together within the piece. One should be particularly cautious in interpreting the differences between diatonic and nondiatonic notes in participants' reproductions. Although in the original full sample with Eddie (Figure 5.2) the difference is striking, in the reduced sample it is less so (Figure 5.4) and several diatonic scale degree classes appeared to fare even worse than the nondiatonic notes. There are obvious problems of sample size here, and in the reduced set several scale degree classes occurred infrequently. It should also be noted that the nondiatonic notes did not really represent inappropriate or dissonant aspects of the piece. Usually they reflected common chromatic practices, for example, the use of diminished seventh chords. It seems fair to say they represent an additional level or type of complexity, however, and one that goes a bit beyond the standard harmonic patterns of a key. It is in this sense that Eddie and the other savants seemed to render the preludes in a more canonical or prototypic fashion by systematically deleting this information, Eddie doing so more than the others. Thus, at the more general level all savants appeared to have a particular affinity for the tonality of the music they heard. The particular modal expression of this tonality, major or minor, appeared to be of more consequence for the adult savants than it was for Eddie.

Four sighted adult pianists from the earlier studies were also given the preludes to perform. None of these subjects had encountered the preludes previously as part of their musical training. The procedure for listening to and reproducing the material varied somewhat for these comparison subjects. The 24 preludes representing the complete set were divided into three trial types. Eight trials were identical in procedure to those given the savants; a piece was simply listened to and then played. On the remaining 16 trials additional information was provided; on 8 occasions the subject was told the key of the piece before the trial began and on 8 trials the complete score was made available while the piece was being heard, though as in the other conditions the listener had to play the piece from memory. The particular type of trial was randomized across the 24 prelude set.

These conditions were designed to consider several analogues to the particular skills possessed by savants. It was expected that the "listen only" condition would prove quite difficult for all participants without absolute pitch. This follows from the performance of the sighted normal adults on the chord and melody reproduction tasks described in earlier chapters. Those without the ability to identify pitch information quickly and efficiently simply did not do very well, and the aural presentation of the preludes presents a similar

TABLE 5.2
Distribution of responses: Adult comparison group

	Listen			Key information			Score		
	Match	Cons	Error	Match	Cons	Error	Match	Cons	Error
M.B.	.75	.21	.04	.76	.23	.01	.75	.21	.04
P.M.	.06	.60	.34	.10	.62	.28	.74	.19	.07
G.J.	.01	.70	.29	.03	.71	.26	.33	.57	.08
H.H.	.07	.56	.37	.19	.72	.09	.25	.56	.19

kind of challenge, albeit in a more musically coherent setting. The 8 trials with the provision of key information were suggested by the ready grasp of tonal structure exhibited by Eddie and the other savants. Would providing a tonal context beforehand help the aural encoding of those without absolute pitch?

The eight trials with score available represent the more conventional situation for the sighted musician, and these trials should naturally yield the most accurate performance. In addition, however, the provision of score information may simulate the degree of specificity that is obtained aurally by the savant. For example, the score should help to identify specific notes as they are heard, thereby fixing them better in memory, as well as assisting in the analysis of chordal elements in a piece. Recall that these tasks seemed to be particularly difficult for those without absolute pitch. There is also evidence to suggest that in reading musical scores the mature musician shows the kind of attention to overall structure exhibited by musical savants in their aural perception of music. Sloboda (1976) asked musicians to sight read passages that had been altered to contain unlikely or inappropriate notes. Musicians erred more often on these than on the more conventional neighboring notes in their renditions, suggesting they were making inferences based upon the general structure of the passage. Attention to more general characteristics such as phrase boundaries is also indicated by sight reading performance (Sloboda, 1978). These characteristics of sight reading suggest that mature musicians routinely extract information about tonality and melodic structure. Thus, when the score is available the adults in the sample should show error patterns similar to those found in the savants.

Subjects in the adult comparison group heard and played the preludes with the physical set-up described previously and performance was again transposed via appropriate software to musical staves. In the first analysis, all notes played in a given rendition were scored as either being a match to the original, consistent with the key of the original (but not a match), or an "error," that is neither a match nor consistent. Matching responses were again determined on a measure by measure basis, with a 50% criterion for accepting any specific measure as in the preceding analyses. Table 5.2 presents these data in summary form. Several differences are striking. First M.B., the subject with AP, showed very similar levels of performance across the three conditions, and clearly outperformed the other adults. For the three adults without (extended) AP, the condition under which the preludes were heard was clearly important. Very few matching responses were found in the listen only condition; in fact, the overall consistency index (% matching and consistency responses) was often little better than chance, (roughly 58% or so). The use of averages here is a bit misleading in that considerable variability across preludes marked the performance of P.M., G.J., and H.H. under the listen only and key information conditions. These three participants identified the correct key on many of the preludes, thereby making very few "error" responses. For other preludes performance was at chance levels, or in a few cases, significantly below chance, suggesting a transposition of key in the rendition. (In these cases subjects' renditions were then transposed to the original key before matching responses were scored.) Although the provision of key information helped some, it was not enough to raise matches or decrease error responses considerably. Even H.H., who showed significant improvement on both counts when given key information, was far from optimal in her performance. It seems clear that providing a specific tonal context beforehand is not enough to allow performance equivelant to M.B. or the savants.

As expected, providing the score to the non-AP subjects resulted in quite respectable performance in many instances and the remainder of the analyses concentrate on their performance under this condition. Figure 5.5 presents the scale degree distributions of all notes in the renditions when subjects were allowed to examine the score. These distributions varied significantly across subjects ($X^2 = 59.5$, $p < .01$). Although in broad outline each subjects' distribution follows that of the original, comparison of each with the original key using the goodness-of-fit statistic revealed significant variance with respect to the original for all. A glance at the table suggests primary sources for the discrepancy were the seventh degree and non-diatonic notes. These appeared considerably more often in subjects' renditions than in the originals. Turning to matching accuracy, Figure 5.6 presents these data for the subjects H.H., G.J., and P.M. when the score was available. Of the three non-AP subjects, P.M., and G.J. were significantly more accurate than H.H. Relative accuracy across the scale degrees also varied for these three participants ($X^2 = 28.0$, $df = 14$, $p < .01$). Examining the data in a bit more detail, it appears the primary source of individual variation was performance on scale degrees not defined by the tonic triad. Separate X^2 comparisons revealed no differences among H.H., P.M., and G.J. on the relative accuracy for these 3 degrees (although, of course, overall accuracy varied) while significant differences among them existed for the remaining notes ($X^2 = 17.4$, $df = 8$, $p < .05$).

As noted earlier, M.B. performed quite well under all three conditions. Figure 5.7 portrays this performance as a function of scale degree. Interestingly, matching accuracy was slightly lower when key information was made available than in the other two conditions ($z = 4.3$, $p < .01$). In post-test ques-

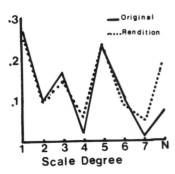

FIGURE 5.5. Note distribution, score available trials, non-AP subjects.

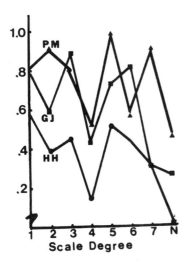

FIGURE 5.6. Matching accuracy, non-AP subjects.

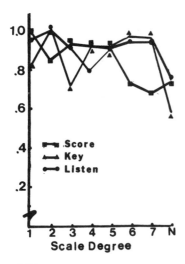

FIGURE 5.7. Matching accuracy, M.B.

tioning M.B. remarked that the key information tended to distract him a bit from "just listening to the music." There is some indication the provision of key information may have led M.B. to modify his responding a bit. He played very few notes not consistent with the key under this condition, and his accuracy for nondiatonic notes was somewhat lower as well. At any rate, it is clear that across conditions nondiatonic notes were more difficult for M.B. as they were for H.H., G.J., and P.M. In each case the difference in accuracy for nondiatonic notes versus the average of the diatonic scale degrees is marked and statistically reliable.

It was originally intended to examine differences in accuracy as a function of mode (i.e. major versus minor key preludes) because this had appeared as a significant source of variability for the adult savants. Unfortunately after the data for the sighted comparison sample were collected, an error in counterbalancing was discovered. The proportion of minor preludes varied considerably across the three conditions, with 6 of the 8 "score available" trials being minor preludes. If anything, this imbalance probably reduced differences among conditions for the non-AP subjects in that they had more detailed information for those preludes the savants found most difficult. However, it prevented a comparable examination of major–minor prelude differences in this sample. An indication of a similar kind of major–minor difference is suggested by the error scores, or key consistent responding by the non-AP subjects under the listen and key information conditions. It was noted earlier these trials elicited quite variable responding by the non-AP subjects. On some trials they were very consistent with the key of the original, on others they were not. The latter occurred more often when they were trying to reproduce minor preludes (33% of the trials) than when they were working with preludes in a major key (13%). A more detailed analysis was possible for M.B., the AP adult whose performance across the various conditions varied much less. Considering only the "score available" and "listen" conditions, where overall performance was equivalent, preludes in a major key elicited more accurate matching than those in a minor key ($z = 3.6$, $p < .01$). The available evidence, then, suggests the comparison adults were like the savant adults in being more accurate in major than in minor mode selections.

The results of the short term memory experiments suggested some additional dimensions of all subjects' performance that might be examined. Recall that the savants excelled especially when notes were presented simultaneously (i.e., chords). Would this superiority be evident in their reproductions of the preludes as well? This question was examined in several ways. First, each measure of every prelude was designated as either primarily melodic or primarily chordal in nature depending on whether the majority of notes in the measure was sounded simultaneously or successively, measures with equal numbers of simultaneous and successive notes being disregarded. Next, corrected protocols were examined to see whether the type of measure, melodic or chordal, was a factor in accuracy. Turning first to the adult sighted musicians H.H.,

G.J., and M.P., it is apparent this characteristic of the musical information was very important. Although very few segments of the preludes attempted under the "listen only" and "key information" conditions were rendered with greater than 50% accuracy, (cf. Table 5.2) most of those so rendered were primarily melodic (57%) even though melodic measures were less common in the sample of 16 preludes comprising these conditions. This preference for successively presented information persisted when the score was available. Seventy-eight percent of the material from melodic measures was accurately reproduced for these participants whereas for chordal measures accuracy was only 58%.

By contrast, for the savant sample the accuracy for the two types of measures was nearly identical—77% for melodic measures and 75% for measures primarily containing chords. There was some individual variability among the savants in this regard, C.A. doing considerably better on the melodies than the chords (.89 versus 74). Nevertheless it seems clear the savants, Eddie included, were at a distinct advantage in processing and rendering chordal material. This is most clearly seen in a subset of four preludes (#s 8, 12, 14, and 17). These were part of the set heard by the adult comparison subjects with the score available and also heard by the savants (naturally with no score). For the sighted adults melodic information was reproduced more accurately than chordal (65 vs. 51%), whereas for the savants the reverse tended to be true (77 vs. 82%).

The final analysis considered how the location of information in the prelude affected recall. Location or "serial position" effects had emerged as important sources of variability in participants' performance in Chapter 4. For the sighted adults H.H., P.M., and G.J., primacy effects were again in strong evidence. Considering first the scorable measures from the "listen" and "key information" conditions, the majority of these (63%) were from the first rather than last part of a prelude. For the "score available" trials, accuracy was high enough to permit examination of performance on a measure-by-measure basis. Comparison of performance on the first two, middle two (for longer preludes), and last two measures revealed a strong primacy effect, or heightened accuracy on the first measure of a prelude (84%, 57% and 54% for the first, middle, and last measures of these preludes). This general pattern was present in each of the sighted musicians. The savants presented a different picture. Comparable analyses of the 12 preludes heard by the savants D.W., C.A., L.L., and Eddie yielded accuracy rates of 79%, 71% and 79% for the first, middle, and final measures of these preludes. There was some individual variability in these data. A primacy effect was suggested by the scores of D.W. (72, 63 and 64%), but for the remaining three savants performance at the initial and terminal measures was more nearly equal. Again, perhaps the best source of comparison is the set of 4 preludes heard by the savants and by the adults with the score available. For the sighted adults accuracy decreased from 82% to 53% from the first to last measures; for the savants as a group performance decreased only slightly from 82% to 80% with some variability among the savants again apparent in this smaller sample. D.W. remained at variance with the rest of the savants in showing a marked primacy effect (79% versus 50%).

The discussion of these additional analyses so far has omitted reference to the adult with absolute pitch, M.B. Did the pattern of his errors resemble the other sighted adults or the savants? Both, it turns out. As we have seen, M.B. recalled as well with the score not available as when it was. His aural memory for the preludes was at least as good as the savants. Given the evidence of his facility for recalling chords as well as note strings, it seems reasonable to expect him to do equally well on the melodic and chordal aspects of the preludes. In the full set of 24, his accuracy for these two kinds of measures was 93% and 88%, respectively, suggesting a slight advantage for the melodic material. There was some suggestion that this varied depending on the listening condition. For the score available and listen conditions melodic measure recall was higher than chordal (95% versus 91% when the score was available, 96% versus 83% for listen only), while the reverse was true for key information (83% versus 90%). Recall that the key information condition caused a bit of a conflict in M.B. Considering this, it appears M.B. resembles the remainder of the sighted sample a bit more in the relative accuracy for chords and melodies, although his recall of the former is clearly on a par with the most accurate savant. With respect to positional aspects of the material, M.B. clearly resembles the other sighted adults, rather than the savant sample. His recall is consistently better for the items appearing first than for those heard last, (94% for material in the first two measures, 82% for material in the last two). Although not quite so marked as the other sighted adults, it was statistically reliable ($z = 7.5$, $p < .01$) and consistent across the three listening conditions.

In summary, the experimental conditions used with the sighted adults suggest an analogy to the kind of information savants are able to extract from aurally presented music. Roughly speaking, the degree and kind of specificity available to savants is equivalent to that available to the mature musician with the musical score in hand. Like the musical score, the savants' representation of music includes more general key designation as well as specific harmonic and melodic content. Moreover, it appears that in forming his internal musical score the savant employs the same general kinds of selective encoding as the sight reader. Both are biased toward note values that are most characteristic of the overall harmonic structure of the piece, and there is some suggestion that both are affected by compositional mode. It was also clear the designation of key structure in the abstract, so to speak, did not help the non-AP subjects in achieving the ready appreciation of key structure seen in the savant. Evidently, while key (and mode) are theoretically dissociable from actual content, in practice effective recall requires accurate encoding of both levels of information as a joint enterprise.

This is not to say that savants literally must have the equivalent of musical scores in their head. There are probably many ways of representing auditory information internally just as there are different models for representing visual information (Kosslyn, Pinker, Smith, & Schwartz, 1979). Musical scores employ a series of more or less arbitrary conventions for constructing a visual-spatial representation of an auditory-temporal pattern (Sloboda, 1978). Learning this equivalence can be a slow and arduous process (cf. Appendix A). There are many aspects of music that are realized only partially or imperfectly in a score and others that may be communicated more effectively. Scores may be more limited with respect to dynamic information, but they allow one to see the piece as a whole in a way that aural presentation alone may not. It is also quite likely the musical savant with absolute pitch and the classically trained sight reader attain expertise by different routes. Even so, the present results suggest the essential harmonic and melodic structure of music is a core aspect of music representation in either case.

There were also some clear differences in the pattern of performance seen in the savants and the comparison group. The former seemed a bit more comfortable with the chordal components of the music they heard, whereas the latter showed a clear preference for successive note groupings. There are probably several reasons for this difference. The savant skill in analyzing and retaining chords has already been discussed at length, and the current result represents another example of that skill at work. Even providing the additional visual information to the sighted sample did not allow them to overcome this disadvantage. Perhaps a difficulty with the visual representation of chord information is that it does not provide the kind of note articulation available in arpeggios. Scoring conventions require less space in the simultaneous than in the sequential representation of a note combination and to some extent the aural confusion of information among notes is preserved in the visual form. Second, many of the melodies encountered in the preludes were successive transpositions of note groups similar to those encountered in the grouping condition of the melody reproduction task (Chapter 4). Having accurate information about the basic note group, the adults were as adept as the savants in following it through its various transformations.

The sighted adults also differed from the savants in their memory for information from the beginning versus the end of the preludes. For savants this difference was small; for the comparison subjects it was substantial. It is noteworthy that the individual differences in primacy effects seen here reflected those found in the short term memory studies in many respects. Thus, D.W. and M.B. showed significant primacy effects in the earlier chord sequence study whereas Eddie, C.A. and L.L. did not. That pattern is repeated here. Each of the sighted adults also showed a primacy effect in the earlier melody experiment as well as here. C.A. and L.L. showed somewhat less marked primacy effects for these note strings while Eddie showed less accurate recall of the earliest items. Earlier, we argued that Eddie's better recall for the most recent items in melody strings could reflect difficulties in retaining precise positional information about earlier items. Possibly the structure of the preludes helped in this respect. Most of the preludes contain repeated or transposed examples of a basic motif. Understanding the general structure of the prelude, then, might make it easier to locate modulations in a way not possible for many of the note strings. In other words the preludes may have provided some additional temporal markers not present in the earlier material.

The presence of positional differences in accuracy seems a more straightforward manner for some of the remaining participants, not for others. Responses of H.H., G.J., and P.M. to post-test questioning suggested a common reason for their primacy effects. Even with the score available, the rate of information transmission was too fast; by the time they had achieved a reasonable "fix" or grasp of the earlier items, the later ones had already gone by. Also, the requirement to reproduce what had just been heard may very well have erased any trace of the most recent items given that these would be the last played in the rendition. In standard short term recall tasks, any advantage for the last presented item can be severely curtailed by requiring report from first to last (Greene, 1986). The problem might simply be one of encoding speed and efficiency, similar to that discussed in the previous chapter. By the same token, the superior performance for the savant group on the later items may reflect their ability to keep up with the information flow, storing successive parts of each prelude in a manner which made them less susceptible to interference from other items either in encoding or recall.

There remain D.W. and M.B., both of whom show excellent general recall of the preludes as in the other AP participants, yet primacy effects, as in the non-AP subjects. The reasons for this difference are not apparent. Among the AP subjects, M.B. and D.W. have the most extensive formal training. Perhaps this training has led them to adopt a more conventional first-to-last analysis of pieces in a manner that would preserve the earlier information. It may also be relevant that pragmatic language skills are much less developed in Eddie, C.A., and L.L. than they are in the remaining participants. In any case, it should be kept in mind that the distinctiveness of D.W. and M.B. is relative; they resemble the other AP subjects (and are distinguished from the non-AP subjects) in showing exceptional recall of the material in these coherent musical segments on the basis of aural input alone. They also resemble Eddie in many crucial aspects, particularly in their attention to the essential tonal structure of a piece and in their ability to use that tonal structure in reproducing it. Recall that the preludes represented the first formal sample of Eddie's music making. Consequently, it appears that this structure extracting skill is at least a very early, if not fundamental, component of savant expertise.

"Unconventional" Musical Forms

Given their performance on the chord sequences and random note strings of Chapter 4, it is not surprising Eddie and the other savants were able to reproduce the brief preludes with a considerable degree of accuracy. They appeared to be especially adept at discovering the basic tonal structure of a piece, whatever its key signature. In many respects their knowledge was as precise as that obtained by a mature musician on examining the printed score. However, the preludes themselves were quite simple compositions; harmonically conventional and with melodic elements that often reflected some of the more obvious note relationships of the key being used. A more challenging set of compositions was recently presented to the adult savant N.P., by Sloboda, et al., (1985). N.P. was given two pieces; a conventional tonal composition taken from the classical repertoire, and a "mildly atonal" 20th-century piece by Bartok that utilized the whole tone scale. The classical composition was taken from one of Grieg's collection of Lyric Pieces for piano (Opus 47 #3). It begins in A minor, and introduces a simple melodic line supported by a rhythmic ostinato in the bass. Subsequent variations of the theme are accompanied by a series of chords with passing notes. There is eventual resolution in the key of A major. The Bartok composition is distinctive in several respects. Framed by a whole tone scale on C, different sections of the work have different pitch centers. The opening C whole tone scale is soon harmonized with an A whole tone scale to produce a series of parallel minor thirds. Subsequent sections introduce other whole tone pentatonic collections with the parallel interval motive recurring throughout. Each piece was first heard by N.P. in its entirety. Subsequently, sections were played again and he was asked to reproduce them using a format much like the listen-and-play technique we had used with Eddie.

Comparisons of N.P.'s reproductions suggested some marked differences in his sensitivity to the contrasting musical idioms. Whereas the reproduction of the classical piece was quite impressive, with few mistakes or additions, the Bartok composition was another matter. Here, there were many more stumbles and pauses in N.P.'s playing. On one trial there was not even an attempt at a reproduction. When the same pieces were given to a nonretarded adult with approximately the same number of years' experience with the piano, a different pattern of results emerged. For the comparison subject the piece by Greig was a real challenge, and far less than half was reproduced successfully. The whole-tone composition of Bartok proved to be the more easily mastered of the two for the comparison pianist, although performance was still less than perfect. Sloboda, et al., (1985) suggested this indicates some real limitations to the kind of musical expertise present in the savant, the savant's musical precocity extending only as far as the more conventional musical structures and rules.

The conclusion that savant musical expertise is quite restricted with respect to idiom is consistent with descriptions of the rather restricted range of musical interests savants are frequently described as having (cf. Chapter 1). The conclusion is not so consistent with the results reported by Charness, et al., (1988) and replicated to a large extent in Chapter 4, where savants appeared to extract scale information in a whole tone as readily as in a conventional diatonic idiom. As instances of the whole-tone format, a short string of notes and a complete composition differ considerably. As remarked earlier, it was open to question whether the savant participants truly grasped the structure of the whole-tone scales used in the note strings of the short-term memory trials. For one thing, the strings were quite brief, and for another, the format provided few opportunities for the participants to exhibit generalized knowledge of scale structure. Perhaps if Eddie were given the more extensive whole-tone composition used by Sloboda, et al., (1985) he too would find it relatively intractable.

The next experiment was designed to test this notion. Bartok's whole-tone composition and the conventional classical piece were given to Eddie and to the savant C.A. in a manner similar to that used with N.P. The adult pianists, P.M., B.A., and M.B. again provided comparison data. In the original report (Sloboda, et al., 1985) the conditions of administration varied somewhat for N.P. and their comparison subject, A.S. The procedure adopted with the present sample was that used with N.P. The complete set of trials was given to Eddie, and the others received a reduced set.

After transcription to musical scores, the subjects' renditions were evaluated using the criteria applied to their renditions of the 24 preludes. As before, no measure was given credit unless as least half the notes in the measure had been reproduced correctly. The application of this rule to the renditions of the Bartok passages was a bit difficult since many measures contained so few notes. Consequently, the 50% rule was augmented with the stipulation that any two adjacent notes also had to be appropriate either with respect to interval or sequence to be scored as correct.

The accuracy scores for each participant are presented in Tables 5.3 and 5.4 for the Grieg and Bartok compositions, respectively. Accuracy scores have been summed across successive 4 measure lengths for each piece. Comparison data from N.P. and A.S. (Sloboda, et al., 1985) are also presented after having been rescored using the current criteria.[1] Every participant received the same initial trial with each composition. Thereafter the number and length of the trials varied somewhat. Consequently formal comparisons were restricted to first trial performance while descriptive statistics were used to summarize the remaining data. Turning first to the conventional composition by Grieg, all participants on the first trial gave a reasonable rendition of the opening 8 bars. Actual note matching accuracy was highest in Eddie (75%) and lowest in C.A. and P.M. (39% and 38% respectively) with the others falling in between. Thus, the overall accuracy was a bit higher in the savants (.57) than in the comparison subjects (.52) due to the performance by Eddie. The differences between Eddie and the remaining participants, and between M.B., B.A., and C.A. versus P.M. were significant ($z=8.48$, $p < .01$ and $z=2.1$,

---

[1] I wish to thank Dr. John Sloboda for making the original data available to me.

TABLE 5.3
Matching accuracy, Lyric Piece, E. Grieg

Trial	Eddie					C.A.			A.S.*				
	1	2	3	4	5	1	2	3	1	2	3	4	5
Meas													
1-4	.88	.91	.67			.62	.74	0	.72		.64	0	0
5-8	.60	.91	.91			.15	.53	0	.15		.15	0	0
9-12		.84	.86				.16	0		0	.36	0	0
13-16		.93	.98				.15	.17		0	0	0	0
17-20			.82	.84				0					0
21-24			.66	.81				0					0
25-28			.35	.68				.15					0
29-32			.60	.61				.20					0
33-36			.15		.62			.19					
37-40			.45		.58			.18					
41-44					.72								
45-48					.69								
49-52					.67								
53-56					.77								
57-60					.76								
61-64					.82								

Trial	M.B.				P.M..			B.A.			
	1	2	3	4	1	2	3	1	2	3	4
Meas											
1-4	.50	1.00	.95		.45	.59	.52	.47	.85	.86	
5-8	.58	.98	.60	.24	.45	.29	.73	.65	.85		
9-12		.91	.93		0	0		.47	.81		
13-16		.82	.78		0	.15			.64	.82	
17-20		.33	.32				0			.64	.22
21-24			.58	.32			0			.15	0
25-28			00	.57			0			0	0
29-32			00				0			0	0
33-36			00				0			0	
37-40			00				0			0	
41-44											
45-48											
49-52											
53-56											
57-60											
61-64											

*From Sloboda, et al., (1985), data for N.P. not available

$p < .05$ respectively). Although comparable raw data for the savant N.P. were not available, Sloboda, et al., (1985) reported that his rendition of the first 8 bars was exceptionally accurate.

After the first trial, the performance of the various participants begins to

TABLE 5.4
Matching accuracy, Mikrokosmos, B. Bartok

	Eddie					C.A.				
Trial										
	1	2	3	4	5	1	2	3	4	5
Meas										
1-4	.38	.62	.85			1.00	.92	.69		
5-8	.47	.40	.20			.73	.67	.20		
9-12	.27	.18	.45			.73	.23	.36		
13-16				.35	.73				0	0
17-20				.17	.17				.17	.17
21-26				.16	.20				.28	0

	N.P.*					A.S.*			
Trial									
	1	2	3	4	5	1	2	3	
Meas									
1-4	.46	.46	.69			2.9	1.00	1.00	
5-8	.07	.53	.46			.60	.60	.60	
9-12	.18	.27	.45			.36	.45	.50	
13-16				(0)[a]	.81				
17-20				(0)	.35				
21-26				(0)	0				

	M.B.					P.M.				
Trial										
	1	2	3	4	5	1	2	3	4	5
Meas										
1-4	.77	.77	.92			.31	.31	.31		
5-8	.27	.40	.27			0	.20	.27		
9-12	.05	.54	.32			0	0	.23		
13-16				.35	.42				.15	.19
17-20				.17	0				0	0
21-26				0	.16				0	0

	B.A.				
Trial					
	1	2	3	4	5
Meas					
1-4	.77	.85	1.00		
5-8	.67	.73	.73		
9-12	.50	0	.68		
13-16				(0)[a]	0
17-20				(0)	0
21-26				(0)	0

*From Sloboda, Hermelin & O'Conner, (1985).
[a]No response attempted.

diverge. Sloboda, et al., (1985) reported that their savant N.P. easily mastered successive sections of the Grieg composition. For Eddie, too, introduction of successively larger and/or different chunks of the original did not impair performance to any great extent. Even for the more extended sections accuracy remained well above 50%. For the savant C.A., the second trial elicited a fair rendition of the first 16 measures. At trial 3, however, performance deteriorated considerably, and the session was terminated. It should be noted that these trials came at the end of a very long testing session, and fatigue likely played a role in his flagging performance.

Turning next to the comparison subjects, performance on subsequent sections of the Grieg was quite variable. For M.B. and B.A., subsequent sections always elicited a measure of accuracy, their performance often equalling Eddie's. The only exception to this was the series of modulations and transitions occurring on trial 3, measures 28–40. (Note that Eddie also found these a little difficult.) At the other extreme, A.S. showed a marked deterioration in performance after the first trial. On trial two, the procedure varied slightly for A.S., who heard only measures 9–16 rather than 1–16. Nevertheless, interference from the earlier trials prevented her from rendering the passage with any degree of accuracy. A third trial resulted in some improvement, but thereafter accuracy for no measure reached the 50% criterion. P.M., too, found the selection by Grieg quite confusing after the first 8 bars. Although she managed to produce the gist of the first portion in each of the first three trials, very few measures thereafter reached the 50% criterion for consideration.

As noted earlier, Sloboda, et al., (1985) described a marked difference favoring the comparison subject's renditions of Bartok. This advantage for A.S. over N.P. is also seen in the evaluated data (Table 5.4), although the difference is perhaps not so great as that reported by Sloboda, et al. A word about differences in scoring procedure may be helpful at this point. Rather than the note for note match used here, Sloboda, et al. concentrated on more general aspects of performance—pauses, skips, melodic inversions, and the like. Our respective gauges concentrate on different aspects of the performance. Thus, the performance by A.S. was smooth and regular, but the introduction of the second voice (measure 7) is lowered $\frac{1}{2}$ step resulting in a series of major, rather than minor third intervals. The new line is entirely consistent with this lowered pitch center though not identical to the original. N.P., by contrast, did not make this "interval error" though his performance was more halting and irregular.

In any case, in the larger sample, differences between savants and comparison subjects are much less pronounced. Indeed, individual differences within groups are more pronounced than those between. The highest overall performance on the first trial is found in the savant C.A., the lowest in the comparison subject P.M. Even omitting P.M., the performance of the comparison subjects is only slightly better than that of the savants (49% versus 43%). After the first trial individual performance patterns again emerge. For

Sloboda's pianist A.S., performance remains at a relatively high level, but with the transposition of the second whole-tone scale, as mentioned before. Five of the remaining 6 subjects show improvement over the first three trials. Only C.A. fails to improve on his initial (very accurate) first trial rendition. At trial four a new section was given to all but A.S. This section introduces two new melodies beginning on G^b and E^b, and follows with a return to the pentatonic melody on A. All participants found this a real challenge and in no one did performance on this section equal that on the first. Once again, however, differences within each group appear to be as marked as those between groups, although the data are very limited.

It is intriguing to consider how A.S. might have fared, had the second section (trials 4 and 5) been attempted. Note that like A.S., the comparison subject B.A. gave very accurate renditions of the opening measures. Thereafter, however, she apparently experienced massive interference. On the fourth trial, no response was attempted, and the fifth trial elicited a very limited reproduction with no measure reaching criterion. Thus, part of the reason for the superiority found for the comparison subject A.S. over the savant N.P. by Sloboda et al. may have been due, in part, to restricted sampling.

Of particular interest, naturally, was how Eddie would react to this relatively novel musical idiom. Eddie showed clear improvement during the course of his first exposure to Bartok. By the third trial his performance was on a par with the other participants. He seemed to assimilate the new material on trials 4 and 5 rather better than most. During the trials he showed keen interest while listening, and he clearly enjoyed the challenge provided by this new musical sound. In contrast to earlier listen and play episodes (e.g., the short term memory series of the previous chapter, and the preludes of this one) his responses were much longer than the original on every trial.

Mention of the length of Eddie's renditions raises the question of scale or idiom preserving features of subjects' responses when they were not actually replicating what they had heard. These nonmatching responses were examined to see if attention to general scale structure was evident as it had been in the earlier experiments. The most direct way to do this would be to see if participants' errors conformed to the diatonic and whole-tone scales in the two compositions. Unfortunately the nature of the music prevented treating errors in this manner. After measures 1–8, the piece by Grieg undergoes a series of harmonic modulations that introduce many chromaticisms with respect to the original A minor scale. This means that characterizing errors as scale conforming versus nonconforming is less useful than was the case with the preludes or note strings. It is noteworthy that A.S. and P.M. evidently had much more trouble with these modulations than Eddie, although all participants except N.P. became somewhat confused by them. Since the first 8 bars of the Lyric Piece constituted the clearest information about its key structure, examination of subjects' errors was restricted to that section, and can be summarized quite easily. All participants showed essentially perfect key consistent responding for these measures, indicating the extraction of essential key information was no problem. (Subject A.S. had the additional advantage in having been told the key and starting note of the piece at its outset.) On subsequent measures there is considerable divergence from the basic A minor scale among all participants as they tried to capture the later harmonic variations. Clearly those with absolute pitch were more successful at doing so (Table 5.3).

Examining scale consistency in response to Bartok's whole-tone composition presents a similar problem. As mentioned earlier, the original C whole-tone scale is soon followed by a series of different pentatonic whole tone collections presented separately and in combination. This means it is not practical to characterize notes as appropriate to a given scale, since there are several. One way to examine the idea of whole-tone scale consistency is to consider successive notes in the renditions. Do they correspond to the intervals suggested by the scale itself, and thereby preclude the use of half-tone successions (e.g., from E to F or G to Ab)? In the original composition such a half step melodic motion occurs at only one point in the piece. Consequently subjects' renditions were examined to discover whether they had followed this implicit rule in their renditions. For all but one participant half step successions were very rare, averaging between 2 and 3 per trial. The exception was P.M., who also had the most difficulty capturing the basic constituents of the piece (cf. Table 5.4). P.M. averaged 20 half-tone successions per trial in her renditions.

Another way to characterize rule following is to examine renditions for the presence of biases in the direction of a diatonic scale interpretation of the whole-tone passage. One region where this might be most easily detected is the note a perfect fifth above the tonic. This is a pivotal note in diatonic constructions and as we saw in Chapter 3, assumed some importance in participants' renditions of unconventional and conventional chords. In whole-tone scale construction, on the other hand, there is no perfect fifth and in the opening bars of Bartok, the value is never present. Were participants likely to include it anyway in their renditions? It seems not. The first 3 trials (which were restricted to the first 12 bars) were examined once again for the presence of the note "G" in the upper line and "E" in the lower because these represent the perfect fifth components to the C and A conventional diatonic scales, respectively. These notes appeared very seldom in Eddie, N.P., A.S., M.B., and B.A. (never more than twice in a trial), a bit more often in C.A. (3 times per trial) and relatively frequently in P.M. (6 times per trial). In other words, the primary difference was once again between P.M. and the other participants rather than between the savants and the comparison group. After the session P.M. commented that she had a very difficult time getting a good grasp of the basic structure of the piece by Bartok, but not that by Grieg. In any event, both error patterns suggested that in these respects at least, the savants were as adept as the comparison subjects in discerning the kinds of regularity implied in whole-tone scale usage.

What can one make of the varied patterns of response to these different musical idioms? As noted earlier, Sloboda, et al., (1985) interpreted their original results as indicating savant skill was limited to more conventional musical forms. The present results do not seem quite so straightforward, as savants Eddie and C.A. did well on the whole-tone composition. Before attempting to place these results in some general context, however, it is important to note that the compositions vary in respects other than tonality. As befitting a composition from the romantic period, the Lyric Piece has a much denser texture, chords of 4 and 5 parts being the rule. The whole-tone composition, by contrast, usually employs only 1 or 2 voices. The harmonic goals of the modulations in the Grieg are relatively predictable, centering on the A-minor key signature; the key changes in Bartok less so. Different technical demands are also apparent. In some sections Bartok requires a somewhat unusual overlap of the hands. Parts of the Grieg span well over an octave, but this is rare in the Bartok. It would be virtually impossible to find two pieces matched on everything but tonality; whole-tone compositions are rare enough. Such control rarely occurs outside the especially constructed materials of the laboratory. Comparison of the two kinds of compositions will be suggestive at best, and it will be difficult to attribute any overall differences in performance to tonality per se.

Having said this, however, the results of the earlier chapters point to certain of these factors as being particularly significant. The savant ability to disentangle complex harmonic configurations has been repeatedly demonstrated. In many respects Grieg's Lyric Piece is perfectly suited to such a skill, being essentially a study in complex voice leading for simple harmonic modulations. The Bartok passage presents a different king of challenge. Here, one must discern a basic melodic line that undergoes a series of transpositions and/or modifications. The results of the immediate memory experiments suggest that under certain conditions, savants and comparison musicians are equally adept at detecting such a "theme and variations" structure within a simple line. It may be this melodic organization, as much as the use of the whole-tone scale, which distinguishes the pieces for the listener. P.M. experienced difficulty in extracting the basic melodic line and consequently performed the most poorly of all participants on the Bartok passage, although she had encountered the whole-tone idiom occasionally in her musical experience. In contrast M.B., having both the "absolute pitch" found in the savants and a sensitivity to melodic features, was able to produce quite acceptable versions of both pieces.

Beyond this, is there any evidence savants have a special problem detecting whole-tone based regularities in music? The answer appears to be not necessarily. Based on the limited type of error analysis performed, savants appeared to be no more likely to violate the implicit rules of the whole-tone passage than the comparison subjects. Moreover, for Eddie at least, the whole-tone piece clearly was a novel and interesting challenge. At the first trial he began experimenting with the pattern of intervals it contained. In later sessions with his teacher the complete piece was taught to him and it became part of his active repertoire for a time.

This is not to say that savants are able to assimilate whole-tone material with the apparent ease they exhibit for more traditional modes. Both Eddie and N.P. seemed a bit halting in their first renditions of Bartok, but not Grieg. A further piece of evidence of a more anecdotal nature is available for the savant L.L. L.L. also was given the Bartok composition, but only in the complete version on a single trial. Nevertheless, he enthusiastically supplied a rendition. Unfortunately, the rendition was so filled with chord embellishments that I despaired of trying to analyze it. His rendering of the Grieg, also after a single presentation of the complete selection, was much more recognizable. L.L. may have a tendency to modify music toward more traditional lines (although recall that his renditions of simple whole-tone melody lines were entirely consistent). It is also quite likely that savants have had less exposure to more unusual musical idioms, such as whole-tone technique. Thus it is difficult to determine the extent to which preference and familiarity are involved as well as competence at abstracting underlying structure. However, the present results suggest savant skill or interest is by no means restricted to the traditional diatonic scale.

Long-Term Retention

As noted in the first chapter, one of the more remarkable aspects of Blind Tom's musical talent was his extensive long-term memory for music. His active repertoire was estimated to contain thousands of pieces. His ability to commit new material to (long term) memory with ease was also allegedly exceptional, although there is some question whether a single exposure to a piece was sufficient to ensure its long term retention (Tutein, 1918). Little is known about the active repertoire of other savants, although Minogue (1923) mentioned that XY's was quite extensive, and Harriet's detailed knowledge of music history is noted by Viscott (1970).

A large active music repertoire among concert performers is not unknown of course. For example, the classical pianists Anton Rubenstein and Josef Lehvinne were capable of presenting extended concert series from memory without a repetition in the overall program. In the latter case this was apparently achieved with very little effort (Schonberg, 1987). Estimates of Rubenstein's and Lehvinne's repertoire are informal, being based on a consideration of their concert schedule and programs during their most active years. The evidence for Blind Tom's repertoire is even less well specified though it seems likely his ability to recall musical material was indeed very good.

It is very difficult to make accurate estimates of long-term memory, particularly over the periods involved in building and maintaining a musical repertoire. The time span alone is usually prohibitive. Rarely does a situation permit objective monitoring of memory over a period of years. There are also difficulties in keeping track of relevant intervening events; how much has the material been recalled or rehearsed in the interim? What kinds of opportunities for retroactive interference presented themselves while the material was in long-term memory? How accurate was the original encoding of the material? Information about such issues is necessary before one can make a reasonable estimate of how much of what was originally known in an area is still available in long term memory (Bahrick & Phelps, 1987). It is not surprising there are so few studies of long-term memory that provide data relevant to these issues. However, the opportunity to work with Eddie over a period of years permitted such an examination of long-term memory, albeit of a very restricted musical sample. Recall that the 24 musical preludes discussed at the beginning of the chapter represented the first formal musical experiment with Eddie. Over the two month period during which the complete cycle of preludes was presented, a format for repeating some of the preludes in later sessions was adopted. Eight of the preludes were given names and requested, first by name, and if Eddie did not respond accurately, with a cue consisting of the opening notes of the prelude. The original objective of assigning names to these preludes was to strengthen associations between words and music. If the prelude was not successfully recalled it was replayed. Recall of most of the remaining preludes was also occasionally requested but with no labelling. In other words, only the musical cue was provided because the prelude had no assigned name. Over the course of several months, a log was kept of the number of times each prelude was successfully cued or demonstrated. As it turns out, the number of times a prelude occurred varied considerably, from zero to 10 times. No attempt was made to equate the preludes assigned to the various conditions for content or difficulty. Indeed, as already noted the preludes were reproduced at initial hearing with considerable fidelity, and each prelude was presented several times in the initial session to increase its chances of being well encoded.

In the ensuing months Eddie's attention was turned to other music. His piano lessons with Nancy had begun, and his sessions with me began to explore some of the facets of short-term memory described in the earlier chapters. The preludes had no formal role in these sessions, but occasionally, one (or snatches of one) would appear in his spontaneous playing. One year after the original presentation I decided to test recall of the preludes in more detail. I introduced each of several sessions with a comment that we were going to "play some of the old songs" and after introducing the first bar of a favorite of his (one that had appeared spontaneously quite often) asked him to play the song. This priming procedure was then used once for each of the 23 remaining preludes, and Eddie's renditions were recorded. Renditions were transcribed to musical staves by an accomplished pianist. Eddie's renditions were then compared note by note to the originals in a manner identical to that followed in immediate memory assessment, except that reproduction of the first (priming) measure was not counted.

Eddie's recall of the preludes was quite variable. For one prelude (#18) the cuing produced no additional matching material. This prelude also had the lowest accuracy rate in the original memory test (32%). Request for another prelude yielded accurate recall of only a quarter of the original. For the remaining 22 pieces, however, Eddie was able to recall at least half of the original, and perfect recall was found in several instances. The effect of various background factors on recall was investigated in a series of analyses of variance. These considered the relation between long term recall and original immediate recall accuracy, number of subsequent exposures, and whether a name had been assigned. None of these variables exerted a significant effect on long term recall, although there were trends in the directions one would expect. It is noteworthy that even though the named preludes were presented far more often than the unnamed ones (an average of almost 8 versus 2½ times) there was only slightly better overall recall for the named preludes (74 versus 72%).

Figure 5.8 portrays accuracy as a function of scale degree, separately for the major and minor preludes. The dotted lines represent comparison data for the same scale degrees in the immediate memory test. Several aspects of long-term recall emerge in this comparison. First, generally speaking, the relative accuracy for the various scale degrees is quite similar in immediate and long-term recall, particularly the accuracy for diatonic versus nondiatonic notes. (The difference between average diatonic and nondiatonic note accuracy

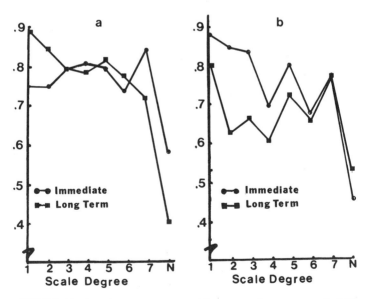

FIGURE 5.8. Matching accuracy, immediate versus long-term recall, Eddie (a = Preludes in major key, b = Preludes in minor key).

was significant in long term recall for both modes). Second, whereas short-term recall measures indicated no difference as a function of mode, in long-term recall, major key preludes now have a clear advantage over those in a minor key (79% versus 69%). This difference did not seem to reflect any special advantage given the major preludes in the interim between immediate and long-term recall assessments. Several of Eddie's favorite songs were in the minor mode, and major mode pieces were prompted no more frequently. Finally there were extremely few "errors" or notes not consistent with the key of the primed prelude (fewer than 1% of all notes played). Nonmatching notes consistent with the key were somewhat more common, averaging a little more than a quarter of notes played, and appeared much more often in the renditions of minor key preludes ($\overline{X}=.38$ versus $\overline{X}=.14$).

As a rough comparison, I also requested G.J. and H.H. to play some of the preludes from memory 6 months after they were first shown them. The procedure was similar to that used with Eddie. I played the first measure and asked them to complete it as best they could. The recall test was restricted to the 8 preludes they had been allowed to examine as well as hear, so their immediate recall of this material had been quite respectable (cf. figure 5-6), though not as good as Eddie's. The results were quite straightforward. Neither H.H. nor G.J. were able to recall any specific content of the 8 preludes heard and seen 6 months earlier. They may have retained some general information about style and tonality. Each was willing to give at least some rendition on most trials, and their renditions tended to preserve the key of the original, but the task was clearly a challenge (and a surprise) for them.

There are probably several reasons Eddie's recall was so much better than that of two accomplished pianists. First, of course, Eddie's original exposure had been more intense. In addition to the repeated exposures occurring in the original session, most of the tunes were reviewed periodically during the next several months. By contrast G.J. and H.H. had only a single exposure with no intervening review. Both ease of original learning and the opportunity for review, even only a single review, are important for long-term retention (Bahrick & Phelps, 1987). Eddie was clearly at an advantage on both counts. Of the two factors, original learning and review, the former seemed the more important for Eddie. Four preludes were heard only in the original immediate memory test, yet accuracy for these (83%) was actually a bit higher than average.

Another factor is suggested by comments made by G.J. and H.H. during the recall session; "I didn't know I was supposed to memorize them" and "They weren't very memorable." Intent to commit something to long-term memory is certainly important for retention, and G.J. and H.H. had no particular reason to commit these pieces to memory. Indeed, it is very useful to be able to forget things we probably will not need later. For Eddie, at least when it comes to music, this distinction between "to be remembered" and "to be forgotten" is likely nonexistent. The music of the preludes was much more memorable in this respect than the titles I had assigned to them. In spite of repeated attempts to get Eddie to recall by name only, successful name-theme associations were made in only about half the cases. Eddie has become much more adept at such directed remembering now, but originally this was not the case.

There is another sense in which those early sessions with the preludes were particularly memorable for Eddie. They were our first times together and they represented one of the first occasions for consistent, interactive music making by Eddie. Their distinctiveness in extra-musical respects probably enhanced the sessions' music for Eddie. Some anecdotal evidence in support of this comes from another memory test I performed with Eddie on the Lyric Piece by Grieg. This was also played in a single session over several trials. As we have seen, Eddie's immediate recall of it was excellent. The piece has never been repeated nor has it appeared in his spontaneous playing. About 6 months after its original presentation, I tried to assess recall with a 1-measure "prime" as I had used with the preludes. Eddie's response indicated no reliable recall of the music. Since then I have tried with successively longer primes, up to the first 4 measures of the original. In no instance has Eddie played any identifiable rendition beyond what he had just heard. It may be that for Eddie, by the time the Grieg was introduced, it too was "not very memorable," and so has faded.

As this example indicates, Eddie's long-term musical memory is impressive, but it is certainly not infallible. It appears to have the same sorts of regularities and lawfulness that characterize long-term memory in general. It is dependent on an accurate, well encoded initial representation. It shows selective recall consistent with the overall structure of the material, and it tends to be constructive or reconstructive rather than literal. One aspect of Eddie's long-term memory is a bit puzzling; the more accurate recall of major than minor key material. Why did the mode effect occur in the long-term but not the short-term memory test? Mode effects were present in the short-term recall of the other savants, and one might expect them to persist in long-term memory. For Eddie, however, immediate recall accuracy in the two modes was nearly identical. Perhaps the emergence of a mode effect reflects Eddie's growing sensitivity to the differences in mode usage in his environment. Or the long-term recall measure could be a more sensitive index of these usage differences. There is also the inevitable problem of sample size to consider. Recall of the minor preludes was quite variable, in 4 cases being less than 60%, in another 4 cases, over 85%. In any event, the mode effect was clearly much less robust than that of chromaticism, which strongly affected both short- and long-term retention.

Discussion

Several questions prompted the research described in this chapter. How sensitive are savants to the rules and conventions that govern the music in our culture? We saw in the earlier chapters that savant recall of musical segments is neither flawless nor literal. Moreover, errors were not random, but were consistent with different structural aspects of what they had heard. To what extent did this selectivity extend to the patterns found in a coherent musical composition? Second, how is savant expertise in the "bits and pieces" or prose elements of music, the chords, melodic and rhythmic fragments examined in Chapter 4, related to their performance of coherent music? Are these smaller units the natural building blocks of musical skill development, as suggested by many formal assessments of musical talent (e.g., Seashore, 1938; Bentley, 1966) or are they essentially irrelevant to the understanding of music, as some have argued (e.g., Serafine, 1987)? Finally, where does savant skill stand in relation to that of the mature, performing musician? Does the savant represent a particular kind of unique or abnormal musical expertise, or does savant musical understanding embody the same kinds of principles as those found in the mature musician?

With regard to the first question, the present results provide strong converging evidence that savants attend to the implicit rules that govern music composition in our culture. This was evident, first, in their renditions of the brief musical preludes. In these renditions, notes consistent with the underlying scale were much more likely to be reproduced accurately. Harmonic structure emerged as a particularly important factor in performance. Scale type differences were also observed, recall of major mode compositions usually being more accurate than that of pieces in a minor mode. Because the latter appears to be the less commonly used in musical composition, this suggests a sensitivity of a somewhat different sort; one perhaps reflecting degree of familiarity with different musical idioms. This does not mean savant skill (or interest) is necessarily limited to more conventional musical idioms. Even Bartok's whole-tone passage elicited largely accurate renditions from the savant participants, although their accuracy was less impressive.

It is also apparent that the musical rules exhibited in savant performance were generative in nature. Some evidence of generative rule usage was also seen in the earlier reproductions of the note strings, where errors more likely conformed to scale structure than not. For the musical selections of this chapter the evidence is more conclusive, in that the longer selections (and resulting renditions) led to more reconstruction and/or improvisation by the participant. If anything, these renditions were more rule consistent than the originals, for example, by the frequent omission of nondiatonic material and reinforcement of the tonic.

The attention to implicit musical rules in both the fragments of Chapters 3 and 4 and the intact compositions here gives considerable support to the contention that the two are intimately related. That is, factors critical in the processing of music on the molar scale of extended compositions are also at work at the molecular level of note clusters and sequences. Evidence from the chord and melody reproduction tasks suggested that subjects with absolute pitch would be particularly adept at disentangling the chord structure, or more generally, the basic harmonic pattern in music. This was borne out in the analysis of relative accuracy for the harmonic versus melodic aspects of the brief preludes. It also was suggested as an important factor in the patterns of response to the Grieg and Bartok passages. There was evidence, too, that individual differences in primacy/recency effects seen in the response to musical fragments had an analogue in the response to intact music. As a group savants showed less pronounced primacy effects than the comparison subjects on both types of material. Among the savants, the strong primacy seen in D.W. on musical fragments was also seen in her response to the preludes. It is interesting to examine Eddie's "profile" in the two kinds of content, fragmentary and intact. On chord and melodic groups Eddie showed a pattern similar to the other savants, excelling at the former. He seemed to regularize a bit more than most, putting in missing fifths, for example, or having difficulty with conflicting contextual cues. On the other hand, he was very quick to pick up strange or unfamiliar idioms, even when these were based on an arbitrary rule. These strengths were also seen in his performance in this chapter. Eddie was superb at detecting regularities in music even when the regularities were realized in a relatively unfamiliar idiom. Irregularities in the form of chromaticisms or melodic minor modulations (e.g., prelude 18) gave him some trouble. He exhibited a remarkably open mind about music whatever its manifestation, and one that seemed particularly tuned to the general principle at work.

The experimental analysis of musical cognition (Sloboda, 1985) is replete with examples of organizing principles behind the perception and performance of the mature normal musician. Their appearance in Eddie and the other savants indicates that in this respect they are more like their fellow musicians than unlike them. The most direct support for this contention came from comparison of the savants and those asked to reproduce musical passages after being allowed to examine the score as well as hear the music. In both cases, subjects were intent on (and largely successful at) capturing the general character of the piece. Wolfe (1976) suggests that in the superior sight reader, the primary concern is discerning the general gist of the music and the recurring pattern or regularities that occur within that general context. This orientation leads to less concern about individual note accuracy such as that seen in one preparing a piece for recital. Indeed, such minute attention to detail might be inimical to successful sight reading. Interviews with successful sight readers indicate this may be a conscious strategy—check the key signature, look for a repeating bass figure, note the chordal cadence (Wolfe, 1976). The suggestion here is not that similar conscious strategies are being applied by the savant, although they may be. Rather, given that these strategies refer to structural aspects of the music, they are used in the encoding and retrieving process. The means of uncovering these regularities in music may or may not involve formal training. In the savant this seems not so important. What is critical is some regularity or patten recognizing and reproducing facility on the part of the musical cognizer. Eddie and the other savants appear to have this in full measure.

The discussion thus far has omitted any reference to the rhythmic dimension of music. There are several reasons for this omission, the primary one being practical. Whereas note chroma matching was a fairly straightforward procedure with the available data-transcribing software, note or interval duration matching was not. To do so would have involved adopting a set of more or less arbitrary rules for determining rhythmic units, and assigning starting and ending points to phrases. While it seemed reasonable to do this in the earlier temporal fragments, when chroma was not involved, here both the length and the nature of temporal variations made this determination difficult. For example, how should one consider the hesitations and abrupt starts that characterize "on line" recall of the musical extracts?

To some extent this ambiguity in rhythm determination probably reflects some fundamental problems in extracting a basic rhythmic pattern from an ongoing stream of events (cf. Lee, 1985). It may also indicate something about the different roles that rhythm and tempo can play in musical interpretations. Eddie often seemed disposed to modify rhythmic as well as harmonic elements in his renditions. However, although his harmonic modifications were more often of the tonic triad reinforcing variety, rhythmic ones sometimes changed the basic pattern, usually in the direction of increasing syncopation.

Informally, there seemed to be nothing distinctive about the rhythmic accuracy of any participant in the "preludes" or "whole-tone" experiments. All captured the basic rhythmic pattern of the original, some (especially Eddie) seemed to play with it a bit. For all participants, the primary referent of the listen-and-play instructions seemed to be the melodic and harmonic character of a piece. Similarly, terminating an attempt more often seemed to result from a failure to retrieve chroma rather than rhythmic information. Of course this could have reflected the rhythmic simplicity of the selections. It could also mean, as suggested in the preceding chapter, that rhythm usually has a subsidiary role in conventional musical forms, and that rhythmic facility (among pianists, at least) is more difficult to distinguish. In this restricted sense the results of the musical pieces agree with those of the musical fragments in suggesting nothing exceptional about rhythmic skill in the musical savant.

In his classic study Revesz (1925/1970) describes a series of tests of immediate and long-term memory for music in the child prodigy, Erwin Nyiregyhazi. Though using different stimulus materials, in many respects the broad outline of the tests is similar to that described here, and a comparison of results may be instructive. These experiments were conducted during roughly the same chronological age span (6–11 years old) as Eddie. After a series of trials examining Erwin's short term memory for musical excerpts, Revesz concluded that while it was very impressive, it was rather more so for melodic than harmonic dimensions of the pieces given (Revesz, p. 96). As mentioned earlier

(Chapter 3), Nyiregyhazi was able to render isolated complex chords with great precision, and this conclusion about more extended musical excerpts may reflect an attentional bias or preference on Erwin's part (he apparently loved operatic arias) rather than a particular performance limitation.

Erwin was also compared on optical versus acoustic memory, either being allowed to examine the score or only listen to it played. Even at his tender age, optical exposure was better than acoustic. In the latter case even single melodic lines were sometimes reproduced only after considerable repetition. Throughout the series, Revesz was impressed by the young pianist's grasp of the overall structure and tonality of the pieces he saw and/or heard: "Erwin, with the greatest ease, memorized melodious pieces harmonized in a simple manner" (Revesz, p. 90). However, as with the participants of the studies in the present chapter, deviations or irregularities in tonal structure apparently caused some difficulty: "In the case of musical pieces of a strange character, such as melodies with complicated accompaniment and peculiar harmonies, his memory did not prove itself equal to the task" (Revesz, p. 90). A change in the direction of more sophisticated understanding of musical structure was observed over the years in Erwin's harmonic modulations during improvisation. At first these were restricted to closely related keys, or were rather abrupt. With musical development came a more sophisticated and complex technique for effecting transitions between even distantly related keys (Revesz, p. 118–121).

Even more impressive was Erwin's long-term memory for material. Once learned, a piece remained in his repertoire virtually intact. In an intriguing comparison, Revesz contrasted the short-term and extended memory (24 hours or more) of Erwin and an adult, classically trained pianist who also had absolute pitch. On the whole, the adult reportedly was more accurate on short-term recall after limited exposure. On measures of long-term recall of the same material Erwin was the more accurate of the two. In some instances Revesz reports Erwin's long term recall to be more accurate than short term recall of the same material (p. 94).

In broad outline the results of the tests given the prodigy Nyiregyhazi are consistent with those of the participants described here. Superior pitch naming skill confers a great advantage in encoding and recalling new music. Absolute pitch is by no means the whole story, however. In addition, there is a sensitivity to harmonic and melodic conventions in the music so that new material embodying these conventions is easily mastered. And real mastery it is, for long-term as well as short-term recall excels.

There are also some differences. Erwin's superior "optical" recall at the ages of 6 and 7 suggests a prodigious acquisition of sight reading capabilities as well as an outstanding ear. He was introduced to printed music scarcely a year before the experiments reported by Revesz were begun. Erwin also had the benefit of more formal and extensive music training than is the case with the savants. Revesz notes exceptional, if not prodigious talents in other aspects of Erwin's development too, and he was apparently well suited to the sophisticated musical environment he enjoyed. Even so, there are many commonalities in the early music of Erwin the prodigy and Eddie the savant.

Many of the experiments described in the previous chapters took place while Eddie was taking his lessons, as described in Appendix A. The presence of these lessons means, of course, that there is a potential confounding in the results of the experiments. It was not possible or even desirable to prevent some measure of interaction between the experiments and the other activities we enjoyed together. Lessons and experiments were conducted at different times, and usually by different people. Within our experimental sessions, I tried to distinguish "work" times from "play" times. Eddie's piano teacher and I keep in close contact with each other about his progress, and I was present at many of his lessons. With this perspective, there didn't seem to be any obvious instance in which Eddie's performance in an experiment was the consequence of training during the music lessons. There was no change in the basic pattern of results for those experiments completed before music lessons (e.g., the prelude experiment of Chapter 5) and those after over a year of lessons (the chord and rhythm experiments of Chapter 4). Lessons formalized and elaborated many of the musical ideas Eddie already appreciated implicitly. Within the time span of the experiments, it is unlikely they changed him musically in a more fundamental sense.

Correlates and
Consequences of Savant Skill

The observations of the preceding chapters indicate that the musical skill exhibited by the savant is complex and sophisticated. This skill does not exist in a vacuum, and considering it independently of other areas of functioning neglects the more general role of music for the savant. What is the context of savant skill? What did music mean to Eddie? Was he using it in any special way as a response to his environment? How did people in the environment respond to his music? How did Eddie's musical talent fit in with other areas of his functioning and how did he fit in to his physical and social environment?

These questions are important ones, both practically and theoretically. Practically speaking, it would be useful for clinicians and other practitioners to know what other types of behavior to expect (if anything) when savant behavior is present. Does the presence of savant skill indicate a more favorable outcome? Are certain kinds of problems more likely if savants are encouraged or inhibited by the environment? Does having a savant skill change the way one interacts with one's environment? Theoretically, the correlates of savant behavior are important for several reasons. Current definitions acknowledge an interpersonal as well as an intellectual facet to mental retardation:

> Mental retardation refers to significantly subaverage general intellectual functioning existing concurrently with deficits in adaptive behavior, and manifested during the developmental period. (Grossman, 1977, p. 11)

The two domains of responding to one's environment are related; social interactions affect, and are affected by cognitive functions (Shantz, 1983). For the mentally retarded person, these interactions of social and cognitive factors may assume special important. For example, the experience of repeated failure on cognitive tasks may affect the retarded person's initiative and success in relatively unfamiliar situations (Ollendick, Balla, & Zigler, 1971; Stevenson & Zigler, 1958). Conversely, continued experiences with unstimulating environments such as those found in traditional institutions can have negative consequences for cognitive functioning (Hagen & Huntsman, 1971). For the savant, the interactions of social and intellectual factors may be of particular interest given his unusual cognitive skill structure.

Superficially, it would seem the savant is at a distinct advantage in comparison to his mentally retarded peers. Given the presence of some areas of exceptionality in the savant, one might expect the literature to indicate positive intra- and interpersonal consequences of savant skills. This is often not the case, however. Descriptions of musical savants emphasize the disturbances they experience in many areas of interpersonal behavior. Returning once again to the case material reviewed in Chapter 1, S. is described as exhibiting "weak, shallow and short-lived emotions" and occasionally displaying "excessive boorishness" (Anastasi & Levee, 1960, p. 697). Minogue (1923) noted about her case, "Emotionally, this boy is excitable, egocentric, usually cheerful and obedient, but very sensitive and wholly incapable of a social existence" (p. 351). The most extensive behavioral report is again provided by Scheerer, et al. (1945) who describe L. as being severely delayed in social development when taken to nursery school as a young child. "He barely notices the presence of other children [and] does not play with any child or participate in group activity . . . Aside from his consistent love of music and his dependency on his mother, there is little emotionality of normal depth and coherence" (p. 4). By the age of 11, L's behavior had changed considerably, due to his mother's concerted effort to normalize his social development: "The mother's continuing effects to 'socialize' his conduct . . . led to demonstrable improvement. Conformity patterns appear, at the same time his social response repertoire increases and his temper and restlessness diminish" (p. 7). However, a bit later "his emotional responses and human attachments remain shallow and perfunctory" (p. 15). These descriptions certainly suggest some difficulties in social development, and particularly social cognition, among musical savants. They appear to have a difficult time perceiving and responding to the various cues by which people usually communicate emotions and attitudes (e.g., Ekman, 1982).

The presence of pathology in many different areas of functioning is predicted by traditional conceptions of the particular significance music has for the savant. In fact, the prevailing view is that the presence of savant skill is disadvantageous for the child. Some writers have hypothesized that the musical behavior seen in the savant is a consequence of various pathological conditions. For example, the intense interest in music seen in the savant Harriet G. (Viscott, 1970) was attributed to certain environmental and interpersonal events of a traumatic nature which were associated with music during her first year of life. (Recall that Harriet G. apparently spent a great deal of time in a crib next to the piano while her mother was busy giving voice lessons.) Traumatic events of a less specific sort are postulated for savants by Sherwin (1953) and Bergman and Escalona (1948). Sherwin, for example, suggests that savant behaviors represent the expression of diffuse prior need states or conflicts for the child. A general set of pathological circumstances underlying savant behavior is also proposed by Nurcombe and Parker (1964). These authors suggest that, for a variety of reasons, the child has been inappropriately channeled or forced by his environment to spend all of his time on a single activity such as music. In this respect, the savant is thought to share some of the characteristics of the child prodigy (e.g., Wallace, 1986). In both cases, family pressures may result in a pathological channeling of the activities and interests of the child with consequent distortions in other areas of development.

A second perspective holds that savant behavior is inherently pathological. This approach contrasts with that above by having an internal focus for its analysis. Thus, the pathology is thought to indicate a certain type of defect in psychological processing rather than a series of environmental pressures or traumas. The savant's preoccupation with music has been characterized as obsessive in nature (e.g., Nurcombe & Parker, 1964) and this obsessiveness has been seen, in turn, as typical of savants (Lewis, 1985). There is certainly some support for this view in descriptions occasionally encountered in savant histories. O'Connell's (1974) savant was fond of repeatedly playing a series of diminished seventh chords as a kind of musical representation of the cardinal directions. Scheerer, et al., report that their savant for a time appeared "fixed on a certain operatic selection, repeating it over and over for days" (p. 8). The savant's sensitivity to sounds has also been interpreted as pathological in nature. Bergman and Escalona (1948) propose that such sensitivities indicate a weak protective barrier between the child and the environment. This, in turn, can lead to a greater susceptibility to trauma or to the erection of premature ego defenses to deal with the problems resulting from the sensitivity.

Not only is savant behavior frequently seen as indicative of pathology, it has also been suggested that savant skills affect subsequent development adversely. Several mechanisms for such an effect have been proposed. Robinson and Vitale (1954) see many of the interests of the savant as asocial. Time spent on such solitary behaviors as practicing music or calculating sums is time away from the broader social environment. When carried to excess, as it often appears to be in the savant, normal social development is hindered. Savants' skills therefore aggravate any pre-existing difficulty in establishing normal social relations. Others suggest that savant skills have adverse intrapsychic consequences. The savant child is seen as having only limited intellectual and attentional resources at his disposal. Expending these resources on savant interests means less time or attention available to be spent in other areas of cognitive development (Cain, 1969; Viscott, 1970). Again, a certain measure of unevenness in development is predicted. Probably the most extreme example of such unevenness is the case of Nadia (Selfe, 1977), an autistic girl with precocious drawing ability. According to Selfe, as Nadia's language became less echolalic and her social interactions improved, her drawings lost their early sophistication. Selfe concluded that Nadia's early drawing skill was closely linked to her difficulties in communicating with her environment. As communication improved, drawing became less central in Nadia' interactions with her environment, and less a focus of personal expression. Cain (1969) also suggests that typical savant interests entail passive or noninteractive information acquisition, which is not conducive to more advanced levels of development.

In summary, the presence of musical skill in a savant has been held to reflect developmental disturbance in three different ways: by indicating pathology in the events of early childhood, by indicating the presence of an information processing system which is overly sensitive to such trauma, and finally by indicating a channeling of interests in a manner inimical to balanced development. Given the number of problems hypothesized to be associated with savant behavior, it should come as no surprise that at least one model has proposed a close link between savant behavior in the retarded and extreme forms of psychopathology (Nurcombe & Parker, 1964) the implication being that the presence of savant behavior indicates an especially poor prognosis for the individual.

Of course, one might expect to see some measure of pathological behavior in the savant. Mentally retarded persons are generally at risk for a wide range of disturbances in functioning (Reiss, Levitan, & McNally, 1982). However, such a close tie to extreme forms of pathology would mean savant behavior in the retarded is not something to be encouraged. Some concerns about such a tie are found in the case histories. L's parents were worried that his excessive interest in music prevented him from pursuing other activities. L. L's foster mother strictly curtailed his time on the piano. As mentioned earlier, Sacks (1985) reports a case of calculating savant twins who were separated to prevent them from exercising their talent with each other. In each of these cases, it was assumed that there were dangers in the savant's preoccupation with his area of interest.

In large part, the conclusions just reviewed are based on case descriptions with limited comparison data. The comparisons most frequently made note the similarities of savant personality characteristics and those of psychotic (Nurcombe & Parker, 1964) or autistic (Sarason & Gladwin, 1958; Scheerer, et al., 1945) people. However, the definition of savant syndrome suggests samples of the mentally retarded as the more appropriate comparison group. Such data could address whether savant behavior is associated with additional pathology, other things being equal. Attempts to approach the question in this fashion have been rare. Thus, Duckett (1977), after an extensive review of documented cases of savants (of all kinds), concluded that slightly less than half of the 43 cases were considered to be emotionally disturbed. This figure may seem high, but compared to normative rates of mental disorders among the retarded, it is not extreme (Reiss, et al., 1982). Duckett (1977) also provided a formal comparison in an analysis of maladaptive behavior in 25 savants. The savants in this sample included calendar calculators and people with special mechanical, reading, or memory abilities as well as those gifted musically. No formal assessment of savant skill in any area was attempted; instead, subjects were nominated by institutions participating in a general survey. Comparison subjects also came from these institutions and were matched to the savants on age, IQ, and sex. (Not surprisingly, given the results of the review presented in Chapter 1, only two of the savants were women.)

Conflicting results emerged from the analysis of these 2 groups on 3 different measures of maladaptive behavior. When institutional records were examined, the savant group's records were much more likely than those of the controls to include examples of emotional disturbance and school misbehavior. Clinical judgments based on personal observations made by Duckett yielded a similar result; 60% of the savants were judged to be disturbed, compared to only 28% of the control group. The third measure used was the AAMD Adaptive Behavior Scales (Nichira, Foster, Shellhaas, & Leland, 1974) completed for each subject using institutional staff as informants. Here the savants actually performed better than the control group on academic achievement. Of the 24 AAMD Adaptive behavior scales, savants performed better on two scales measuring such skills as the ability to handle money and to tell time. The savant subjects also had significantly higher rates of abnormal stereotyped behaviors and unacceptable and eccentric behaviors according to these ratings. Duckett concluded that idiot savants are "more like their peers than unlike them" (p. 311), and that past characterizations of savants as exhibiting extreme levels of maladaptive behavior were unwarranted.

Duckett's study did not differentiate types of savant skills, and it is not clear whether the pattern of strengths and weaknesses she observed apply equally to all types of savants. In an attempt to determine this, we (Monroe & Miller, 1988) examined social and emotional adjustment in a group of retarded subjects nominated by area institutions for their exceptional musical interests and skills. Control nonmusical subjects were also chosen from participating institutions, using the criteria suggested by Duckett. In addition, all subjects were given a formal test of basic music discrimination skills (Bentley, 1966) as well as two brief measures of cognitive functions (vocabulary and immediate memory). As expected, the music measure strongly discriminated the two groups with very little overlap in total scores. Overall, neither AAMD behavior scale distinguished the two groups, though the savant group exhibited less evidence of maladjustment on the Reiss scales of maladaptive behavior (Reiss, 1987). There were indications that the two groups differed in specific areas. Savants presented significantly fewer conduct problems, but were marginally more likely to engage in stereotyped behaviors and to be socially withdrawn. We also discussed the study's aims and hypotheses with the teachers after all data had been completed. Interestingly, the majority of the teachers had intuitive hypotheses quite different from our own, predicting that the musical group would show more strange or aberrant behavior, agreeing with historical thought in this area. Why should there be such discrepancies between the various measures and descriptions of savant adaptive behavior? One possibility is that the individuals in the Duckett and the Monroe and Miller studies are not really comparable to the cases reviewed in Chapter 1 (i.e., previously documented cases representing extreme levels of skill). On the basis of traditional notions, this difference in skill level could be related to differences in pathology. For example, if the level of savant skill seen in the case descriptions represents an obsessive preoccupation with a very limited content area (Viscott, 1970) or if excessive attention to one interest by the savant inhibits development in other areas (Nurcombe & Parker, 1964), pathology might be expected only for those showing exceptional savant skills. However, 3 of the nominated savants in Monroe and Miller (1988) also participated in the experiments of the preceding chapters (subjects D.W., N.Y., and C.N.). It is clear from their performance profiles that their talent was remarkable, yet these three subjects showed no greater pathology than the remainder of the nominated savants.

Another reason for the conflicting picture of savant pathology might lie in the measures themselves. AAMD scores represent evaluations of specific behaviors by observers who are frequently in contact with the subject. Unless accompanied by careful operational definition, general clinical judgments of the sort used by Duckett (1977) are often quite unreliable (Matarazzo, 1983). The case material similarly seems to rely primarily on general clinical impressions. It may be that such impressions are simply not representative of savants' behavior, and that relative to their nonsavant, retarded peers, savants actually show better levels of general adaptation. It is also possible that both the objective test results and the case/clinical conclusions are valid, reflecting different aspects of savant behavior. The AAMD adaptive behavior scales assess both achievements in specific content areas (language, various self-help skills, etc.) and various types of antisocial or socially unacceptable behavior. Clinical impressions may be primarily based upon the latter, therefore agreeing with the AAMD results of Duckett (1977), but not of Monroe and Miller (1988).

Finally, it is highly likely that savant skills differ considerably in their social consequences. In this respect, the musical savant probably has a significant advantage. Music has expressive and communicative qualities that are readily appreciated by others and performing music provides a means of contact with others (Cooke, 1959). This was clearly the case for many of the savants described in Chapter 1. Blind Tom performed for a variety of audiences. L.L. had just returned from a tour of Japan when the experiments in the earlier chapters were conducted. More modest accomplishments were reported for several of the other savants, who occasionally played with professional musicians. Several participants of the Monroe and Miller (1988) musical group were members of a blues band. By contrast, the social interactions associated with savant skill expression for calendar calculators are generally restricted to demonstrations of their skill to each other or to the occasionally interested passerby (Sacks, 1985).

This brief review indicates a diverse and, at times, confusing picture of the social correlates of savant behavior; it is likely that no single characteristic "savant pattern" of social interaction is likely to emerge. Moreover, the concerns about "pathological" consequences of musical interests described earlier are in marked contrast to the assumptions of many techniques which use music as a primary therapeutic tool with disabled children (e.g., Nordoff & Robbins, 1971; Alvin, 1978). These music therapies are based on the assumption that music has the potential to provide an important nonverbal medium for stimulating many different areas of development. The positive effects of these interventions are thought to extend considerably beyond the improvement of musical skills. It is difficult indeed to accommodate the view that music activities are therapeutic with the idea that exceptional musical skill is pathological.

Nevertheless, previous work did suggest several central issues of concern in examining Eddie's general social and cognitive development. First among these was the channelling or limited resource notion of savant behavior; the idea that the continued exercise of a savant's special interests would probably be at the cost of development in other areas. This became a very real issue soon after I was introduced to Eddie. Should additional help be sought for his musical interests, and if so, what kind? I arranged for a professional musician to start seeing Eddie, thereby opting for a "music first" approach to this part of his education. Were some of the school consultants justified in their criticisms of our planned piano lessons and playing sessions on the grounds that Eddie would become "fixated" on the piano? Conversely, might one find evidence of "spill-over effects" or generalization from savant skills resulting in improvement in other areas of development? Second, were there particular problems or issues associated with Eddie's special talent? Would he exhibit any special barriers to growth? How would he respond to attempts to modify and challenge his competencies in different areas?

The sources of information used in answering these questions were varied, consisting primarily of notes and recordings of interactions with Eddie over the past 4 years. Eddie was also formally evaluated each year by the staff at the center he first attended, and these reports provide additional data regarding his general development. Finally, interviews with school staff and family members suggested how Eddie's special talents and problems have been perceived by those who interacted with him on a daily basis. Table 6.1 contains a summary of the formal staff evaluations over a 2-year span while Eddie was participating in music sessions with us. The first evaluations were made shortly

TABLE 6.1
Callier-Azusa performance, (in year equivalents)

	Eddie			Comparison			
				DN-a	JB-b	LK-c	AC-d
(Years) CA=	6	7	8	9	11	14	15
Motor							
Posture	2.8	3.5	3.5	3.5	2.2	3.0	2.5
Locomotion	1.7	3.0	3.0	4.0	4.5	2.6	3.0
Fine Motor	3.7	4.5	4.5	5.0	1.9	4.5	4.6
Visual Motor	2.0	3.0	4.2	2.3	0	0	3.3
Perception							
Vision	1.3	5.0	5.0	5.0	0	0	5.0
Audition	2.3	2.2	2.5	2.2	1.8	2.5	2.5
Tactual	3.0	7.0	7.0	7.0	1.8	7.0	3.2
Daily Living							
Dressing	3.0	3.5	3.5	4.2	1.9	3.0	3.5
Pers. Hygiene	2.8	4.5	4.5	5.0	2.7	4.5	4.5
Eating	2.8	3.5	3.5	4.2	3.5	4.8	4.7
Toilet	4.0	6.0	6.0	4.2	3.5	6.0	6.0
Cognition							
Cognition	1.2	2.7	3.0	2.1	1.0	2.3	2.3
Reception	1.2	3.3	3.3	1.7	1.9	4.5	3.3
Expression	1.3	2.5	3.0	1.7	2.7	3.3	1.9
Speech	1.5	2.0	2.5	2.2	2.0	2.2	1.5
Social							
Adults	1.3	2.0	2.0	2.2	2.0	2.0	1.8
Peers	.5	2.5	6.0	2.0	1.3	2.0	1.3
Environment	1.0	1.8	6.0	2.9	1.3	5.0	.5

a—enrolled at age 3 with devel. 12-24 mo. range.
b—enrolled at age 5 with devel. 12-18 mo. range.
c—enrolled at age 6 with devel. 24-36 mo. range.
d—enrolled at age 4 with devel. 12-18 mo. range.

after the onset of music sessions, which occurred about 16 months after the corrective surgery had been performed for his congenital cataracts. The scores are from the Callier-Azusa scales, an instrument for assessing various components of social and cognitive development in multiply handicapped children (Hansen, Young, & Ulreg, 1982; Stillman, 1978).

The data in Table 6.1 reflect improvement in many areas of development during the time the piano became an integral part of Eddie's life. Within the first year, major gains were evident almost across the board, with some progress exceeding the average expected rate of development (12 months). Especially prominent are gains in visual and tactual perception, social areas of cognition, and social responses toward peers. These were indicated by successful performance on such tasks as matching objects tactually and visually, localizing stimulation to body parts, constructing objects from materials and subsequently remembering their location, and imitating the role of an adult or teacher in an appropriate situation (e.g., directing activity of a peer). During the second year, Eddie's progress remained substantial though the rate was not quite so dramatic. One of the reasons for the decline in rate may be the nature of the items which comprise the Callier-Azusa scales. They are designed to be particularly sensitive to differences at lower developmental levels (Stillman, 1978). By the second testing session, all appropriate items in the vision and tactual perceptual area were passed and the scores consequently reached the highest level possible. (Ironically, the auditory perception area, one of Eddie's strengths, has a very low ceiling of 2.5 years on the scale.) The daily living item cluster also has a relatively low ceiling, and except for eating, not much improvement could be expected. Eddie's finickiness about food and eating continues to this day. Prominent gains continue in the second year in visual motor coordination, and two social areas, peers and environment. The latter two clusters contain such items as selecting certain playmates for games, wanting to win games and internalization of social rules appropriate to a setting. These represent the most advanced levels assessed by the scale.

Comparison data are provided by 4 other students at the school. These children were among the highest functioning at the school, and like Eddie, participated in a simple preschool curriculum as part of their daily schedule. Unfortunately, comparable earlier Callier-Azusa scale scores were not available for these students. Instead, the chronological ages at the time of Callier-Azusa evaluation and age and estimated level of functioning at the time of entry into the program are noted to give some idea of their rate of progress in the program. These cases indicate general progress in the program Eddie attended is usually very slow. Two children were functioning almost as well as Eddie at the last assessment; however, they were 13 and 15 years old at the time of last testing, whereas Eddie was not yet 8. A year earlier, a different instrument (The Maxfield Bucholz developmental scales) had placed A.C. roughly at the same level as that shown in Table 6.1. D.N. is perhaps the most similar to Eddie in growth rate. He entered the program at age 3 with an assessed level of social functioning at about 1½ years. His progress since then has been slow, but steady. These cases provide only a general framework for evaluating Eddie's development. Still, it is clear that Eddie, in the 2 years of active music-making, had oupaced most of his classmates. Particularly impressive are his gains in different aspects of social and cognitive development, where at the end of the evaluation period, he was the highest functioning child in the class. His improvement led to a reevaluation by the local school system and subsequent placement in a public school special education classroom, which he currently attends.

The gains made by Eddie on the Callier-Azusa scale were reflected in changes in his behavior during the school day. At the end of the 2-year period, Eddie recognized (mostly by voice), named, and greeted most of the staff and his classroom peers. He showed delight in noting the names of things (including letters and numbers) and in completing the various puzzles and games provided by the staff. He often recognized and commented upon the activities of others (e.g., "Lana's crying") and was learning to take his turn at group games. Even his speech, which proved in many respects to be the behavioral area most resistant to change, lost much of its echolalic character over the 2-year period.

It would be inappropriate to conclude Eddie's remarkable improvement at school was caused just by our music lessons. His improving vision and the efforts of his dedicated teachers played major roles in his success in the program. However, it also seems quite evident that at the very least, the introduction of a "musical curriculum" did not delay or prevent growth in other areas. On the contrary, there is considerable anecdotal evidence to suggest musical experiences provided an important context for more general development. In some instances, we intentionally structured music lessons in order to promote growth of some basic perceptual and cognitive skills and these are described in more detail in Appendix A. At other times, change seemed to occur as a natural consequence of the musical experiences themselves. The following examples may suggest ways in which music experiences affected development in other domains.

One obvious concern was Eddie's language development. At the age of 5½, Eddie's language was monosyllabic and/or echolalic. During our earliest weekly music sessions, Eddie spoke very little, though by the end of the first month, he would greet me by name. Our conversations consisted primarily of my reminding Eddie to listen while I played, naming the piece (usually I supplied a name if it didn't have one) and responding to his playing with verbal approval. On following weeks, I would then ask by name for various selections previously heard. If the response was incorrect, I would supply the correct tune and its title. Within 2 months, Eddie would reliably repeat the names of the tunes I requested, although often not with the appropriate melody; the first notes of a song were much more reliable cues than the song's title. More formal lessons began several months later (Appendix A). During these lessons, Eddie's language use increased gradually, first involving naming notes and tunes, and later including comments on the pieces and requests or instructions to the teacher during the lesson.

As Table 6.1 indicates, Eddie's general expressive language development continues to be quite slow. His conversational speech often has a disconnected quality, incorporating (apparent) snatches of dialogue from television programs and advertisements. Such discourse is not uncommon in cases of severe speech disturbance (Fay & Butler, 1968). It was our impression, however, that Eddie's conversations were much more coherent when they pertained to music. Here are transcriptions of three brief, typical conversations with Eddie during his eighth year.

(A) (Before a piano lesson. Upon returning from a vacation with his Mother.)

N.N.: What did you do on vacation, Eddie? Did you go on an airplane?

E.: Yes.

N.N.: With your Mom?

E.: Yes, to New York.

N.N.: Oh, you went to New York. Did you see your Grandma?

E.: Yeah.

N.N.: Is she sick or better?

E.: I want to go in the car.

L.M.: You want to go in the car?

E.: In the cake.

L.M.: In the cake?

E.: Oh boy!

L.M.: What else did you do on your trip?

E.: Connecticut.

N.N.: You went to Connecticut?

E.: Connecticut.

N.N.: Who went with you, did S_____ go?

E.: Yeah

N.N.: Did R_____ go?

E.: Yeah

N.N.: Did L_____ go?

E.: Yeah

    (In fact, only Eddie and his Mother made the trip).

(B) (In the car on the way to the University.)

L.M.: What do we have to do first, Eddie?

E.: Seatbelts.

L.M.: Right, let's put on the seatbelts. Now, shall we go?

E.: Yes (car starts). Here we go! Leon?

L.M.: What?

E.: What time is it?

L.M.: It's twenty minutes after nine.

E.: Nine, sixteen. How do you play that? Let the king come. Let the king come through. Leon!

L.M.: What Eddie?

E.: The king is _____ (unintelligible)(cough).

L.M.: Do you have a cough?

E.: Yeah.

L.M.: It's not really bad, is it?

E.: She had a thousand dollars. She's going to, Leon.

L.M.: What are you looking at, Eddie?

E.: At the red light. (We are stopped at a traffic signal.)

L.M.: At the red light?

E.: White, black—Oh, there is a car.

L.M.: That's a pretty car.

E.: Yeah, one car. The red car. See the red car?

L.M.: I don't see it Eddie.

E.: Oh, look at this _____ (unintelligible). They have it sometimes. And then there's a _____ (unintelligible). What's that? (Points to tape recorder).

L.M.: A little machine.

L.M.: A little machine.

E.: At the University? Downstairs. That comes first. Oh, here comes another one.

L.M.: Another what?

E.: And then comes the first king. And he saw _____ (unintelligible). And they saw one little kid, one little calf.

(C)   During a music lesson (on the recorder).

N.N.: Now here's a tune we played last week. We'll do it as a round, OK? (Plays the first phrase of an English folktune.)

E.: Now start, Nancy. (They play the round through once.) I like that. I will go first. (They play the song through again.) Show me C$^\#$ Nancy.

N.N.: You have to put your fingers like this. (Moves Eddie's fingers to appropriate positions. They move to the piano.)

E.: Nancy, shall I play um—(starts playing).

N.N.: What do you call that?

E.: Duet in F (the piece was one of the sections of a Mozart Duet from previous week). Shall I play um—new song (theme from "Bewitched").

N.N.: What's that?

E.: Bewitched.

N.N.: Is that on TV?

E.: Yes. Leon, where's J____ (referring to someone Eddie met during the previous lesson).

N.N.: She's working. (Eddie repeats the "play and name" game for several more tunes.) Can I show you something?

E.: What?

N.N.: Here's the second part of the Duet (plays). Can you do that?

E.: (Plays without comment).

N.N.: Very good, now listen again.

E.: (Listens, tapping to beat with foot and then plays again).

N.N.: Now play together. (The Duet is played successfully, after which we applaud.)

E.: "I did it!"—Now, we do this next week?

The three brief conversations vary markedly in their coherence. When not at the piano talking about music, Eddie's responses often contain nonsequiturs and/or snatches of dialogue from other contexts. Talking to Eddie at these times often leaves one with the impression that he is on a very different wave length. Eddie clearly likes to converse, and he dutifully "takes his turn" in conversations. However, the confusion caused by his disjunctiveness frequently leads to lapses in the conversational flow. During the music lessons, by contrast, the subject matter of Eddie's speech is more connected, silences are less frequent and topics change in a more natural fashion. Eddie's conversations during music also typically contain more complex and active constructions than they do elsewhere. During the music session, he is more likely to make requests, ask questions or comment spontaneously (and appropriately) on a situation.

In retrospect, Eddie's use of more sophisticated language in musical contexts should have come as no surprise. Music is the area where Eddie's knowledge is greatest and his desire to understand and communicate most intense. Too, musical lessons like the one described above provide a concrete context with a familiar agenda or scenario. Knowing this certainly must help in maintaining coherence in a conversation. Indeed, much of our daily working knowledge uses learned sequences of events or "scripts" (Schank & Ableson, 1977). In time one could see Eddie constructing other "scripts" describing events more peripherally concerned with music making. For example, at one point a routine of bi-weekly trips to the University for recording sessions was established. Toward the end of this period, Eddie became fond of naming activities next in sequence during the trip (seat belts off, now we take the elevator, etc.).

Appendix A contains additional examples of how musical activities provided an opportunity for developing expressive language as well as cognitive skills of a more general nature. In summary, neither we, nor his school teachers could see any indication that Eddie's interest in music inhibited cognitive development, and we strongly suspect music played (and continues to play) an important role in facilitating cognitive growth.

Eddie's musical interests and skills also influenced the scope and nature of his social interactions. Not surprisingly, compared to the other children at his school, Eddie was exposed to more varied social situations. Although one-to-one adult–child interactions characterized school routine, Eddie, by virtue of his particular status, enjoyed special times with different teachers who would voluntarily take him to the piano for a practice session, in addition to our weekly sessions. Once knowledge of his special talent became more widespread, he probably received more than his share of attention from school staff. Staff members would sing songs with Eddie and play or request certain pieces. This experience enriched the kinds of interactions he had with the staff. In addition to being a student, he was an accompanist and a fellow musician. Visitors to the school also occasionally sat in on a session with Eddie, sometimes to play, sometimes just to listen. Eddie's talent also led to varied experiences outside of school. His playing in more public concert-like formats has developed gradually over the past 3 years. At the outset, he played primarily alone or in more intimate situations—with his family or with us in the "piano room" at school. These sessions typically took place against the background of the usual noise and commotion at his home or school. His first "official" concert as a piano student before a strange audience occurred about 6 months after we started seeing him and was something of a disaster, although in an interesting way. When it was Eddie's turn to play, the sudden silence that fell over the room confused him. He remained at the piano, quietly waiting for something to happen. When we encouraged him to play, he did so, but by touching the keys lightly so that the silence would not be broken. Later during the post-concert socializing, he found his way again to the piano and played several of his favorite pieces fortissimo. Clearly the social structure of the concert was a new experience for him. Several such concerts later, Eddie has become accustomed to the routine, waiting his turn and playing with abandon when he has the stage. (He still forgoes one bit of concert etiquette, applauding himself as well as the other participants after playing.)

Eddie's interpersonal behavior also changed during the course of our sessions at the piano. At first, Eddie was more "reactive" than "active" in our interactions. I would play, ask him to play, then I would play, and so forth. Soon, Eddie became fond of volunteering pieces from past sessions, and eventually sessions included ensemble as well as solo pieces. (The development of ensemble techniques is described in some detail in Appendix A). We were very interested in using musical dialogues to enhance Eddie's sensitivity and initiative in social situations. Eddie took the cues and direction that we provided with little effort. At this point, he is a willing ensemble player, and particularly enjoys exchanging blues and jazz riffs with a partner on the piano.

This delight in musical "conversations" has also been noted in other savants. J.L. (Charness, et al., 1988) is fond of playing duets with one of the staff members at his residence. I observed a particularly heartwarming example of musical interaction during the "challenge" portion of one of L.L.'s concerts. This part of his concert requests members of the audience to challenge L.L. by playing pieces they have learned, his task being to repeat the piece after a single hearing. (Recall that a similar routine formed part of Blind Tom's concerts.) During this particular challenge session, a young lady succumbed to stage fright during her attempt to play and sing a piece for L.L. Undaunted by her distress, L.L. accepted the "challenge" with enthusiasm, reconstructing the piece from the fragment she had played and exhorting her to sing with him. The resulting improvised duet was a considerable success with the audience (and the young lady) largely due to L.L.'s uncanny ability to "shadow" her singing on the piano (including several unexpected key modulations!).

Examples such as these reflect savants' self-confidence about their ability. L.L. accepts all challenges with alacrity, and during our testing session, occasionally exclaimed, "I can do that" after hearing a segment of our testing materials. Eddie's satisfaction in accomplishment is well-documented in Appendix A, and the other savants who contributed the data for the evaluations in the earlier chapters were, for the most part, very willing participants, obviously enjoying the game of trying to perform our test pieces successfully.

There is growing evidence that such feelings of effectance provide an important motivational basis for exploring and mastering one's environment.

Research by Harter (1978) indicates retarded children typically exhibit less mastery motivation than do normal children of the same mental age. Moreover, mentally retarded subjects demonstrate less pleasure over successful mastering attempts. This, coupled with the usual life history of social deprivation found in the retarded, leads to an attenuation of intrinsic motivation, according to Harter. The history of relatively frequent experience of competence as well as the social reinforcement associated with savant performance is likely to augment savants' self-esteem. Indeed, for Harter, self-esteem enhancement is one of the major consequences of problem-solving success combined with appropriate reinforcement (Harter, 1978, 1981). Low self-esteem has been linked to a variety of maladaptive behaviors such as over-dependency, withdrawal and self-derogation (Wells & Marwell, 1976) whereas high self-esteem has been associated with more mature and/or socially desirable behaviors (e.g., Coopersmith, 1967). Active, confident exploration characterizes savants' interaction with their musical environment. For example, Eddie's recent introduction to bongo drums resulted in an intense and spirited session during which he tested them for different sound and rhythm combinations. L.L. and C.A. are busy learning several new instruments. (This enthusiasm was sometimes a mixed blessing. I had to cover the control panel of the synthesizer during the formal part of the testing sessions with C.A. and Eddie once they realized different sounds were possible from the instrument.) The kinds of success savants usually have in things musical suggest it is one area where curiosity is strong at the beginning and is continually nourished by the environment. Unfortunately, those who characterize Eddie's playing as a "gift" or "miracle" praise him for what he is, not what he does. Harter (1978) suggests that praise for specific behaviors and for trying is the most prominent contributor to the social enhancement of self-esteem.

The presence of musical talent is not without its problems and the foregoing does not mean Eddie's musical experiences were invariably trouble-free. Eddie's family is proud of, if somewhat mystified by his unusual talent. Most of the time they enjoy his playing. However, Eddie's enthusiasm for piano playing at home can result in conflict with other members of the family when he wants to play while they are watching television. Savants' single-mindedness about playing was noted earlier (Chapter 1). In Eddie's case, a sort of compromise has been reached by his family, limiting his playing to commercial breaks while they watch a program. He devises accompaniments for the advertising jingles! More seriously, Eddie's sensitivity to and interest in his sound environment can result in an apparent information overload. These occasions most often occur when the ambient sound becomes confusing and discordant or where a piece presents an especially demanding challenge. Several attempts to get Eddie to play at school for Christmas concerts were a limited success for this reason. When under such stress, Eddie reverts to stereotyped behaviors that were more common at an earlier age (hand waving, eye poking, etc.) or he simply sticks his fingers in his ears. Currently, our response to this problem is to be sensitive to such sources of stress and to curtail them when they appear to be developing. Eddie's reaction to frustrating situations has also changed over the years, now taking a more problem directed form, though not always in a way we would like. A frustrating session with the recorder recently resulted in its being thrown out the window. His lesson books also get a pre-emptory toss every now and then when he loses interest or patience with a lesson. In some respects, even this represents an advance over earlier reactions of withdrawal and behavioral stereotypy. Still, as an important part of Eddie's life, music has the capacity to evoke unpleasant as well as pleasant experiences.

In summary, there appears to be very little empirical evidence that the development or enhancement of special skills in the musical savant is likely to promote pathology. If anything, the data presented in this chapter indicate the opposite effect is more likely. Eddie seems to have "bloomed" generally as well as musically over the past 4 years. It is curious that such strong expectations that music might become pathogenic in the savant are expressed in the literature. There appear to be several reasons for this pathological "bias." Historically, music has often been considered irrational, even demoniacal at times (Attali, 1977). Savant skills in general may be subject to a certain amount of "guilt by association." There are many behaviors displayed by savants that are indeed pathological or abnormal in some way. One reasonable hypothesis is that the savant behavior has much in common with these manifestations of pathology. As we have seen, links between savant skill and pathology have been proposed from both etiological and functional perspectives. In the next chapter, we will explore some of these hypotheses in more detail. For the present, consider a case where the same kind of musical wizardry is seen against a background of normal cognitive and social development. This describes many musical prodigies of course, and pathology is rarely involved in describing these cases (Revesz, 1925/1970). Assuredly, the presence of special talents may bring with it special problems in terms of adjustment, acceleration, and the like (Feldman, 1986). However, there is nothing intrinsic to savant skill necessitating the designation of pathology. The same cannot be said for other aspects of the cases encountered, for example their persistent echolalia. In fact, there is considerable evidence indicating a link between language disability and emotional disturbance in the nonsavant (Beitchman, Nair, Clegg, Fergusen, & Patel, 1986; Cantwell & Mattison, 1979). Could not such language disabilities play a major role in the emotional disturbance attributed to savants?

Alternatively, one could conceive savant skills as representing an area of relative normalcy against a background of disturbance. As such, it is likely to be affected by such disturbances, but the implications for development (and treatment) are quite different. This view would suggest that continued exercise of savant skill provides an important normalizing influence on development, one that should be encouraged. In any case, the evidence indicates that music is an important vehicle for communication and a source of satisfaction for savants.

The comparison groups often used in describing savants probably reinforce the idea of an association between savant skill and pathology. These groups often include severely disturbed children, as noted earlier. In contrast, our assumption has been that the most appropriate comparison is with those for whom the primary diagnosis is mental retardation. This is not a view shared by all (e.g., Nurcombe & Parker, 1964); however, it follows from the usual definition of "idiots savants," a special or exceptional skill against a background of mental retardation. Because other types of disturbance or disability do not form part of the core definition, they need not enter into the design of appropriate comparison or control groups in savant research. To some extent, this is a matter of different perspectives, the nature of the comparison depending on one's research objectives. However, it seems likely that the consistent use of comparison groups whose central feature is severe pathology would serve to strengthen the notion that such pathology and savant skills are necessarily related as a kind of self-fulfilling prophecy.

There is something unsettling about savant skills. Our interactions with others are based on a set of general notions about each other's competencies, attitudes, interests, and so forth. We try, sometimes not very successfully, to adjust our conversation or expectations to accommodate the interests and intellect of our conversational partner. Against this background of conventional social interaction, there is probably something a bit unnerving about interacting with someone who has savant skills. The combination of unusual sensitivity and severe behavior deficits can make it difficult to predict what the savant will do. It probably also affects the kinds of expectations one has and adjustments one must make in interacting with them. I observed L.L. sitting quietly during a conversation with his guardian about his recent trip to Japan. As different incidents were described, L.L. would smile, apparently in recognition. He seemed to be indicating he understood the general conversation. It's possible he did, but attempts to engage him directly in the conversation were invariably met with echolalic or monosyllabic responses. L.L.'s sister described the frustration expressed by reporters when they try to interview him. It was difficult for them to accept the possibility that someone so skilled at the piano could be so limited in a simple conversation. C.A.'s musical instructors often wonder how much of what they say is "getting in." At times C.A.'s behavior indicates willing and facile cooperation; at other times, he appears intransigent, and it is hard to tell whether this reluctance reflects lack of motivation or failed understanding. Eddie, too, has his unpredictable side and "out of context" comments, questions or behaviors can occur even during piano lessons. His emotional reactions to different situations are often quite intense (he is a young man of very strong likes and dislikes) and images of "the sensitive artist" come to mind at these times. His current teacher at his new school finds him something of a mystery, similar to the other members of her TMH class in some ways, but very unlike them in other ways. When compared to other students or residents at a particular facility, the personal peculiarities of savants may be especially prominent and memorable to those who observe and interact with them. Moreover, it may also be that some of the maladaptive behaviors of savants are more "public" than those of other retarded people. The emotional displays associated with performing (or being prevented from performing) their skill have already been noted. The frequent presence of stereotyped behaviors and echolalic language in savants could also result in patterns of public behavior that would be aversive to many (Berkson, 1983). Together, these factors could make the savant's maladaptive behaviors more memorable and thereby lead to a strong impression of pathology in descriptive summaries of their behavior. Thus, at least some of the maladjustment attributed to savants may be in the eye of the beholder.

There remains the curious case of Nadia (Selfe, 1977). In this instance, there appeared to be a strong developmental link between the disappearance of her exceptional drawing talent and increasing normalization in her social and cognitive development. Was the original drawing ability present at the expense of normal social and conceptual skills? It is difficult to say, of course. For one thing, we have very little information about the subsequent course of Nadia's development. The change in the sophistication of her drawings may reflect, in part, simple changes in current interests and activities. Late in the second year of our work with Eddie, he began to play the piano much less often at home, and according to his mother, seemed to be losing his interest in music. Subsequent events suggested this change reflected Eddie's growing mobility, visual acuity, and ability to explore his environment. He is no longer so single-minded about playing the piano, but his playing is more structured and sophisticated. Similar "plateaus" have been observed in C.A. (L. Ritchy, personal communication, 1987). Second, precocious skills are not static and their development may show periods of regression as well as growth. Bamberger (1982) has described a kind of "midlife crisis" that occurs for the prodigy when early holistically or spontaneously organized skills are reorganized along more formal and analytic lines. These periods may be accompanied by a temporary disintegration of a skill. More generally, children's growing concern about literalness may lead to less spontaneity in their drawings (Gardner & Winner, 1982) and perhaps in their musical activities (Moog, 1976). Possibly the change in Nadia's drawings reflected this growing awareness about her own behavior rather than some substitution of one kind of competence for another. There is also the danger of concluding too much on the basis of a single case. Although clearly a savant, Nadia was also formally diagnosed as autistic, a designation that occurs in a minority of musical savants (Chapter 1). Savant drawing ability, too, is relatively rarer than music or mathematics, on the basis of current evidence (Rimland & Hill, 1974).

These reservations about the general implications of Nadia's development reflect the fragmentary nature of our knowledge and many questions remain. Do different savant skills have different consequences? As noted earlier, the potential for social interaction and reward seems inherently higher in some skills (e.g., music) than in others (e.g., calendar calculating). The cognitive domain of different savant skills also apparently varies considerably. Calendar savants, for example, have very restricted areas of exceptionality (Sacks, 1985). It is likely these differences have varying consequences for different areas of development. Differences in the consequences of different skills have already been implicitly recognized in the development of special therapies for the handicapped. There are many programs of music therapy (e.g., Nordoff & Robbins, 1971) and art therapy (e.g., Wadeson, 1982) for the developmentally disabled, but I am aware of no analogous "math therapy" programs. The most appropriate model of the consequences of savant skill for development might be one in which savant skill type and area of development interact, each skill having its own associated strengths and weaknesses. There are some empirical indications this might be the case. Recall, for example that Duckett (1977) found in her sample of savants higher achievement in personal economics and understanding time, whereas Monroe and Miller (1988) did not. A reasonable hypothesis is that Duckett's results reflect a kind of spill-over or generalization primarily on the part of the calender calculators in her example. DeLong and Aldershof (1988) recently have presented data suggesting manic-depressive disturbances are associated with the presence of special abilities in a sample of adolescents. However, the incidence of musical exceptional skill was very low in this group, and manic-depressive illness does not emerge as a special area of concern in the savant cases described here. In any case, the possible links between the nature of the talent and the nature of associated difficulties deserve attention.

Savants differ in amount of personal investment in their skill as well as their skill level. Our survey of musically talented individuals in area institutions (Monroe & Miller, 1988) revealed a wide range of involvement among those nominated. Some were actively involved with making music nearly every day while others merely seemed to have an especially good "ear" for picking up melodies. Investigation of these differences may help clarify notions about the possible obsessive nature of savant behavior. Pathology may characterize a relatively limited type of savant skill expression. Such data may also reveal the extent to which the differences in talent observed in earlier chapters have corresponding differences in consequences. The presence of musical talent in the retarded does seem to have salutary effects. However, it does not follow that an expanding social or personal environment is the inevitable consequence of musical interests in the retarded child. If the child has an extremely disturbed orientation to his social environment, stimulation of musical interest may not be indicated according to some musical therapists (Alvin, 1978) on the grounds that this may weaken already tenuous ties to others. In our survey of musical interests and skills among the mentally retarded (Monroe & Miller, 1988), there were frequent reports of intense musical interests of a passive nature, for example, listening almost nonstop to local music radio stations. Musical interests of this sort seem much less conducive to the kinds of self-esteem enhancing experiences associated with playing an instrument, although they are obviously rewarding in other respects. In music therapy there is usually a concerted effort to have the client play a more active role in music making (Bruscia, 1987). We know little about factors affecting adoption of more active versus passive expression of musical interests among the retarded. Is it merely opportunity which separates the listeners from the players or are there different motivation systems at work? At this point, it is difficult to tell. Yet this must be of critical importance in determining the social and cognitive consequences of these interests.

7 | The Nature and Origin of Musical Savant Skill

A frequent reaction to hearing Eddie play is to suggest his talent is divinely inspired (cf. also Monty, 1981), or a musical "gift." His talent is certainly special, and his playing reminds one of some fundamental mysteries about music. Like language it is a very human activity, yet unlike language its role in human behavior often seems unclear, or at least controversial (Sloboda, 1985). Moreover, when musical activity expresses itself in unusual ways, as in a savant or a prodigy (Feldman, 1986), it seems much less amenable to explanation by recourse to more conventional models of human behavior. This apparently impenetrable quality of savant behavior has been seen as a fundamental challenge to theories of intelligence (Sacks, 1985) as well as pathology (Treffert, 1988). The results of the previous chapters, as well as that of other recent research in the area (e.g., Charness, et al., 1988; Hermelin, et al. 1987; Sloboda, et al., 1985) suggest a more tractable view of musical savants. They have much in common with fellow musicians. They also have some fairly uncommon characteristics. The evolving picture of savant behavior still seems quite complex, even if less obscure.

The demonstration that savant skills are amenable to analysis is only a first step, and several core issues remain. First, what is the nature of the skill exhibited and second, what leads to its appearance? As noted in the opening chapter, speculations about both the nature and origin of savant behavior have not been lacking. The phenomenon invites hypotheses, but usually they have been of a most general nature. Moreover, the link between the nature of savant skill and its origin has received only sporadic attention, other than the notion that its (supposedly) pathological nature

177

suggests a pathological etiology (e.g., Bergman & Escalona, 1949; Nurcombe & Parker, 1964).

Questions about the nature and origin of savant behavior are dissociable. Useful models of savant expertise need not assume any particular stance with respect to origin. Separate treatment of the two questions has often been a practical matter. Typically, savant skill has been examined considerably after its first appearance and empirical information about its origins is sketchy at best. In this respect Eddie represented an unusual opportunity because we could examine his talent at a very early point in development. The similarities in Eddie and the adult savants were considerable, the points of divergence not unexpected from a developmental viewpoint. Consequently, it seems reasonable to consider the picture of early musical development in Eddie as particularly relevant to issues surrounding the origins of adult savant skill.

In this chapter we will examine these two facets of savant behavior, its nature and origin, with a view toward providing a more integrative model of the syndrome. The model is predicated on two theses. First, that savant behavior represents the operation of normative or conventional modes of information processing, but in a relatively limited domain. There is nothing unique about the kinds of processing seen in savants. It represents a kind of activity seen in many areas of human cognition. What is unusual is the intensity and sophistication with which these more generic cognitive processes are applied in the musical environment. Second, savant skill reflects the confluence of a variety of factors quite early in development. It is unlikely there is an unequivocal relation between any single factor and savant skill. Instead, as in other areas of exceptionality, the unusual achievement develops over time as a consequence of complex interactions among factors.

The Nature of Savant Skill

Do musical savants represent an "amented talent" as Scheerer et al., (1945) suggested over 40 years ago? As we have seen, most of the anecdoctal or summary descriptions of savants' music making have been in accord with this view. Characterizing savants' music as mimicry or as an obsession (Lewis, 1985) does suggest a pathological or severely truncated talent. It is also consistent with the notion that the development of musical sensitivity is severely constrained by limitations in general intelligence (e.g., Seashore, 1938).

The results of the experiments described in Chapters 3, 4, and 5, together with recent studies by Sloboda et al. (1985) and Charness et al. (1988) present a different picture, one in which the savant compares favorably with the mature musician. Like the mature musician, the savant is sensitive to the various rules reflecting the structure inherent in musical composition. Among the aspects of structure savants responded to were scale or musical alphabet (Deutch, 1982), harmonic regularity, recurrent patterns and musical modes. Reviewing briefly the evidence for these conclusions: Scale sensitivity was seen in Eddie's greater accuracy for note strings constrained by conventional scales than for those randomly generated and in the general tendency for savants (as well as the more accomplished comparison subjects) to omit or modify material not consistent with the key signature of a selection. It was also evident in savants' key consistent responding. When notes were not literal replications of what was heard, they nevertheless preserved the key of the original. Sensitivity to harmonic regularity was seen in the chord sequence experiment, where savants were much better able to reproduce chords that were harmonically conventional than those which were not. Grouping effects were observed directly, in the reproduction of structured versus unstructured strings described in Chapter 4, and indirectly, in the savants' high degree of accuracy on the brief preludes. Finally, mode appeared as an relevant factor in savants' sensitivity to selections written in major versus minor keys. Idiom sensitivity in a more general sense was also evident in savants' ability to respond in a scale consistent fashion to the selection written in a relatively unfamiliar whole-tone principle. In summary, savants showed structure preserving music making whenever they were given the opportunity to do so.

In this sensitivity to rule and structure these musical savants have much in common with savants in other domains. Two other areas of savant accomplishment have received some empirical attention recently, calendar calculation and hyperlexia. The emerging picture for these types of savant behavior is in many respects similar to that for musical savants. Calendar calculators can provide the day of the week for any given calendar date with a minimum of effort. Horwitz, Deming, and Winter (1969) found that one of two calendar-calculating twins apparently was using a "master" 400-year calendar, which repeats itself in the conventional (Gregorian) calendar system. His brother's calendar calculating skills did not exhibit this feature, being restricted to a 300-year span roughly centered on the present. Hill (1975) and Rosen (1981) also reported patterns indicating structured knowledge in calendar calculators. Variation in errors and latencies in answers given to a range of calendar dates suggested several constraining principles at work. Among these was the strategy of using the current year or a certain month of the year as an anchor point. In a detailed examination of 8 calendar calculators, O'Conner and Hermelin (1984; Hermelin & O'Conner, 1986) found different kinds of regularity across subjects. Answers were usually faster and more accurate for dates in the past than for those in the future, but being able to provide accurate answers for dates in the future indicated the skill was not simply a detailed memory for past events. Different cyclic patterns inherent in the structure of the Gregorian calendar were evident. In addition to the 400-year cycle mentioned earlier, there was the use of 28-year calendrical cycles. Some patterns of answers also suggested the use of the congruence of weekday—date assignments for different pairs of months during the course of the year, and the advance of a given date—day on successive nonleap years (i.e. if January 1 is Sunday this year it will be Monday next year). Individuals varied considerably in their implementation of these regularities, particularly the less obvious ones. O'Conner and Hermelin suggested these results point to (implicit) rule discovery and use rather than rote memory as the core ingredient in calendar calculating skill.

A similar conclusion comes from examinations of hyperlexia, the ability to read and recall text at a level considerably above what one would predict on the basis of general cognitive achievement (Goldberg, 1987). Hyperlexic readers are sensitive to the orthographic and phonological rules that are used in constructing and decoding written language (Goldberg & Rothermal, 1984; Healy, Aram, Horwitz, & Kessler, 1982). They are also better able to decode fragmentary or perceptually degraded written material than their peers (Cobrinik, 1982). Moreover, they can apply general word reading skills to artificially constructed "pseudo words" (Goldberg & Rothermal, 1984), and are able to extract meaning from individual words (Snowling & Frith, 1986).

Although the sophistication observed in the subjects of these empirical studies is occasionally attributed to rote memory factors (e.g., Horwitz, et al., 1969; Hill, 1975), more often it is not. Rather, as in musical savants, there is evidence of a sensitivity or appreciation of some of the fundamental rules operating in the organization of the domain. In each case subjects are able to use the information in a manner similar to that shown in mature levels of expertise. The calendar calculator's discovery of regularities in numbering systems used in calendars resembles rule usage evident in other areas of exceptional mathematical calculating (Smith, 1988). The attention to phonological and orthographic regularities shown by the hyperlexic is also evident in the mature reader (cf. Tzeng & Singer, 1981).

There are also some important, perhaps profound differences among these various kinds of savant skill. Both calendar calculators and hyperlexics display serious constraints or limitations in their respective areas of expertise. Calendar calculators may be able to perform impressive feats with their calendar knowledge; their talent rarely extends to other areas involving mathematical regularities. Except for rare ability to perform mental multiplication (Sacks, 1985), calendar calculating savants are more often inept at even simple mathematical concepts (though not invariably so, see Steel, Gorman, & Flexman, 1984). Hyperlexics, too, display some severe limitations in achievement. Although able to decode print rapidly, they are deficient in extracting its meaning, particularly in larger units of text. Individual words may be meaningful to them but connected ideas in a paragraph or the gist of a story are not (Huttenlocher & Huttenlocher, 1983; Snowling & Frith, 1986). Savant calendar calculators are certainly not mathematicians and hyperlexics are not superior readers in the more comprehensive sense of the term. The term "splinter skill" is quite apt in these cases.

Based on the results of the present research, this is not the case with the musical savant. The musical savants revealed no particular "holes" or deficits in their performance. In its pattern of sensitivity the savants' music making was essentially indistinguishable from the adult comparison subjects, particularly those with absolute pitch. In this respect the musical savant appears to diverge considerably from other types of savants in more nearly resembling the intact version of the skill in question.

This conclusion rests upon several assumptions deserving some additional consideration. First, it assumes the set of tasks used in these studies represents a reasonably comprehensive sampling of musical skills and activities. Admittedly, they are severely restricted in methodology and many of these limitations have already been discussed (Chapter 2). In addition, the basic experimental procedure required a relatively passive approach to music. Participants were required to listen and then repeat as faithfully as possible what they had just heard. (Ironically, the procedure would seem ideally suited to the kind of "tape recorder" talent the results so strongly disconfirm.) Participants' music making on their own initiative has not been considered. The omission is primarily motivated by practical issues. It is easier to analyze performance in relation to a given standard than spontaneous or improvised music (e.g., Sloboda, 1985; Sudnow, 1978). The savant participants are active music makers, and all but one played pieces from their own repertoire when given the opportunity to do so between experimental tasks. N.Y. demurred, and because she often plays impromptu concerts for her friends at the facility, this reluctance is not characteristic.

Is the savant sample seriously deficient in improvisatory or compositional skill? It is difficult to say. As far as could be determined, there had been very little training in this direction for most of the sample, although some is currently underway with C.A. (Ritchie, 1987, personal communication). Until very recently L.L. had never been observed to create a composition on his own, according to his sister, although he gives his renditions of standard works a distinctive personal style. At the end of our second session together L.L. offered to play a new tune of his own making, called "The Hotshot Blues." This was a first, according to his sister. The result was a piece that followed conventional blues form through successive choruses, but though fairly generic as to type, the basic theme was not recognized by anyone. It was indeed a new piece as far as we could tell. Eddie's improvisatory skill was one of the singular aspects of his playing from the start. Some features of Eddie's improvisation are described in Appendix A. For the present, it is clear that musical savant talent is not necessarily restricted to the more passive aspects of music. Additional evidence supporting this conclusion has been provided recently by Hermelin, et al. (1987).

There is one respect in which savants are clearly at a disadvantage in comparison to their musical peers. They find it very difficult to talk about their music. Comparison subjects, particularly the adults, conversed easily about their attitudes regarding different musical styles, periods and composers, as well as being able to describe what general aspects of music making they found easiest and most difficult. Not surprisingly, given their level of training they were also familiar with the language of music theory. The savants could name favorite pieces and composers, and sometimes global categories; popular, blues, and so forth but little beyond this.

It is revealing to contrast the limited and relatively simple or global requests and comments made by Eddie about music with those of the child prodigy Erwin Nyiregyhazi (Revesz, 1925/1970). As we have seen, Eddie and Erwin appear to have much in common in terms of the fundamentals of music making (Chapters 3 and 5). However, young Erwin would speak eloquently and at length about his reactions to different composers, his approach to composition and what music meant to him. The extent and depth of this metacognitive side of Erwin's talent amazed Revesz, who thought this even more extraordinary than his playing skills. The very limited language skills of most savants make it difficult to assess this aspect of their musical intelligence. They may also lack a sense of perspective about themselves and their music. As one aspect of a limited concrete (Scheerer et al., 1945) conceptualization of music, they may find it difficult, if not impossible, to even consider these more general issues, let alone discuss them.

This restriction to the most concrete aspects of the domain has also been attributed to other types of savants (e.g., Cobrinik, 1982). To what extent is it warranted in describing musical savants, independent of their problems in using language? This is difficult to determine because the primary evidence for attributing the absence of a "sophisticated abstract" attitude toward music comes from extra-musical sources. As we saw earlier, (Chapter 1) concrete attitudes were ascribed to musical savants (e.g., Anastasi & Levee, 1960; Scheerer et al., 1945) based upon standard cognitive assessment instruments, many of which are heavily language dependent. The confounding of language usage and evidence for an abstract attitude is no coincidence. As a vehicle for describing and communicating information that goes beyond the tangible present, language has no peer.

The absence of abstract understanding was also attributed to the nonlanguage side of savants' personality. Their excessive attention to detail and their desire for consistency in the physical environment has been seen as indicative of a particularistic, concrete, perhaps even obsessive stance toward their environment. This accords well with dictionary definitions of abstract, which emphasize consideration of the general as opposed to the particular, and tending away from the literal. In its verb form, abstract usually means to summarize or consider apart from specific instances. By this criterion, much of the nonmusical side of the musical savant may be concrete or particularistic. However, as applied to savant music making, it suggests a more abstract rather than concrete understanding of music. Their music does not tend toward literalness, as we have seen. If anything the emphasis in their playing is on the more general characteristics of the piece, tonality, basic harmonic relationships, and the like. The tendency towards nonliteralness was evident in other ways. One of these was the ability to provide a rendition independent of the original musical context. L.L.'s challenge sessions, for example, most often contained piano pieces provided by the audience for him to play. Occasionally the challengers played a different instrument or simply sang, but these variations proved no problem. Eddie similarly takes his music from many sources, and the instrumentation of the original seems of little concern, though he may attempt to capture its flavor in his rendition. One Christmas Nancy and I introduced Eddie to the full orchestral version of Tchaikovsky's *Nutcracker Suite*. After each segment Eddie ran to the piano, giving his rendition. These were always faithful to the style and ambience of the original. The *Sugar Plum Fairy* was light and delicate, the *Cossack Dance* exuberant. Eddie summarized the "gist" of each section quite successfully, an example of musical abstracting if there ever was one.

Savant music often does have a direct, nonreflective character to it. This was manifested in the speed of savants' responses to the various experimental tasks. They appeared not to take (or need) much time to organize a response and their replies were almost invariably faster than those of comparison subjects. There was also a characteristic of their playing, more difficult to specify, that suggested a less analytic approach. For example, on the prelude task (Chapter 5) both the adult savants and comparison subjects usually gave renditions quite a bit longer than the original. For the savants these longer renditions had a "theme and variations" quality with some departure from the original usually present by the end of the trial. For the comparison subjects, in contrast, longer versions usually represented successive approximations of parts of the original. There seemed less natural flow in their productions, but a greater attempt to try to match the model of the original (perhaps reflecting a clearer understanding of the instructions). In any event, much of savants' understanding of music in the more traditional music-theoretic sense may not be accessible given current methodology. Rather than concluding there is nothing there, it seems more prudent at this point to leave the question open.

Rule usage is related to the question of "abstract" versus "concrete" dimensions to savant music. Throughout the experiments reported here the regularities and consistencies in savant's music have been related to the rules embedded in musical composition practice. How valid is the additional assumption that savant expertise represents the application of this system of rules in encoding and retrieving musical input? If described as a body of explicit rules, formally applied, this assumption is assuredly wrong. There is little evidence that musical or other types of savants (Hermelin & O'Conner, 1986; Howe & Smith, 1988) consciously apply a well formed set of specified rules to the material of interest. The speed of their response does not suggest the interposition of a complex formal rule structure and evidence of rule application independent of their music making is currently not available.

Hermelin and O'Conner (1986) proposed that rule usage by savants is implicit, but nonetheless very real. Like the child whose language expression and comprehension reflect the rules of syntax, the savant shows "musical syntax" rule use. In both cases, however, formal tuition in, or knowledge of the system of rules is not necessary. A child need not take a course in syntax in order to use it appropriately. For Rimland (1978), savant performance similarly involves unconscious application of a system of rules, possibly made automatic as a consequence of continued application. The attribution of particular internal representations such as rules when there are regularities in behavior has a long history in psychological interpretation (cf. Gardner, 1985). However, considerable controversy surrounds the extent to which such things as rules exist in any formal or independent sense apart from their particular implementation. Moreover, the criteria for attributing implicit rule use vary considerably.

One group of models, which apparently circumvents some of the problems of rule attribution, are those assuming parallel distributed processing of information (PDP) (Rumelhart & McClelland, 1986). Briefly, PDP models characterize information processing as involving the activation of groups of units corresponding to certain dimensions or aspects of information present in the stimulus array. For example, a PDP model of word recognition during reading postulates groups of units representing different feature of letters (e.g. the presence of lines in different orientations), groups of units representing different letters of the alphabet, groups of units referring to words formed by certain letter combinations and so forth (McClelland & Rumelhart, 1981). Although various levels of activation (features, letters, words) are distinguished within the system, the levels are seen as highly interactive. Moreover, parallel or simultaneous information processing characterizes the system both within a level (at a given point in time patterns of activation at the feature level represent arrays of feature information) and between levels (a pattern of activation associated with a given feature activates several candidate letters on the next level; activation of a specific candidate word may, through feedback, augment net activation of its constituent letters). In any particular situation the resultant pattern of activation constitutes a "best fit" corresponding to different possible solutions (e.g., words, shapes, events). When the stimulus array is clear and unambiguous, such a solution may occur relatively quickly and easily. Even under less ideal conditions however, reasonable solutions are possible because the operating principle is one of settling upon the best fit to the information available.

This approach can provide a model of how regularities appear in a person's cognition without resorting to the presence of an independent set of rules controlling those regularities (Rumelhart & McClelland 1986, Chapter 1). It is assumed that what is stored over time are patterns of different connection strengths or associations among different units. Returning to the model of word recognition, the strength of the link or connection between a given feature unit (e.g., one representing a slanted line) to a restricted letter set (A,K,M,N,V,X,Y,Z) rather than other possible candidates (e.g., C,D,E etc.)

becomes established over time. This may describe a rule in one sense, but more importantly, it describes a source of regularity in the array of information provided by the environment which has a matching representation in the activity of the perceiver. It is available without the requirement of explicit formulation, although of course explicit formulation could aid its establishment. Moreover, it restricts possible patterns or candidates at higher levels, for example in "suggesting" some words, but not others. In conjunction with the fact that different levels of information representation are assumed to exist, this means constraining regularities describe activity at different levels of generality or abstractness. The recognition of regularity is not limited to the more elementary units of the system.

Figure 7.1 suggests how such a PDP inspired model of musical processing in the musical savants (and in others with AP) might look given a single input (or a frequency representing a given note). Only three levels are specified, each with a highly restricted subset of units, in the interests of clarity. The model assumes activation of chroma units (e.g., note names) given frequency information as a primary level of information extraction. It is assumed a given pitch elicits a very restricted range of candidate chroma in one with AP, usually that represented by the fundamental frequency of the pitch and perhaps the octave and the fifth as overtones. (In this latter respect it is likely to differ from the experience of the non–AP musician seeing the note on a musical stave.) It is expected patterns of inhibition to other notes at this level will not be particularly strong, given the ability of those with AP to identify concurrent notes (i.e., chords) with relative ease, even when they are dissonant (Chapter 3). On the other hand, the band of frequency information uniquely activating a given chroma will be relatively narrow, given the savants' ability to identify chroma quickly and unequivocally. The frequency-chroma link also suggests a path to eventual development of higher order structures. It represents the establishment of a useful elementary alphabet that provides the units for subsequent higher order pattern extraction. Just as the young reader must be able to identify the basic letters making up the material of primary interest, words and sentences, so must the musician learn to map or represent the notes in a reliable way before he can construct higher order

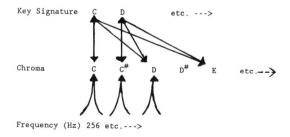

FIGURE 7.1.   An Interactive Model of Savant Processing of Pitch.

groupings in music. This model suggests the savant has a ready means of doing so.

At the next level, the presence of chroma information (e.g., the note "C") in turn activates several candidate key signatures; C, G, F Major, and so forth and not others, for example, D Major. The restricted set of key signatures would affect subsequent patterns of activation at the chroma level; hence activation of chroma values consistent with the "suggested" or candidate key would be augmented, those inconsistent or chromatic with respect to the key inhibited. That something like such activation and inhibition occurs is suggested by errors of commission and omission seen by the savants in the note string and prelude experiments (Chapters 4 and 5). A similar model suggesting specific links between chroma categories and scales has been proposed recently by Bharucha (1987).

A frequent suggestion in music theory is that the three levels, frequency, chroma, and key or scale are linked in a natural way (cf., Bernstein, 1976). Thus, in addition to specifying certain core or central categories (chroma) by its fundamental frequency, a note suggests relations among sounds at another level in its series of overtones. These may be embodied in the definition of a musical scale for example, in including the note a perfect fifth above the tonic as a scale degree, as in the conventional major and minor scales, or not, as in the whole-tone scale. Relations among fifths and tonics within a diatonic framework in turn may describe higher order structure in relations among keys (Shepard, 1982). The extent to which some frequency-chroma-scale links are more "natural" or "inevitable" than others has been the subject of a long and often acrimonious debate in musicology (Norton, 1984). The important point here is that they may represent a pathway by which a young musician with a particularly good sense of chroma identification could start establishing a more complex system for extracting patterns in music. It may be no coincidence that Eddie often uses the dominant as a kind of pivot note when changing registers in his left hand accompaniment or that L.L. is so fond of reinforcing octaves in his renditions.

Other candidate classes over time would involve recurrent temporal patterns or prose elements of music (Bernstein, 1976), harmonic cadences, and the like. In each case, the activation of candidate families concerning different aspects of music would serve to augment processing of information contained in some subsequent patterns, and not in others. In such cases, rule following as well as inference (Rumelhart & McClelland, 1986, Chapter 3) might be evident in the subject's music making, but without explicitly formulated rules.

Intuitively, at least, the PDP family of models is very attractive as a way of characterizing the kind of talent seen in musical savants. As a technique for realizing stimulus structure in a hierarchically organized mental representation, PDP models have an affinity for general conceptual models stressing hierarchical representations of music (e.g., Deutsch, 1982). The models are also advantageous in that they could tie the general representation of music in the perceiver to its processing in any particular situation. Thus, it is not necessary to assume any particular separate facility or operation in the musical perceiver. The tendency to extract higher order pattern information in music is intrinsic to music's representation in the savant's mind.

The parallelism in PDP models was originally suggested in part by severely limiting constraints in processing if one assumes we always process information one bit at a time (Rumelhart & McClelland, 1986). It seems apt for music as well. Even the fast and efficient individual chroma encoding attributed to musical savants in Chapters 3 and 4 seem insufficient to account for savant performance. It is not enough to be able to process single notes quickly. Considerable parallel processing within the system must also occur; activating multiple chroma units given complex sound arrays like chords; activating potential or candidate note configurations as well as currently sounded chroma units, and so forth. This concern about more general dimensions as well as individual notes seems to characterize the accomplished sight reader, for example (Wolfe, 1976), and is characteristic of a parallel distributed system.

Several of the more venerable issues in discussions of exceptional musical talent lose some of their import given a distributed processing framework. The issue of whether savant music is "abstract" or "concrete" becomes essentially irrelevant. Various degrees of abstractness are inherent in the hierarchical representation of music. The question becomes not whether musical savants have any abstract representation of music, but what kinds of abstraction are being used in their representation at successive levels in the system. As we have seen, many of the candidates for abstraction suggested for the accomplished normal musician apply to the savant as well. How such a complex representation could exist for music with little evidence for more general conceptual sophistication also becomes less mysterious, at least in principle. Not requiring a general, complex executive function for successful implementation, a distributed processing system can nevertheless perform highly sophisticated processing of a given input. Thus, domain specific kinds of expertise tend to be the rule rather than the exception. Finally, whether processing of music is fundamentally determined by elementary stimulus discrimination (bottom-up) or general plans and representations (top-down) is also moot. A reductionist model, which sees some elementary frequency discrimination skill at the core of exceptional music talent, is likely to be on the wrong track. The limited evidence of Chapter 3 suggested the discriminative skills of savants were quite good. However, on simple same/different discriminations of pure frequencies such as those given on the Seashore (1938) or Bentley (1966) tests of musical aptitude, savants may be no better than their nonmusical peers (Monroe & Miller, 1988). The results of Chapters 3 and 4 do suggest it is very useful to have a readily available stimulus encoding system such as that apparently at work in absolute pitch. In this sense some special elementary units are strongly implicated. In turn, it seems clear sophisticated processing cannot occur without significant contributions from more abstract or general levels of representation (Serafine, 1987). The skills of savants, in other words, include critical bottom-up and top-down elements.

PDP models are not without their critics, of course, even among those who find much of value in the approach (e.g., Massaro, 1988; McClelland & Rumelhart, 1986). The absence of central controlling functions or executors to moderate more general changes in cognition or direct subject-initiated programs is seen by some as particularly problematic. How does one describe Eddie's spontaneous music making and evident creativity without recourse to more general executive processes? Possibly it is the relative lack of executive control over music making (i.e., better skill at processing given input than creating or reflecting upon their own) that characterizes many savants. May this be what really distinguishes the young prodigy Erwin Nyiregyhazi from Eddie and the other savants when they were children? If so, how important is this deficit in the kind of talent found in savants?

Problematic too, are certain characteristics of savant performance. For example the acquisition of appropriate higher level representation units in a PDP system is usually assumed to take place over some time as a result of considerable practice. How is it the savants were (apparently) able to extract the whole-tone scale from the excerpts given them with presumably very little experience with the idiom? How are they able to translate encoding of the complex sound array into performance with so little effort? As noted earlier (Chapters 1 and 5) the link between perception and performance is exceptionally strong in the savant. There is nothing in PDP models to prevent such a linkage, in fact models of language processing propose a similarly strong link (McClelland & Rumelhart, 1986, Ch. 15). However, describing this performance aspect of savant skill would require elaboration of the representation.

The view being presented here contrasts with recent characterizations of savant skill as representing a particularly active memory subsystem. For example, Goldberg (1987) suggested the savant is superior in declarative and deficient in procedural memory: "It is as if savants know, but are unable to use or manipulate their knowledge" (p. 41). Waterhouse (1988) saw savants as having an extraordinary high-fidelity pattern discerning ability. For Rimland and Fein (1988) the problem is rather the kind of knowledge memory available to savants. They are characterized as being episodic and literal in their representation rather than semantic. Treffert (1988) saw a similar kind of problem in the savant: a reliance on a noncognitive habit formation system rather than a cognitive memory system. This restriction to a particular type of memory or memory subsystem means savant performances will lack many characteristics of performance in the domain seen in their normal skilled counterparts. For example, it may be restricted to a catalogue of facts or bits of knowledge without a more general organizing scheme and/or a means of implementing them. Or, the "facts" may exist without a rich connotative context to give them (personal) meaning. Because the type of processing is restricted, the knowledge in the domain is truncated.

The alternative is that the representation of the domain by the musical savant is essentially like that of their normal fellow musicians. In this regard, the present view is quite similar to that of Charness et al. (1988) who concluded that their musical savant J.L.'s skill "is comparable to the skill that normally intelligent musicians develop in the sense that . . . both acquire cognitive structures that code (and enable reproduction of) selective aspects of musical information as opposed to nonabstractive, sensory representation" (p. 291). The primary difference in the savant is a limited domain of expertise rather than a limited or truncated representation within the domain (with the aforementioned qualification that musical savants don't appear to be able to reflect on and discuss their skill very well).

These varying views of savant skill may actually not be so incompatible. There are differences in levels of analysis. Rimland and Fein (1988), in the tradition of Scheerer et al. (1945) considered a constellation of characteristics in the (autistic) savant, not just their demonstrated skill. Possibly, the hypothesized memory subsystem deficits become more prominent when considered across domains, or in some areas of functioning (e.g., language) than others. Another issue is the domain of savant expertise. As suggested earlier, (Chapter 6) music savants may share only some of the attributes of other savants. We shall return to the possibility that music represents a "special case" shortly. For the present, it is noteworthy that the more recent investigations of musical savants suggest a large amount of overlap in general skill structure with nonretarded comparison subjects (Charness, et al. 1988; Sloboda, et al. 1985). This does not seem to be the case with other savant skills (e.g., Goldberg, 1987).

What processing model will best capture the particular skills and weaknesses of musical savants remains an open issue. However, it is important to remember all of these models talk about savant skills in the context of normal memory mechanisms. Whatever model emerges as the best fit, it undoubtedly will point to some basic similarities between musical savants and other musical "experts".

The Origin of Savant Skill

Earlier it was argued that there was no single etiologic factor in savant case histories clearly pointing to the eventual appearance of musical talent. The same can be said for the additional subjects studied here. All have a severe visual deficit, but this is not invariably the case with savants. Varying degrees of language disability and associated physical handicap have also been noted as frequently associated with the appearance of savant skills in the past (Hill, 1978), but not invariably so. The one apparent additional characteristic of all savants, what we have called extended absolute pitch, itself has a complex and probably varied etiology. Consequently, although it has emerged as an important mediating or associated factor, its status as the causal agent is suspect.

There is also the problem of predicting the absence of the syndrome. Most musical savants are male, visually impaired, and have a history of language disorder; yet this combination of factors does not ensure the appearance of savant skill. These characteristics may be present in someone who is unexceptional in any area. One solution might be to extend the list of causal factors, perhaps adding social withdrawal (Rimland, 1971) or obsessional tendencies (Lewis, 1985) as necessary prerequisites. This would reduce the likelihood of one's having a savant skill. At the same time, such an extended list is likely to be too exclusive, failing to predict the occurrence of savant skills in Eddie, for example, for whom social withdrawal or obsessional tendencies do not seem to be a problem.

A viable model of the emergence of musical savant skill must, in addition to capturing central features of the syndrome, generate a candidate population that is neither too inclusive nor too restrictive. Most single factor or even simple list explanations are inadequate on this basis. Thus, even if it is true that musical savants often practice extensively, a massed practice model of savant skill (e.g., Ericcson & Faivre, 1988) is unsatisfactory. J.L. evidently did practice extensively (Charness, et al. 1988), but Eddie did not. Many others have likely practiced extensively with unexceptional results. Models suggesting an exclusive link between savant skills and various forms of extreme pathology (e.g., Nurcombe & Parker, 1964) are suspect for a similar reason.

More attractive are models which suggest predispositions toward having savant skills (e.g., Waterhouse, 1988). This is similar to the idea of risk factors (Brown, 1981) in predicting developmental outcome and shares many of the advantages of the "at risk" approach. These models can generate limited target samples, depending upon the weighting given various factors. They also have the flexibility to allow for the effects of mitigating circumstances. By doing so, they may modify the expected occurrence of various types of savant skill along the lines indicated by empirical evidence.

One set of predisposing factors is suggested by the kinds of associated cognitive deficits found in savants, especially their language disability. Savants as a group appear to have an extremely high incidence of language disability in their histories. In fact it approaches 100% (Table 1.1). Might not the set of factors associated with this disability also play a pivotal role in the development of savant skills? An association between language disability and enhancement in nonlanguage areas is predicted by some conceptions of cerebral differentiation of function. Primary language functions for both speaking and understanding are localized in the left hemisphere in most people. A complementary set of functions, including many associated with music, are usually more lateralized to the right hemisphere (Bryden, 1982). Most of the time the various functions of the cerebral hemispheres coexist peacefully, with one's general cognition representing coordinated contributions from both hemispheres as deemed appropriate for task, situation, and so forth. On the whole, however, there appears to be a left hemisphere predominance in the determination of output. This left hemisphere bias or control is often evident in different characteristics of people's responses to a situation, for example, in the frequent use of solutions that rely heavily upon language (Levy, 1983).

This differentiated and coordinated approach to one's environment can be disrupted in several ways. One way is to increase processing requirements so as to exceed available resources or capacity (Friedman & Polson, 1981; Hellige, Cox, & Litvac, 1979). Not being able to attend to all of the relevant information in such cases, we become selective and this selectivity may advance certain ways of processing at the expense of others. For example, most people find it hard to attend to the music in a concert and others' conversations at the same time. We usually find ourselves opting for one or the other. The example also suggests the relative power of language in such situations; background conversations when we are trying to listen to music can be very annoying. Background music when we are trying to carry on a conversation is usually much less so, unless it is very loud. Note that in these situations we are indirectly giving precedence or priority to one type of processing. To the extent this processing is cortically (laterally) differentiated, we are thereby favoring one lateralized function over the other.

A second kind of imbalanced situation is more permanent. If there is some kind of dysfunction present in the cerebral structures associated with a given domain, several potentially biasing consequences are possible. First the dysfunction limits the ways one has of dealing effectively with the environment. Second, the relative absence of a function also means the relative absence of its inhibiting or moderating effects on other complementary functions. A language dysfunction thus can have several consequences. It precludes or at least reduces the effectiveness of an important vehicle for understanding and communicating with the world. At the same time it may make more likely the expression and enhancement of other, nonlanguage ways of relating to the world.

It is easy to see how this general picture could be tailored to fit the case of the musical savant. Thus, the dysfunction occurring in the savant's language severely restricts ways of meaningfully interacting with the environment. Music is an alternative, and one that might be spared from damage to language areas of the cortex. The absence of an intact language system would also limit the amount of inhibition by language over other areas. Music interests and talents would be allowed to flourish unimpeded by any competition from language.

The idea of music somehow commanding all of the intellectual resources of the musical savant is by no means new (Lindsley, 1965). The advantage of the cerebral lateralization model is that it relates the relative enhancement and compensation to a more general model of cerebral functioning, and one with considerable clinical and experimental support. There is much to recommend a lateralization explanation of musical savants on other grounds. Cerebral lateralization of higher cognitive function is rarely, if ever, an all or none phenomenon. Rather, there is a gradient of specialization, and this gradient means a wide range of variation in possible dysfunction or enhancement. The appearance of savant skill thus might reflect the subtle interplay of dysfunctional language areas and intact nonlanguage areas. Considerable variation in savant skill has been suggested by Treffert (1988).

Models based on cerebral lateralization can also account for more specific aspects of the musical savant syndrome. In addition to the relative intactness of music itself, there is the evidence for differential achievement in the various components of music. As noted in Chapter 5, the higher level of performance for tonal than rhythmic aspects of music is consistent with the evidence that these components may be lateralized to different hemispheres. There is also the evidence that affect seems to be more often spared in savants than not, though the emotional display may not be socially appropriate (Chapter 1). Aspects of affect expression and perception are apparently more often under right hemisphere than left hemisphere control (Bryden, 1982).

There is also the striking preponderance of males among musical savants; a sex difference ratio favoring males by about 6:1. Males outnumber females in the population of retarded people at large (Richardson, Koller, & Katz 1986), but the sex difference is still much greater than one would expect on the basis of the larger group. Treffert (1988) proposed that this sex difference marks another link to cerebral lateralization of function, one originally outlined by Geschwind and Galaburda (1985). During prenatal cortical development, the rate of cortical maturation is modulated by hormones, particularly sex-linked testosterone. Elevated levels of testosterone may even have hemisphere specific effects associated with the sequence of development in the brain such that the maturation of the left hemisphere is slowed more than the right. As a consequence, the left hemisphere is less likely able to assume its usual role as the locus for many important language and executive functions. The predominance of some reading disabilities, notably dyslexia (Geschwind & Galaburda, 1985) and possibly hyperlexia (Healy, et al. 1982) among males may reflect such effects. Perhaps not coincidentally these reading anamolies may coexist with musical savant skills (Chapter 1). The model also suggests right hemisphere skills other than music might be enhanced, for example, certain spatial abilities. There is some evidence supporting this contention (Chapter 1). Finally, there is the relatively specific evidence of left hemisphere dysfunction in several of the cases. J.L. is a right hemiplegic and L.L. has some motor impairment on the right side. Computerized tomography of J.L. indicates considerably more cortical atrophy in the left hemisphere (Charness, 1987, personal communication).

A further curious sex-associated difference was apparent in the participants in our sample. Among the retarded subjects the two females' conversational language skills were much better than any of the males, Eddie falling somewhere in between. Among the three comparison subjects with absolute pitch, K.L, B.A., and M.B., the first two, both female, had no history of language delay or difficulty, whereas the male M.B. was severely echolalic at an early age

(Chapter 2). There is evidence language is usually more bilaterally represented in females than males (McGlone, 1980). Perhaps the hypothesized left hemisphere dysfunction occurring in musical savants is particularly debilitating if the savant is male.

The cerebral differentiation hypothesis has recently been amended to consider another possible neuropsychological substrate of savant behavior (Rimland & Fein, 1988; Treffert, 1988). Noting the intense concentration of attention often exhibited by autistic savants as well as their excessive concern and often, knowledge about their spatial environment, Rimland and Fein (1988) suggested this may reflect a reliance on a memory system mediated by the hippocampus. This is in contrast to the more usual situation where several memory systems, one mediated by the amygdala and one by the hippocampus combine in a cooperative fashion to form long term memories.

As attractive as these neuropsychological accounts of savant skill are, they have some shortcomings, as their originators readily acknowledge. One problem is that skill or deficit does not map so neatly onto cerebral hemisphere or memory subsystems as the preceding descriptions would suggest. There is considerable evidence, for example, that the lateralization of various aspects of music depends on training, experimental task, and material (Bever, 1983). It seems to be represented differently in the skilled musician than in the novice, for example. Whether it might be represented differently yet in the savant is not known. A similar problem exists with respect to the "hippocampal link." Functions of processing systems associated with the hippocampus and amygdala are currently a matter of considerable controversy (e.g., Olton, Becker, & Handelmann, 1979). Until the issues in the controversy become clarified, it will be difficult to make more specific links between memory structures and functions in the savant.

The neuropsychological models can also be faulted for what they fail to consider. Thus, the language deficit observed in musical savants usually has a specific form, with echolalia mentioned in the overwhelming majority of cases. This may be significant on two counts. First it indicates language is not completely absent, what one might actually expect if music only develops in savants when there is no competing language. The most gifted musical savants are not mute. Second, it suggests that although savants have considerable facility in the phonetic, and perhaps, syntactic aspects of language, their semantics and pragmatics are severely disturbed. This kind of deficit seen in the savant resembles Wernicke's aphasia (Luria, 1966), a fairly localized language dysfunction. It suggests damage must be quite selective for savant behavior to occur.

There is another sense in which the language-music tradeoff model needs modification. Clearly musical prodigiousness of the sort seen in savants is common among many renowned classical composers (Schonberg, 1981) with no accompanying severe language deficits. More importantly, as we saw in Chapter

6, musical precocity need not mean many language functions cannot recover, at least to some extent. Eddie's pragmatic language usage is improving, slowly but surely, with no negative consequence to his musical growth.

An interesting development seems to be occurring in L.L. that indicates music and language in the savant are not mutually exclusive. Until very recently L.L.'s responses to conversational attempts have been monosyllabic or echolalic. Our first informal testing sessions were characterized by this nonresponsiveness. His music during these times has been skillful and expressive, but it has been confined to renditions of songs and melodies of others. He has evidenced very little inclination to compose. As mentioned earlier this has changed and in our last session he announced and played an original composition for us. During the last several months his language has changed dramatically as well. He is now beginning to make requests, comments, and to respond in a much more sophisticated fashion to questions. At the end of the last session, which was held shortly before Christmas, we conversed about what he wanted for Christmas. His responses were reminiscent of Eddie's, at times disjointed and replete with phrases from radio and TV. Still, this represents a significant improvement over his earlier language use (Larsen, 1987, personal communication).

Other aspects of the savant syndrome are also not addressed in the neuropsychological approaches. Why do so many savants have a severe visual deficit? Why does the evidence of special sensitivity to music appear in development when it does? Why is the keyboard almost invariably the instrument of choice among savants? What is the significance of the presence of absolute pitch among musical savants? How can one accommodate the extensive practice evidently required by J.L. and C.A. to reach the level of skill acquired effortlessly by Eddie?

An approach to these issues is provided by a developmental analysis of the emergence of savant skill. Within this framework, it is important to consider the nature of the developing child, including the period or stage of development, the nature of the particular skill domain and the range of environmental input. Developmental models suggest that it is as a consequence of continuing interactions involving these factors that a given achievement emerges (Brown, et al. 1983). What follows is a sketch of the developmental period when savant behavior typically emerges. Next we will examine some of the characteristics of music as a domain which encourage precocious achievement. Finally, we will consider some of the particular attributes of the emerging savant on the one hand, and the musical environment, on the other, which make savant skill development more likely.

The special sorts of interests and talents exhibited by musical savants appear at a very early age. Reports of special attention to music or attempts to reproduce the sounds in the environment as early as the second and third years of life are common (Chapter 1). This very early attraction to music seems to typify musical prodigies in general (Scott & Moffett, 1977). Indeed, manifestations of exceptional talent make their appearance earlier in music than in other areas (Stanley & Benbow, 1986).

There also appears to be an upper limit to the developmental period during which a musical savant skill might be expected to flourish. The latest introduction to music in the savant sample was in the early elementary school years (age 6 to 8, approximately). This upper limit is approximate on several accounts. First, it may reflect factors associated with opportunity for expression rather than a manifested predisposition. Thus C.A., who was not introduced to a musical instrument until age 8, nevertheless showed an intense interest in the sounds of his environment at a much earlier age (Chapter 1). A second issue centers on the use of chronological age as the appropriate marker for delineating a developmental period. Against a background of delayed development, the appearance of quickly developing musical talent even at chronological age 6 or 8 indicates relatively early emergence. In these cases it might be more meaningful to speak of an optimal period for manifesting talent in relation to other developmental milestones, such as walking or talking.

With these considerations in mind, the optimal period of emergence for musical savant skill roughly corresponds to the preschool period of development. What achievements of this period might favor the expression of musical interests? There are many candidates. The preschool period is one of often spectacular accomplishment in many areas; cognitive, social, and emotional. The variety and magnitude of these accomplishments have made the preschool period the object of intense empirical and theoretical attention over the years (e.g., Brown, et al. 1983; Donaldson, 1978). Citing a particular subset of factors as providing "the" developmental context for savant skill emergence is risky, at best. In fact, perhaps it is the fact of massive developmental change in the general sense that makes a musical talent more likely to emerge at this time.

However, considering musical understanding as primarily a cognitive achievement (Serafine, 1987; Sloboda, 1985) may restrict the domain considerably. Here several achievements during the normal course of development stand out. First, the child acquires the natural language(s) of his culture. At the beginning of this period, at age 1 or so, the child may be able to produce many of the sounds of the surrounding natural language but only an occasional word. Five years later, the typical child has mastered the fundamental grammar of the system, speaks distinctly enough to be easily understood, and has a vocabulary of 14,000 words (Templin, 1957). A second acquisition has been described by Gardner and Winner (1982) as a "first draft" understanding of the environment. This understanding goes considerably beyond the sensori-motor or practical understanding often seen in infancy (Piaget, 1952). It involves such accomplishments as a system for classifying events and objects in the environment, one which includes hierarchic ordering along a dimension of generality (dogs vs. animals and the like, Rosch, Mervis, Gray, Johnson, & Bayes-Brehm, 1976). It also involves the establishment of a set of important conceptual distinctions about the environment. For example, the preschool child comes to distinguish between real and apparent, animate and inanimate, "my" perspective and "your" perspective, and so forth (Flavell, 1985).

The distinctions, like the classification systems, sometimes miss the mark, and much research has been directed toward examining those errors of understanding in the preschool child (e.g., Donaldson, 1978). Hence the appropriateness of the term "first draft" in describing the provisional nature of the child's knowledge. The important point to note is that as with language, the various aspects of understanding provide the foundation for later elaboration and refinement (Flavell, 1985). Some additional indication of the magnitude of these changes is that they are accompanied by marked changes in brain organization, especially that concerned with long distance "coherence" or coordination of activity over the occipital, temporal and frontal areas in the left hemisphere (Thatcher, Walker, & Guidice 1987).

Not surprisingly, musical understanding and performance in normal children typically undergoes a series of changes during this period (Hargreaves, 1986). There is some evidence of attention to the patterns of sound (Chang & Trehub, 1977) as well as imitation of specific pitches (Kessen, Levine, & Wendrich, 1979) before the end of the first year. Whether these represent differentiated responses to the musical aspects of these sound patterns is debatable (Sloboda, 1985). By 18 months however, there is clear evidence of attention to specific melodies (Hargreaves, 1986) as well as spontaneous song making. The general pattern to emerge over the next four years is an increasingly sophisticated music perceiving and making capacity. At first, there is primary attention to the global outline of a melody and rhythm with gradual matching of contour and eventually specific intervals and tonal relationships. By the end of this period the young child has developed the ability to appreciate the primary distinguishing features in a tonal framework (Trehub, et al. 1986).

Several aspects of this normative picture are curious, particularly in comparison to early musical behavior in the savant. The first of these is the apparent early disregard for particular pitch qualities seen in the younger child. Thus Davidson, McKernon, and Gardner (1981) describe $1\frac{1}{2}$ to 2-year-old children's songs as often having a glissando quality with little concern for pitch matching. This contrasts with the intense interest in matching specific sounds often described in the earliest expression of music in savants (Chapter 1). Second, there appears to be a waxing, and then waning of some aspects of musical behavior during this period. Moog (1976) describes movement in response to music as being more prominent earlier in the preschool years, though it may be more variegated later. There is also a decrease in spontaneous or original songs at about age 4, as children more often opt for the melodies of their culture, possibly because the latter are usually more consistent and well formed (Winner, 1982). Such eventual reluctance to respond to and make music, (if it is indeed reluctance) certainly does not describe the course of events in the musical savant.

There are many parallels between development of musical cognition and more general cognition during the preschool year. Often these parallels are explicitly incorporated into models of musical development. For Dowling (1982), coming to understand the tonal structure of music is much the same as learning the syntax of one's language. Davidson et al. (1981) suggested musical understanding follows in broad outline the stages of cognitive growth described by Piaget (1952). Hargreaves (1986) also saw the relevance of concepts derived from Piaget, for example assimilation and accommodation, in describing the child's gradually coming to use the musical conventions of his environment.

Although music may be one facet of the general cognitive picture, it is not the case that cognitive development proceeds in a single, monolithic movement. Instead it is probably more accurate to speak of loose assemblies of skills or "understandings" about the environment (Flavell, 1985). Development in different areas may proceed independently, especially at first. For example, functions of early speech may be quite removed from (other) forms of cognition, particularly early in childhood (Vygotsky, 1962).

This relative independence occurs even within relatively restricted domains. Thus language acquisition involves

1. phonology—learning the sound units of the language
2. semantics—associating words with their referents, objects, events, ideas, emotions and the like
3. syntax—learning how words representing different meanings can be combined into longer statements
4. pragmatics—learning appropriate communicative conventions for using the system.

Development in these various areas can be highly asynchronous (Leonard, 1982). Indeed, there is increasing evidence that acquisition of some language components may proceed in the virtual absence of others. It is possible to have reasonably normal phonological development in the face of severe pragmatic and semantic disability (Fay & Butler, 1968). The converse, severe phonological disability with more normal pragmatic and semantic aspects, is also true (Mayberry, Wodlinger-Cohen, & Goldin-Meadow, 1987). Actually, one need not go so far afield to find a convincing separation of sound and meaning in language. Kuczaj (1983) described the various word and sound games that mark the early preschool years when the child is alone—so called "crib speech." This speech is marked by many repetitions and often has a "variations on a theme" quality, the variations only bearing partial resemblance to those occurring in the language environment. Kuczaj (1983) suggested these word games might have several functions. First they may represent an attempt by the child to explore and master recent language constructions without the added requirement of trying to communicate. Second, they might simply be fun to hear and reproduce. Motivation as well as achievement may vary for different components of the emerging language system.

Next, let us consider the nature of the domain in which musical savants excel. Sloboda (1985) has presented a lengthy discussion of the many similarities between language and music as systematic bodies of human knowledge. They are ubiquitous cross-culturally and are largely human activities. As we have seen they both have a normative developmental history. Some basic distinctions in development also apply to each. Distinctions between comprehension and production or among levels of literacy are relevant to both domains. Indeed, in our teaching of Eddie there was a direct attempt to capitalize on the similarities between note reading in musical literacy and letter reading in language literacy.

Sloboda (1985) argued that the similarities extend to the structural organization of the domain. Just as language is conventionally analyzed into basic sound units (phonemes), music has its basic sound unit—the note or chroma. In language, phonemes are combined to produce words, which in turn yield sentences, paragraphs and completed text through a series of generative rules. In like manner the notes of music are combined to produce phrases, motives, symphonic movements, and so on again through a series of generative rules. Within each of these levels Sloboda finds many parallels in terms of models of psychological processes. Thus, at the level of the phoneme as at the level of individual chroma there is a tendency to make sharply defined perceptual judgments. Perception is categorical. At higher levels of organization in both domains one can find analogous effects of structure and redundancy reflected in subjects' ability to process and recall the information presented. Finally, at the most general level Sloboda sees many similarities in the fundamental idea of deep or underlying versus surface structure in language and in music.

Perhaps the most enthusiastic proponent of a music-language link is Bernstein (1976), who suggested many exact parallels between the two, both structurally and developmentally. More often, however, dissenting voices are heard, the issue being how exact the analogy is. For example, some question the application of transformational grammar to music (West, Howell, & Cross, 1985). Particularly problematic is deciding whether a sentence or phrase is legitimate. In language the rules for this are usually quite clear, in music much less so. West, Howell, and Cross (1985) also point to a kind of acid test that can be applied to linguistic utterances much more easily than they can be applied to musical ones. "Does it make sense?" in language means, among other things, whether one understands or acknowledges the referents (meaning) of the various words in the sentence as well as how they are related to each other in sentence structure. Cultural conventions about the referents of different words and the referents of word combinations, in short about meaning, make it possible to resolve disputes about understanding, at least in principle.

Music is another matter. It has no words, or units referring in a consistent fashion to events, objects, and people in the environment. This fundamental semantic property of language is present in music only in a highly abridged or idiosyncratic form. For Cooke (1959) various note combinations or intervals may function as protowords, pointing to different emotional states rather than concepts or things. Davies (1978) considered even this too specific, suggesting that at best different musical conventions may successfully communicate ("mean") different general moods. More specific meaning may occur as a result of personal experiences one associates with a piece, termed by Davies the "they're playing our song" effect. In neither case does the meaning reflect an extensive cultural lexicon or dictionary as one finds in language.

Meyer (1956) argued for two kinds of meaning in music. One kind derives from the sorts of associations we have just been describing, and is termed designative. A second, termed embodying, is internal to music as a formal system for generating and relating sounds. For Meyer a given composition has meaning or makes sense in two ways: It may remind one of something else or it may be internally consistent or pleasing. As Meyer notes, arguments about the designating versus embodying principles in musical composition have been going on for centuries, and in part define various periods in the Western classical tradition. The important point is that as a closed system, music can be understood or analyzed solely in terms of its internal rules and regularities. In this it has much in common with mathematics or games such as chess. As these additional examples suggest, being a closed rather than an open system does not necessarily diminish the attractiveness of an area. However, it will reflect different kinds of skill requirements for one mastering the domain as well as different functions or uses of the resulting expertise. Gardner's (1983) perspective suggests that the appearance of prodigies in such areas as chess and music reflect this "closed system" aspect of the skill domains. Not requiring extensive experience in the larger world of events, objects, and people, expertise in music or chess does not have to await an accretion of knowledge within this larger context (cf. also Hargreaves, 1986).

It is also important to consider the specific form of the musical system to which children in our culture are exposed. Even with the extensive expansion of musical forms and rules of composition in the 20th century, it is safe to say the primary musical language of Western culture remains firmly grounded in diatonic structure. Moreover, the structure itself is further constrained in practice. Two of the seven classical diatonic modes provide the basis for the overwhelming majority of compositions in this tradition (Norton, 1984). Within these modes particular scale usage tends to be further constrained.

Conventional diatonic music is well defined. At the level of scale construction, many of the constituent notes of the conventional major and minor scales are reflected in the harmonics of the tonic. Thus third, fourth and fifth scale degrees occur as relatively prominent harmonics. Moreover, particular scale components have figured prominently in harmonic conventions of the

Western classical tradition for over 300 years (Bernstein, 1976). The nature of the scale and its elaboration is in some respects embedded in the sound complex itself. The various scales of conventional diatonic modes are further organized in terms of shared chroma and tonic-dominant relationships in a highly consistent pattern (Shepard, 1982). These relationships are implicitly acknowledged in adults even without formal musical training (Krumhansl, 1983). Not only is conventional music a closed system, it is one with regularity as a highly salient feature of the system's operation in musical practice. There is evidence of further simplification when the music is specifically intended for children. Dowling (1988) examined children's nursery school songs and found they were far less likely to contain chromaticisms than either adult folk songs or songs from the classical repertoire. Together these various factors could make existing musical structure more apparent to the developing savant.

A conclusion that music is simply language without referential meaning is undoubtedly too simple. Gardner (1983) has characterized music as involving a distinctive kind of intelligence in several respects. Among these he cites its ability to elicit distinctive patterns of individual difference, and to show specific effects associated with critical trauma, developmental history, and laboratory task. For example, the maintenance of musical sensibilities after cortical traumas that are debilitating in many other respects suggests considerable independence of the primary musical structures. As is often the case, a sort of middle ground view is probably closest to portraying the nature of things. Language and music may share some processing characteristics, and in fact at some level these may be identical, while in other respects each might go its own way, with its characteristic product as the result. Pribram (1982) offers a view along these lines, suggesting common syntactic processing features in language and music with considerable divergence at the point of referential meaning.

Summarizing the argument to this point, both the timing of savant skill emergence and the nature of music as a knowledge domain may represent a particularly good developmental fit. Developmentally, it is a period when children typically fashion a fundamental understanding of different knowledge domains. The particular domain represented by music is distinctive in several respects. It shares many of the features of language but clearly not all. It is highly structured and very salient. A normal preschooler who never encounters music is quite rare in our culture, although the extent and sophistication of this exposure varies. Against this background, acquisition of some degree of sophistication about the music of one's culture is a normal occurrence. The savant represents much more than the normative or usual kind of developing musical understanding. What kinds of sensitivities and competencies must the savant have to show precocious achievement in the face of mental and physical handicap?

One clue is provided by the presence of prolonged echolalia among musical savants. Perhaps the most dramatic kind of dissociation seen in language is that characterized by extensive echolalia (Fay, 1966, 1973). Echolalia is most often associated with autism (Rimland, 1971) and is also fairly common among the congenitally blind early in their development (Fraiberg, 1977; Mills, 1983). Echolalia is marked by an apparent lack of understanding of the referents of utterances addressed to the child. Rather than responding to the intent of the message "How are you?" the echolalic child repeats the question. In so doing, there is some understanding of the sounds of language, and their expression in sentence form, at least in an imitative sense. One implication of this is that the echolalic child has a considerable sensitivity to his surrounding language as a system of sounds. There is also some knowledge about how these sounds are combined to produce extended sequences. Exactly what seems to be missing is a matter of some controversy. Briefly, one line of evidence points to the pragmatic, communicative function of language, and its role in sharing meanings about the events and objects in the environment (Sigman & Mundy, 1987). The average child's first words, for example, usually occur in the context of shared experiences with the parents; and it may be this social focus which is somehow absent in the echolalic child. Another, possibly related problem is that of reference itself. Understanding that certain sounds "stand for" or refer to certain (classes of) events and objects can be a considerable cognitive achievement for the young child (Macnamara, 1982). First, evidence is emerging that the first extended language use occurs in connection with learning about the important classes of things in the environment. That knowledge comes about as a consequence of repeated perceptual experience with the qualities of things; surfaces, angles, colors, and the like (Cohen & Gelber, 1975). Apparently it is this quiet, attentive classification by the young child which provides the conceptual basis for the emergence of words (Bloom & Capatides, 1987). Parents are usually only too willing to provide names for concepts the child is sorting out (Macnamara, 1982). This process obviously has an important social component; the naming parent and learning child have to be on the "same wavelength" for the parents' labels to make any sense at all. Fraiberg (1977) suggests that this may be a particular problem for the visually impaired child. Lacking vision means that an important medium for finding out about one's world is not available. In addition, it simply may be very difficult for the visually impaired to understand what parents are talking about when they try to communicate with the child. Even such an elementary distinction as "I" and "you" may be difficult to keep clear. Macnamara notes that this pronominal problem is usually mastered through the child's experiencing the different contents in which these words are used. Eddie, at age 9, still occasionally refers to himself by name rather than in the first person. One can imagine the difficulties Eddie must have had in understanding the referent of the comments being addressed to him in his early years. With limited vision and three older siblings, who was "you" at different times? Lacking access to the various visual cues that would clarify the referent, it must have been quite a puzzle when Eddie was younger.

Lacking the usual semantic competencies which accompany language development, the savant might still have competencies sufficient for many of the requirements posed by music. In fact a conception of language and music as partially isomorphic would seem to fit the particular kind of language and music profile seen in musical savants. The cases in Chapter 1 were not completely devoid of language, as we might expect from a compensation or opposing faculties model. Neither did the kind of language vary in a random fashion, as one might expect if language and music were independent. Instead the kind of limited language seen, echolalia with occasional jargon or "word salad," indicate at the very least competence in recognizing and reproducing the sound patterns of language. If a sound-pattern recognizing system were relatively intact, it could learn to recognize and produce sound patterns in either domain, language, or music. In language the additional requirements for consistent, culturally specified reference may make the acquisition far from optimal. Music, having different requirements as to meaning, represents a much happier fit in these instances.

The foregoing theory suggests the musical savant may represent a propitious match between the requirements of the domain on the one hand and the capacities of the subject on the other. Let us explore this notion a bit further and try to construct the kind of matrix which may result in musical savant skills. A second point of contact between the subject and the domain is suggested by the apparent presence of absolute pitch in all well documented cases of musical savants. As we suggested in Chapter 3, this kind of sensitivity could be invaluable in alerting the young child to some of the possibilities inherent in music. Unfortunately we know little about the circumstances under which this kind of sensitivity surfaces. The presence of a genetic factor is indicated by the fact that absolute pitch tends to run in families (Bachem, 1940). On this evidence the kind of sensitivity represented by absolute pitch is very rare, Bachem's estimate being 1 in 10,000 or so in the general population. However, this is certainly not the whole story. There is the limited but very intriguing report by Kessen et al. (1979) of 6-month-olds who were able to duplicate several pitches produced by their mothers after a little training. Moreover, the infants were described as very interested in the task. This ready tendency to mimic notes made by others may subsequently disappear if it is not practiced (Kessen, cited in Dowling & Harwood, 1986). Though this is by no means a demonstration of absolute pitch, the study does suggest quite sensitive frequency specific attention to sound may be more normative at some points in development than suggested by Bachem's (1948) adult samples. This is also the possibility raised by Sergeant in several studies. In one (Sergeant, 1969) absolute pitch was found to be more likely in professional musicians the earlier the formal musical training had begun. The rate of occurrence approached

95% for those whose musical training was begun before age 4. Many factors may enter into this developmental trend. Earlier musical training might be characterized by a different approach than that begun later or there may be earlier expression of musical interests in certain musicians. However, one viable interpretation is that there is a greater proclivity toward the kind of sensitivity seen in absolute pitch early in development. This was the conclusion by Sergeant and Roche (1973) based on the results of an experiment conducted with normal preschoolers. Three-year-olds' attempts to reproduce nursery school songs learned a week earlier were closer to the original key then were the 5-year-olds' attempts. Once again, there are alternative explanations for the age difference observed. The result also seems to contradict other research indicating a general disregard for specific tonal information in young children (e.g., Davidson, et al. 1981). Further empirical research along these lines would be fruitful. The results of Sergeant and Roche (1973) at least suggest that the young child has a capacity for more specific response to musical information than has previously been supposed.

There is also the evidence from the sample of the present study and other case histories. The majority of musical savants are congenitally blind or at least severely visually impaired. A strong genetic component in the absolute pitch of these subjects is highly improbable. However, heightened attention to the sound structure of their environment certainly seems likely. At the same time, because not all blind people have absolute pitch, such enhanced sensitivity need not necessarily lead to absolute pitch skills.

It is evident the developmental research in this area is fragmentary. However, it does indicate a rather fluid situation existing in young children. First, there is a potential for intense and specific information processing of auditory information other than that involved in language. Second, the sensitivity may be enhanced by a variety of factors. One of these must be a congenital, experience-free predisposition. There seems to be no other explanation for the apparent intensity and vividness of the early sound experiences of a Mozart, a Menuhin, or a Blind Tom. Second, competing sources of information, especially the incredibly rich and varied information provided by vision may make the "sound in itself" less salient. Often in development when vision and audition are placed in competition with each other, vision wins (Butterworth, 1981). Another factor might be the discovery that certain types of sounds are symbols for important things and people in one's environment. Developing the full ramifications of this discovery might well lead one away from attention to sounds as of considerable interest and fun in themselves.

How does the (nonlinguistic) sound environment contribute to the savant producing matrix? Beyond the availability of a reasonably rich musical corpus, there must be an opportunity to sharpen one's identification of these sounds. If we are to believe some of the early literature on the training of pitch naming skill (e.g., Copp, 1916), this is a far easier matter for children than for adults (Brady, 1970). There is also the question of opportunity for less directed learning. The overwhelming predominance of the piano as the instrument of musical savants is relevant here. Why the piano? Musical prodigies are by no means restricted to the piano. Availability is surely one factor. Keyboards of some type are probably much more common as musical instruments for the young child. The keyboard also maps its sound producing qualities onto the musical culture in a direct fashion. That is, a reasonably well-tuned piano contains the alphabet of the musical language laid out in a coherent spatial organization. The piano also offers a kind of feedback that is likely useful to the savant. Subtleties of bowing or fingering techniques such as occur with string and wind instruments do not come between the player and a simple melody. The physical constraints imposed by the nature of the very young voice are also not a problem. Finally the piano allows one to explore sound combinations in ways that are at once direct and extensive. Octaves and various harmonics are laid out in a recurring, spatial pattern. There is evidence that receptively even infants may be sensitive to octave relationships (Demany & Armand, 1984). It is a simple matter to strike (and repeat) note groups on the piano to produce and test such interval relationships. In these respects keyboards are very accessible instruments and perhaps ideally suited to the sensibilities and limitations of the young musical savant.

This developmental picture is quite consistent with some of the general characteristics of the distributed processing approach to savant skill presented earlier. First, as we have seen, children usually acquire a basic implicit understanding of their culture's music during the preschool years. Models that attempt to represent implicit understanding are obviously very compatible with this kind of achievement. Parallel distributed systems models are also well suited to well structured domains where the structure can be represented in patterns of association among types of units. Such is the case with music, at least theoretically (Bharucha, 1987). Finally, the cognitive requirements of parallel distributed systems are not excessive from a developmental viewpoint. Because they do not require complex conscious executive functions, they are well within the cognitive capacity of the preschool child.

In summary the model being proposed suggests that musical savants emerge during a developmental period when the young child is hard at work constructing some of the first hierarchically organized systems of knowledge in different domains. In each domain the features of this organization flavor much of what is to come later. With respect to music this knowledge or organization in the savant involves the use of a coding system based on ready aural identification of the pitch alphabet. The adoption of this particular coding system is determined by several factors—its generally greater availability during this developmental period, individual predisposition, and opportunity for enhancement and elaboration. Subsequently the pitch code is used to map and structure the input from the musical environment using assembly skills similar to those seen in other knowledge domains during this period, notably language. Both the intrinsic gratification derived from successfully mastering structural relationships in music such as those involved in tonality, and the social attention from the environment sustain this effort, the former probably more than the latter. Finally, the particular pattern of relationships defined by conventional tonality may represent an especially "available" kind of structure to the musical savant in that it relates alphabet information to higher order representations, such as scales, in a consistent and logical fashion.

Admittedly, this briefly sketched model sounds a bit like a "mulligan stew" recipe for a musical savant; a little bit of this, not too much of that. Viewing musical savants as the consequence of certain conjunctions in development is similar to the general model proposed by Feldman (1986) for child prodigies. In each the talent is seen as dynamic and sensitive to the nature of the domain and that of the environment. Similarly, musical savants do not appear suddenly, at random, and as a finished product. A considerable degree of both complexity and flexibility is dictated by the data.

The model does offer some predictions and directions for additional research. First, it suggests that musical savants are more common, or at least potentially so, than is suggested by the case history data. This greater frequency is expected on several counts. None of the "contributing ingredients," pitch sensitivity, language delay, visual impairment, opportunity for enhancement, is especially rare. In fact some may be normative for certain developmental periods. Second, the existence of factors in combination suggests some latitude in the contribution of each. Thus J.L. (Charness, et al. 1988) required extensive practice to bring his playing to its current level; Eddie needed much less. For C.A. and Judy progress was slow at first and then accelerated (Chapter 1). Larger samples of musical savants reported in the more recent literature (Hermelin & O'Conner, 1987; Monroe & Miller, 1988) provide some support for the notion that musical savants may be more common than previously supposed.

The model also suggests at least one core attribute of musical savants, what has been called extended pitch naming ability. It is necessary here to be quite precise about the prediction being made. It is probably not the case that absolute pitch is a sufficient condition for musical skill of the sort we have described in earlier chapters. Over the past year and a half we have been monitoring the musical progress of another child at the school Eddie originally attended (Miller & Horodyski, 1988). We strongly suspect this congenitally blind child has absolute pitch. Tunes heard one week earlier are almost invariably played in the same key much later, if they are attempted at all. However, his playing has a severely truncated, disjunctive quality, with rarely more than a brief phrase of a new song being repeated. Interestingly, his harmonic accompaniment is most often an open fifth or an alternating tonic-dominant figure in the bass. If we are correct in our assumptions about this child's pitch sensitivity, it clearly has not been sufficient to enable him to master the musical language the way Eddie has.

The implication of absolute pitch in musical savants is also restricted to tonal rather than rhythmic musical achievement. Past studies of musical savants have not examined exceptional percussion skills in savants for whom this is the instrument of choice, although there is evidence such savants exist (Hauser, Delong, & Rosman, 1975; Hermelin & O'Conner, 1987). Based on the evidence in Chapter 4 there is likely considerable opportunity for divergence in melodic and rhythmic skill. There is, of course, nothing in the proposed model which prohibits percussion savants, only that they would likely follow a different developmental course. Much more damaging to the present theory would be the musical savant with no evidence of absolute pitch. Lacking the general conceptual skills available to the nonretarded person, it is difficult to see how a retarded person could grasp musical structure in the way seen in Eddie and the others without some entry vehicle like absolute pitch. It is in this sense that absolute pitch is predicted as a core attribute. For the kinds of aural musical skills demonstrated in previous chapters, absolute pitch is necessary, but not sufficient.

Two other factors also appear critical, although here the evidence is much shakier. Language disability, or more properly, partial language ability, is strongly implicated in the cases we have reviewed. It also seems an important factor on other grounds. Though not communicative in the conventional sense, echolalia does indicate a considerable knowledge of the sounds made in a language and how they are organized. Thus, it may index the presence of a more general sound organizing skill that could be turned to music, given the proper conditions. The boy with the severely fragmented musical skill we described a moment ago has a language disorder even more severe than Eddie's. His responses are usually monosyllabic and distorted due to a marked articulation problem. There is very little echolalia, and his receptive skills are difficult to estimate. Possibly this pattern indicates a more general problem in analyzing and reproducing the structure inherent in complex sound arrays. Research directed to a more detailed examination of music-language links in the musical savant would clarify this issue.

The notion of a sensitive period for the development of savant skills is also indicated by the existing data and the developmental model. Savant skills emerge roughly between 1 and 9 years. We have already described characteristics of the onset point of this period in normal development. The end point is not so clearly delineated or characterized. Perhaps it marks the end of the time when resources are available for forming preliminary or first draft organizations of knowledge. Or, it could reflect the emergence of a new set of interests or developmental tasks for the child (Piaget & Inhelder, 1969). It does appear to be a kind of watershed period as far as the development of musical talent is concerned. Musical distinction among those who begin music training or self instruction much after 8 years or so is quite rare (Sergeant, 1969; Shuter-Dyson, 1968). For reasons discussed earlier, this end point may be especially variable among those in whom considerable developmental delay has occurred. Still, the late emergence of exceptional musical skill in a retarded adult would present a serious challenge to the theory as it stands.

There is, finally, the notion that certain kinds of music might be more accessible to the emerging musical savant. Does the conventional diatonic system as realized on a keyboard provide the ideal musical corpus for the young savant? Perhaps not. Conventional formal introductions to music often begin with simpler scales, usually pentatonic in nature. Some concentrate on vocal and/or rhythmic aspects of music. How might the young savant respond to these? There is also the evidence in the present research that non-diatonic idioms were also highly accessible to the savant sample. Was the whole tone scale sufficiently different as a musical idiom? I also introduced Eddie to a 12-tone row composition at one point. His response was rather perfunctory, much like his treatment of some of the longer random note strings. The piece wasn't pursued, and this is hardly a conclusive test. An expanded examination across different formal and cultural musical idioms could shed some light on this issue. What does the savant look like in cultures with a tuning system and/or scale structure far different from ours? Is it manifested in different kinds of skills and/or sensitivities on different musical instruments? Is it much more likely to be found with digital instruments like the piano than with analogue ones like the violin? Issues such as these are amenable to empirical resolution, and it is in this spirit that this developmental model has been offered. In many instances it is a matter of expanding the data base. Early musical behaviors, particularly precocious ones need closer scrutiny.

Gardner (1983) has described the many factors which led to the notion that individual differences in intelligence are best described as differences in amount rather than kind. The idea that accomplishment comes from general capacity applied to specific content has a lot of appeal. Failure to achieve is a matter of simple capacity or application, success a happy marriage of the two. As noted by Gardner, savants present a telling argument against this view. There are differences in kind as well as amount, and success requires correlations involving talent, domain, and culture as well as capacity and motivation.

Although Eddie and the other savants represent a dramatic exception to the general intelligence model, there is perhaps the danger of making too much of the exception. A general intelligence model may describe the vast majority. There are reasons for thinking this too is in error (Gardner, 1983). One factor might be the data base. As noted in the introduction, most traditional tests of intellectual functioning may fail to identify many kinds of talent. We have suggested that particularly among the retarded, special talents and competencies may be more common than previously thought. Identification of these competencies seems a promising line of research.

Epilogue

Eddie is now 9½ years old. He continues to grow musically, spending more time on technical aspects such as fingering these days, though he is by no means a technical wizard. He is developing in other areas as well, faster in some than others. In reading he is delighted by the word games in books by Dr. Seuss, and he is improving in his ability to pick up the story line. He remains tenacious in his reading interest, more so in language than in music. He expresses a little interest in arithmetic, but this remains an unexplored area for him.

Eddie's conversational language is also improving and month by month he shows new achievements; being able to incorporate past events in a current conversation, appropriate self reflection ("I don't know that") and so on. He often seems to assume you know what he's talking about, a common fault in young children (Flavell, 1985). Still, it seems unlikely he will attain the kind of easy fluency and coherence one expects in a mature language user.

Finding an appropriate educational environment remains a problem, one evidently shared by many others with unusual interests and talents (Feldman, 1986). In Eddie's case the problem is compounded by his frail health and his family's limited economic resources. His past year in a public school has seen some successes, especially in expanding his social environment. There have been notable failures too, particularly in tailoring the curriculum to fit his strengths and weaknesses. Part of the problem seems to be the working assumption that since he has been classified as "trainable mentally handicapped" there isn't very much that he can do. His handicap is viewed as being systemwide.

209

What of Eddie's future? It seems highly unlikely he will develop into a concert pianist, or a professional musician for that matter. Many a child prodigy has floundered on the way to developing a mature talent, and a host of cultural factors enters the picture (Attali, 1977). Whether Eddie becomes a professional musician is in many ways beside the point. In one interview his mother described the young Eddie, before there was a piano available, spending hour after hour gazing out the window. His life is much different now and music has played a large role in this transformation.

Appendix A:
A Music Teacher's Perspective
on Savant Skill

Nancy Newman, M.A.

My first encounter with Eddie was on cassette tape in Leon Miller's office. Leon had described Eddie to me briefly, and I expected to hear a child with a good ear, one who could pick out tunes and perhaps add simple harmonies. To my surprise, the 6-year-old on the tape played in full 4-part harmony with excellent voice-leading. This was much more complex than I had anticipated, and I looked forward to meeting Eddie.

I had explained to Leon that I had no experience working with multiply-handicapped children. He didn't seem to think it important, a response that I only understood much later. My name had been given to him by my graduate department because I had a reputation for being "good with kids," that is, I could get children to enjoy the not-always-pleasant task of learning to play the piano. In meeting Eddie, however, I realized that he needed no such coaxing: He loved playing the piano more than anything else in the world.

My initial impression was reinforced by descriptions from the staff at Eddie's school. If Eddie ate a good lunch he was rewarded with time at the piano; if he did his work he was allowed to play the piano. I had enthusiastic students, but I had never seen a child like this.

Contrary to my apprehensions, Eddie was neither unapproachable nor withdrawn. He was warm and affectionate once he knew my voice and the reason I was visiting. When Leon boomed "hello" from across the room his face would light up, and he would get very excited, rousing from his usual apathetic slump. At the end of each lesson there would be a round of hugs and hearty farewells. Eddie would sign and say "finished" as he had been taught at school and would good-naturedly allow himself to be led out of the piano room, one hand trailing behind, playing yet another song.

I started seeing Eddie once a week in May 1985, and the first question I asked myself was, "What should I do with this child? He has a fantastic ear and memory and has explored the entire range of the keyboard on his own. On the other hand, the usual avenues of learning—sight and verbalization—are almost completely closed to him. What can I do for him?"

Gradually, I determined that there were three general areas that we could pursue: repertoire, symbol recognition, and terminology. These areas corresponded to Eddie's strengths (hearing and playing) and weaknesses (seeing and verbalizing). The sophistication of the material in each area had to be tailored to Eddie's abilities, so we did interesting repertoire and very simple visual and verbal tasks. There has been a great deal of progress in all these areas, but in the account that follows it might seem as if the achievements in seeing and naming are considered more noteworthy than Eddie's considerable talent. From the pedagogic point of view these achievements are significant because they were less easily predicted, but this is not to overlook that they occurred *by means of* Eddie's original ability.

The most unusual aspect of teaching Eddie was that I couldn't use language to give directions, to focus on details, to go over fingerings and rhythms. Imagine piano lessons without these things! At the same time, I didn't want my sessions with Eddie to be a continual round of "listen and play, listen and play"; I wanted to encourage more variety in our interactions. Consequently I decided to teach Eddie the names of the piano keys. This is typically the first item covered at piano lessons. It was three months before Eddie could designate more than one pitch class reliably. I knew he could identify these pitches by *sound*; he could already play a song in any register and in any key (Chapter 1). Once Eddie could identify middle C, he would play all the lower Cs and all the higher Cs as I had shown him, even imitating my squeaky voice in the high register. In another month he could name the Fs and Es easily. By mid-November he could name all the white keys and B flats. Soon he could name the pitch class F$^\#$, and then C$^\#$, G$^\#$, and D$^\#$. In mid-January it became clear to me that he understood the concepts "sharpness" and "flatness" as well as the specific note names. Additionally, he could not only name individual pitches, but he often played and named authentic cadences (V7-I) in every major and minor key.

Note naming usually takes two piano lessons with a 6-year-old. It took 6 months with Eddie, but once he grasped the concept, he took the initiative and applied it in a sophisticated way. He also internalized our routine, and began naming notes at every lesson. Gradually, I dropped this activity in order to spend more time on other things, but Eddie has not forgotten this material.

Note naming was my first substantial verbal/social goal with Eddie. Leon had already identified pieces by name with Eddie (Chapter 5), and he could sing the alphabet, so theoretically there was no barrier to Eddie's eventually naming the piano keys. Furthermore, pitch names are basic to communicating with other musicians, and we continue to use these names in identifying the repertoire that we perform. In the classical repertoire this is the primary way that certain pieces are distinguished, such as "Sonata in C Major." Eddie has always been accurate with these designations, even when his general language was highly unreliable.

During our first sessions I played a variety of piano pieces for Eddie in order to consider his responses and subsequently develop a curriculum. Observing Eddie in this manner proceeded smoothly because he was already receptive to a listen-and-play format. He would also play continuously if he was in front of the piano; he explored the keyboard at every opportunity. Every "lesson" included a time when Eddie would play the piano freely, improvising and rambling in ways that were both familiar and unfamiliar to me. I was able to recognize television themes, salsa bass lines, and current radio hits, but more importantly, I saw how Eddie approached the keyboard. His exploration and memory was primarily harmonic, and yet his sense of voice-leading, as I had first heard on tape, was highly developed. He would keep his left hand poised above scale degrees 1 and 5 of whatever key he was in or whatever secondary key area might be used. Having tiny hands, he did this by shifting his fingers at the 5th degree to the upper or lower tonic, depending on the register he needed. It was clear to me that Eddie had thought about how to use his hands at the piano. Lacking good vision, he relied upon aural and tactile information to find his way around the keyboard. It seems as though his early favoritism for the key of F$^{\#}$ was due in part to its concentration on the black keys; this key "sits well" under a child's hands.

I decided to begin with pieces that are standard in the children's piano literature—something more advanced than the Thompson *Preludes* but not from the adult concert literature. The principle reason for this was simply that Eddie's finger span was at most an open sixth. I wanted some musical situations that would be literally within his reach so that I could reasonably expect Eddie to be precise. Also, this would expose Eddie to the repertoire that most children study while taking piano lessons.

One of the first pieces I introduced was Kabalevsky's *The Clown*. It is a 25 bar ABA form in A major. The A section alternates between A major and A minor, and the B section moves to flat VI and treats F major and minor the same way. These motions are typical of 20th-century tonality, but unusual by the standards of conventional harmony. Eddie was perfectly at ease with them. After I played the piece for Eddie, what he played back for me was the final A section rather than the entire piece. Later, in transcribing tapes of the Thompson *Preludes*, I discovered that Eddie would sometimes play back only the second strain on an 8-bar piece that repeated. This seemed analogous to Eddie's echolalia, that is, repetition of the last item that was spoken. At the time that we did *The Clown*, however, I resolved to try and communicate the idea of first and second sections. I knew that Eddie "understood" these things in a musical sense, but that he didn't know the terms that describe them. I played each section of the piece, designating each section with the appropriate label, and after a few sessions Eddie would announce these labels as part of the piece. He soon put the piece together as a whole, with an obvious understanding of its ABA structure. Later I learned that Eddie re-enacted much of our lesson time at home, taking the roles of both teacher and student. Not only would he name the notes in a voice imitating mine, but he would say "first part" or "second part" before playing a portion of a piece. I was also told that he would re-enact the musical part of the church services the family attended, performing the roles of leader and congregation. For his mother this was proof that Eddie absorbed more than it seemed from his surroundings. Imaginative reconstructions such as these are not uncommon in children, although with Eddie they occurred at a slightly later age and with material that demonstrated his sophistication.

In the middle of November I was told that Eddie could see very large letters. I decided to draw some musical symbols and introduce them to him. On separate 8½" × 11" cards I drew a staff with the five lines each an inch apart, a treble clef, a bass clef, a flat sign, a sharp sign, and the notes middle C, D, and E in the treble clef. Eddie was only mildly interested in this, but he seemed to understand when I associated the appropriate piano keys with the notes on the cards. I left these materials in the hands of Marie Morgan, a teacher at his school, who patiently drilled Eddie on identifying these symbols almost daily.

It was in July of 1986 that an important development occurred. By that time I had added three notes in the bass clef (middle C, B, and A) and the next two ascending notes in the treble clef (F and G). I began putting three notes at a time on the piano's music stand and asking Eddie to identify them from left to right by naming and playing. Then I would take the cards away and ask him to repeat this sequence of notes. He was delighted with this process and could easily recall the three-note pattern. I excitedly called Eddie's teachers into the room to show them what Eddie was doing; he was beginning to comprehend that visual symbols could have auditory meanings.

The materials that I used were not different from the average 7-year-old's beginning piano book—they were merely larger. Once his understanding and memory of these symbols was established, I began to shrink the size of the flash cards, first to lines ¾" apart, then ½", and by September ¼" apart. (A standard size children's book, which we used until recently, has lines ³⁄₃₂" apart.) At every step I expected to reach Eddie's limit, but I found that there was always some way to build upon what he could already do. In determining the next step, there were always two factors to consider: the visual problem and the verbal problem. I had been told that Eddie was not using his eyes as well as the doctors had expected after the cataract surgery. If Eddie's sight was going to improve, he had to learn to use his eyes, to focus upon and identify objects. The school staff found that it was difficult to get Eddie to look at things; for example, familiar people could come within inches of his face and he wouldn't recognize them until they spoke. He was generally apathetic and uninterested when it came to looking at things, and yet there were several incidents that demonstrated that he could be roused to *look*.

For the occasion of his 7th birthday the previous February, the school had an afternoon celebration, as they did for each of the children. The impression I had of these parties was that they were as much for the morale of the staff as they were for the children. Like each child in turn, Eddie seemed to have a vague idea that something exciting was happening. There was cake and ice cream and singing. I arrived just as Eddie was opening his presents, aided by Marie. He seemed more interested in the sound of wrapping paper ripping than in what was inside, like a toddler. Several people had brought him adorable stuffed animals, which he hardly acknowledged. One of the gifts was a hand puppet, and as the adults were sitting around looking disappointed, I put it on and began singing a song with it. Eddie immediately grabbed the puppet. An intern picked up Garfield, the stuffed animal she had brought him, and began singing a song. Again he reached for the toy.

The gift that made Eddie almost beside himself with excitement, however, was a six-foot-long knit scarf that pictured a piano keyboard. It was the only object that provoked an immediate response through *seeing*. Little Eddie was ecstatic when Marie wrapped him in the 9-octave scarf.

As we established a routine at Eddie's school, I began leaving cassette tapes of piano pieces with Marie. If there was time at the end of the day, she would play several selections for Eddie. He would listen to each one and then play a rendition on the piano. In this way the aural part of the lesson could be reinforced during the rest of the week, a concern I had when I first began working with Eddie. He wouldn't develop the necessary technique for complicated passagework if he didn't *practice*, like any other student. It became clear, though, that if Eddie enjoyed a piece he would practice it of his own accord during the week. In those situations Eddie relied entirely on his memory of what we did at the lesson. With cassette tapes he had access to repeated hearings, a valuable resource for any musician.

During our first six months together I introduced selections from *Pour Les Enfants* by Tansman. *The Bear, The Doll*, and *Skating* soon became favorites, so I recorded the entire first set. There are 12 character pieces, ranging from 12 to 32 bars in length and concentrating on one or two technical requirements, such as a rhythmic pattern or repeated chords. They are teaching or even contest pieces, resembling etudes. Eddie learned to play the entire set under Marie's tutelage, scrupulously announcing the appropriate title before each piece.

During this period I introduced duet playing, an activity I do with many of my students. For Eddie I chose the Diabelli Opus 149, *28 Melodious Pieces*. The opening selections are in C major; the primo melodies lie within the range of a fifth and are doubled at the octave. The collection progresses into more distant keys and to a more complicated relationship between the hands. Eddie and I worked through the first three with him listening to the primo part and then playing it while I played along on the secondo part. The bass parts have octaves and thick chords so I didn't consider going over these in detail.

I always alerted Eddie to my intention of positioning him at the high range of the piano, a tangible and immediate verbal assertion. After a while Eddie began imitating my pronouncements with statements like, "I'm going to move me over." One day, when I had returned him to the piano's center, he began playing the secondo part of the 5th Diabelli duet. This was entirely his own initiative—I had never played this part separately for him. He had discerned its rolling triplet figure (in 6/8 meter) and the harmonic motion at the same time that he played the primo part. The piece is in C major and has three 8-bar phrases with a 4-bar closing phrase added to the last. There are optional repeats at the end of each phrase. The harmonic highlights include diminished sevenths on vii of tonic and supertonic (ii) and the secondary dominants of IV and V. Eddie actually preferred this duet to the harmonically simpler ones. He also preferred the bass part of #5 to the completely diatonic primo part.

We continued to do duets in the Diabelli collection, and from that time on I made a point of playing each part for Eddie. We would put the duet together and then trade parts, and I always attached our names to the part we were about to play. I began asking Eddie whether he wanted to play "the high part or the low part," his response usually being incomprehension (expressed by shaking his head slightly) or at best arbitrary partial repetition of the spoken phrase. After three months, however, he demonstrated his understanding of the question, as discussed below.

The other Diabelli duets we played include #9 in G major, #20 (D minor), #26 (A minor) and #29 (E minor). Eddie favored minor keys in his improvising so I obliged him with these choices. Still searching for interesting pieces within his finger span, I presented *Song of the Wanderer* and *My Doll is Lost* (both in A minor) by Bartok; *The Wild Horseman*, *Soldier's March*, *The Happy Farmer*, and *Sicilienne* from Schumann's *Album for the Young*; *Rain on the Roof* and *Playing Soldiers* from *Musical Finds from the 20th Century*; Kabalevsky's *Folk Dance* and *Toccatina* (A minor); *Musette* (D major) from *First Lessons in Bach* and the *Prelude* in C Major from *Book 1, The Well-Tempered Clavier*. This music was in addition to the numerous nursery rhymes from school, TV themes and commercials, and recordings heard at home that Eddie had made a part of his repertoire.

After we had spent a little time together, I felt I had gained some perspective on what Eddie does at the piano. He had reminded me immediately of Blind d'Arnault in Willa Cather's *My Antonia.*[1] Readers familiar with this

---

[1]Cather, W. (1940). *My Antonia* (pp. 122–127). Cambridge, MA: Houghton-Mifflin.

novel will recognize that the historical basis for this character is Blind Tom of Chapter 1. Cather's account of this pianist and his youth bear a strong resemblance in spirit to Eddie. She describes his childhood:

> Several teachers experimented with him. They found he had absolute pitch and a remarkable memory. As a very young child he could repeat, after a fashion, any composition that was played for him. No matter how many wrong notes he struck, he never lost the intention of a passage, he brought the substance of it across by irregular and astonishing means.

(The next sentence reads, "He wore his teachers out.") These words could be used, unaltered, to describe Eddie. Cather's dated portrait has been superceded by Geneva Southall's excellent monograph detailing the political situation, but her appraisal of his musicianship and early determination is not without insight.

Eddie has shown determination and perseverance at the piano too. It was not until after we met that Leon got a full size piano for him to use at home; prior to that he had only toy keyboards and limited access to the piano at school. Even so, Eddie used his hands very skillfully and sensibly at the instrument, always toward a musical end. No other physical activity is as graceful or controlled as Eddie's fingers on the keys. He hasn't put the same effort into anything else, which is not to say that he won't do so at some later point.

Coupled with Eddie's acquired dexterity is his outstanding sense of pitch. There are two primary aspects of pitch memory for the musician: absolute and relative pitch. Eddie is proficient and comfortable with both of these organizing principles. The first involves the "raw data" of timbre, register, and frequency range (cycles per second). The latter is essential in tonality and in any hierarchically structured music. It allows the listener to assess pitches with reference to their distance from the tonic or from a tonal center. There were several incidents early in our sessions that demonstrated Eddie's flexibility. One occurred when Leon played a cassette tape of a classical guitarist. After hearing the first selection, Eddie played a rendition of the piece remarkably true in spirit to the original. He rolled his chords slightly to evoke the strumming of the guitar and his chord voicings were comparable to those on the recording. Leon played a second selection and Eddie played along, seemingly unperturbed by the discordant ensemble. The juxtaposition of guitar, recorded on mediocre quality cassette tape and played back on an institutional tape recorder, with the idiosyncracies of the available piano was more than a little grating. My experience had been that people with absolute pitch find it annoying or confusing to listen under such conditions. Tempermentally Eddie was neither fussy nor demanding, but how did he make musical sense of this? It was clear that he allowed his sense of relative pitch to take precedence, playing in the key closest to the original and coping with the inconsistencies with forbearance. I later realized that Eddie confronted situations such as this one constantly. At home he plays along with records and TV, and it is rare for the sounds of electronically recorded and acoustic instruments to match precisely.

The scenario just described stands in contrast with another aspect of Eddie's playing: He easily modulates anywhere a singer leads. He demonstrated this on numerous informal occasions at school with wandering vocalists. Indeed, it soon became apparent to us that Eddie enjoyed key changes. Sometimes he would spontaneously play one of the old Thompson *Preludes*, modulating up a half step or whole step with each repetition. This is not only musically acceptable, unlike the meanderings of amateur singers, but it is a standard feature of pop songs. It is frequently used in arrangements of Christmas carols and folk melodies to add interest to the repetitions of short songs. Eddie's versions of such tunes were often in this style; it is an appealing sound. Also, Eddie seemed to explore modulations in his improvisations because they afforded a purposeful opportunity for probing the piano.

Would this flexibility with absolute and relative pitch help Eddie to be a polished performer, or would the inconsistencies that invariably arise with wind, brass, and string instruments be of no consequence to him? For instrumentalists and singers, being "in tune" is a perpetual concern. I decided to postpone answering this question because Eddie's instrument is the piano, and the player has no control of its mechanical workings; one simply makes do. Later, when Eddie took up the recorder, this question arose again, and I obtained at least a partial answer.

During the first six months of 1986 Eddie's sociability improved dramatically. Every time he used language in a direct, appropriate way we were astonished; these behaviors occurred against a general background of non-interaction. The individual events that I describe here might be similar to stories told about any growing, developing child. With Eddie, however, we had the additional element of unpredictability—and consequently, of momentousness.

In mid-January it became clear that Eddie had internalized the routine of the lesson, and one day he guided himself through it in my presence. When I arrived for the second lesson of the new year, Eddie said, "I would like to play *Sparks*," and proceeded to do so. When he finished with that he said, "Now I would like to play *The Bear*," and performed that too. After these pieces he said something about "C" and began to play C in every octave, including major and minor cadences. Eddie named and played nearly every pitch in this way, and on his own initiative. Next he asked to play a duet. I asked if he wanted to play the one in D minor or in E minor, and I wasn't sure that he understood me. However, he was ready to play the E minor duet after he responded, "E minor" to my question. We played it, traded parts, and played it again.

We were still working on the Diabelli Opus 149 duets at this time, although it was becoming clear to me that Eddie needed something more sophisticated.

The style had become so familiar to him that he could learn new selections very quickly. After one or two hearings of a new piece Eddie was able to reproduce the harmonic progression, melody, rhythm, and figuration,–that is, the main ideas. I found something more challenging for him with the Brahms Opus 39 *Waltzes*.

For the most part, waltzes are outside the experience of children today, though they have little trouble learning the style. As I expected, Eddie had no difficulty reproducing the triple meter, quarter-note pulse, and dance-like spirit of the selections we played. We used Brahms' simplified arrangements, which are better suited for small hands. In the primo part of the first waltz (B major) the left hand primarily doubles the right hand at the octave. The Diabelli pieces use octave doublings too, but the *Waltzes* use more difficult keys and harmonies. Eddie had no problem with the signature of five sharps in the first piece, nor did he falter with the chromaticism of the melody.

When we put our parts together we ran up against a new challenge, a hemiola. Brahms offsets the heavy downbeats of the first half (1–2–3, 1–2–3) with a hemiola opening the second half. The primo continues with a pattern in three while the secondo plays a pattern in duple against it (1–2, 3–1, 2–3). The result is that at every 6 beats the patterns coincide, but Brahms extends the hemiola to 12 beats, or 4 bars, and then repeats the entire pattern (another 4 bars) transposed up a fourth. At first Eddie would "break down" in this section, faking his way until the original, rhythmically clear material returned in the closing phrase, at which point he could join in again. How could we improve our performance? I had him play the primo part alone, so I knew that he could handle it technically. It was clear from his behavior that he wasn't content to simply "get through" his part, which is what most inexperienced players aspire to. He wanted to know how the parts fit together musically. Next I played the secondo and primo for him, four measures at a time, and then played the melody from the primo with the bass from the secondo to give him an impression of how the hemiola worked. After this we were able to play our respective parts together, beginning to end, and it was our favorite duet for a while.

We also worked on numbers 2,3,4,5, and 9 of the Opus 39 during the first half of '86, when Eddie was 7 years old. He played the primo parts mostly, which were more suited to his size, but we would switch occasionally because he obviously enjoyed playing the bass and harmony. Eddie surprised me with his understanding of pick-ups and entrances. He could count a little, but he couldn't add or subtract. We hadn't worked much on recognizing note values visually. The comprehension of rhythmic notation requires rapid recognition of symbols because the "meaning" of duration is only revealed in groupings and in context. The reading exercises that I did with Eddie at this time concentrated primarily on getting him to focus on an object or a few symbols rather than on eye motion. Also, Eddie grasped straight-forward rhythms quickly and easily by ear, and his tempi were steady, so we hadn't done much counting aloud. However, when we first began playing the Brahms *Waltzes* it was necessary to "count off" in order to begin together, and when I did so Eddie understood exactly what I was doing. The primo of the first waltz, for example, begins with a three eighth note anacrusis (one, two, AND THREE AND . . .). I still don't understand how Eddie connected the numbers to the beats, but he did.

During this period Eddie played various renditions of *Für Elise* for a variety of reasons. It was frequently requested by new people who observed Eddie, probably due to the fact that McDonald's was running a television commercial campaign that used the main theme of its rondo form. Eddie delighted people by playing the commercial version, which segues from *Für Elise* to the McDonald's song ("It's a great time, for a great taste . . ."). I taped *Für Elise* in its entirety and asked Eddie to play it for me occasionally, but I pursued other pieces with more rigor.

One piece that I did spend some time on was Kabalevsky's *Toccatina* (A minor). One of my students had played it at a recital that Eddie attended the previous autumn, and I played it for him at a lesson shortly after that. He expressed only mild interest in it, and I didn't introduce it again until late February. Also, I was waiting for his hands to grow in order to assure that he could span the parallel first inversion chords in the treble part. This piece has its melody in the bass (left hand) and 3-part ($^6_3$) chords in the right hand. Eddie's initial response was to play the lowest notes of the chords with his left hand, so that it was necessary for the right hand to reach only a fourth rather than a sixth. After a while I noticed that Eddie was playing all three notes of some chords with just the right hand, so I used this occasion to convey to Eddie a "technical" idea. This was probably the first time that I was able to communicate the thought, "It would help your playing if you used your hands this way." Various instances that apply this notion are usually a large part of piano lessons, but without visual and verbal cues, and with Eddie an already capable player, I rarely had the opportunity to communicate such ideas. In the present situation, I held Eddie's left hand in mine and played the right-hand part, letting him imitate each section with only his right hand. Then I played the left-hand melody, allowing him to "fill in" the chords with his right hand alone. He was completely cooperative and seemed to understand the idea, because he incorporated it fairly consistently when he played the piece on his own.

There were two other incidents that indicated that I could begin to convey technical ideas to Eddie. The first involved a short piece call *Playing Soldiers* by Rebikov. I had introduced it briefly once before, and when I happened to play it again a few months later Eddie did something unprecedented: He watched my hands. The piece has an ostinato that spans an octave in the right hand. It is a highly patterned rhythmic figure four measures in length. After this figure is introduced, the left hand enters by crossing over the other hand. The melody, played by the left hand, is basically a descending scale which must cross through the right hand ostinato. When Eddie took his turn at the piece this time he used his hands precisely as I've described. Previously he had distributed the ostinato between his two hands; now he watched what I did and copied it. This is one of the first times I observed Eddie use his eyes for something that was rewarding to him, mastering a song. His original exploration of the piano was primarily tactile and aural, but he was discovering that he could learn something about the instrument by looking.

Another incident occurred when I introduced the Bach *Prelude* in C major from *The Well-Tempered Clavier, Book 1*. When I played this piece for Eddie I used the sustain pedal out of habit, without realizing that Eddie would want to get the same timbre. He attempted to do so by perching on the edge of his chair and stepping on all three pedals with both feet. Of course this didn't accomplish the desired effect. Because of his height, he couldn't sit back in the chair and still reach the pedals; in this position he couldn't lift his feet to "change" the pedals. The result was a blur, and when he stopped, I tried to demonstrate to him that he needed just one foot on one pedal. I even took him under the keyboard to show him the pedals, but he really didn't understand and played the piece again with this same unique sonority.

A few months later I introduced the piece again, and Eddie was able to grasp the one foot, one pedal idea. Furthermore, he easily added one pedalling per chord as he played the piece, responding to the directions, "down, up-down." What had changed? He had grown a little taller and could maneuver with the necessary leverage, though he still had to perch on the edge of the chair. The real difference was that he was beginning to take verbal directions and to look at things.

While Eddie was making some useful observations about the instrument, he began noticing pictures of keyboards on the sheet music I used. This was quite amusing because he would ignore everything else in the picture. He would pretend to "play" these pianos, singing and naming the keys represented in the pictures. I attempted to interest him in other aspects of the illustrations, but he was not nearly so enthusiastic, and I usually had to name the objects before he could identify them.

We started a little game around this time that was both visual and personal. Eddie had gotten to the point where he recognized me from the distance of a few feet. In our first few months together I could come within inches of his face, and he wouldn't notice me unless I spoke. His growing awareness of the visual environment had increased this distance considerably, or so I thought. One day I found that Eddie didn't recognize me at the usual distance; after a few minutes, I realized what was different. I had put my long dark hair up, off my shoulders. I know from experience that even my full-sighted students think I look strange without my hair; I discovered that Eddie was very dependent on this strong visual cue. In the weeks and months following I would come closer to him, without speaking, to encourage him to discern who was present without the most obvious cue. Eventually this was successful. Of course, as soon as he recognized me he would start to touch his own hair and crane his neck to feel his hair on his shoulders. I'd tease him a little bit, saying, "What do you want, Eddie? Do you want me to take my hair down?" After a while he'd say, "hair down," and I'd oblige. Eventually I insisted that he said, "I want you to take your hair down," or something that resembled a full sentence. When my hair came down, he'd laugh and look around at it, sometimes arranging it on my shoulders. Once when it all fell to one side he said, "now take the other one down," so I corrected the arrangement. I later learned that his mother and older sister had long hair when he was younger, which probably accounts for some of his interest. We play this game to this day, unless it's extremely hot and taking my hair down would be unbearable. When I make this excuse to Eddie he accepts it good-naturedly.

This game seemed to encourage Eddie to express his wishes verbally, something that was a rare event during that first year. One day my former piano teacher, Abe Stokman, and his wife Arlene, came to visit Eddie at a lesson. At one point Leon and I were conversing with the Stokmans while Eddie was playing the piano on his own. Trying to hear the conversation above the piano, I gradually became aware that Eddie was quietly but persistently calling, "Nancy! Nancy!" I was shocked. I went over and asked him what he wanted, and of course he wanted to play something together; he wanted attention. Eddie had never called my name to get my attention prior to this, I realized. The Stokmans were not aware of how significant this was, but Leon and I knew it was a step forward.

I had left tapes of the Brahms *Waltzes* with Marie Morgan, taking care to record both the primo and secondo parts. Other pieces that I recorded included Kabalevsky's *Slow Waltz* and *Sonatina* (A minor); more selections from Schumann's *Album for the Young*; sonatinas by Beethoven, Clementi, and Pleyel; *Solfegietto* (C.P.E. Bach); and a number of other pieces that I didn't expect Eddie to play but that he might enjoy. Among others, these included Beethoven's Fifth and Sixth Symphonies and selections by Dave Brubeck, Thelonius Monk, and Erwin Helfer, a Chicago blues pianist. Marie also taped music for Eddie, especially pretty arrangements of popular love songs and ballads. My feeling was, and still is, that exposing Eddie to a variety of styles would help him to communicate musically with a variety of people. His familiarity with any particular type of music doesn't seem to make him less enthusiastic about other styles.

In fact, after a while one or both or us got tired of every duet having triple meter and dense harmony, so we switched to something lighter. In the summer we worked on arrangements of Schubert's *Marche Militaire* and several Joplin rags. Again, one of my students had played the Schubert piece in recital, and Eddie really enjoyed its strong rhythms. The simplified arrangement we used had fewer octave doublings but almost as many sections as the original. It was too long for Eddie to "get" in one or two hearings, so I played small sections for him, under tempo for the sake of clarity, and asked him to repeat them for me. As usual, he cooperated with this method and was not confused when we put the sections together; his sense of the overall harmonic motion of the piece, coupled with the momentum of the other part as I played it, enabled him to reassemble the piece. We accomplished this primarily nonverbally. I listened for the parts where Eddie was unclear on the basic musical idea, and if it was a substantial portion, or something easily communicated by example, I'd play that phrase for him again and then give him a turn. My decisions about what to review were very different than those for a sighted, verbal student. Rarely did I insist on literal repetition. If Eddie played a melody in three different variations, they all served the purpose equally well, and here was audible evidence of his creativity. I tried to select for review the passages where Eddie seemed confused, the questions being, for example: How does this return to tonic? How many repetitions of this figure are there? What passing chord is used here? How are these chords voiced? These questions were never articulated by Eddie, nor could he point to a place on the page, or say simply, "How does the next section go?" I had to imagine his questions as well as try to find a way to give answers.

I tried to use a limited vocabulary when I broke the music into its component parts, using the basic terminology that musicians must understand in order to talk to each other, such as *section*, *part*, and the designations *A* and *B* to distinguish original from contrasting material. These words are abstractions, because they are applied to all pieces, yet within a particular piece they are tangible—they serve as labels for specific passages. Eddie seemed comfortable with this. If we were working on a piece and I said, "Play the B section," he never brought in the B section of another piece just because I had labelled *it* "the B section." Similarly, he was always comfortable with the designation of pitch being both general and specific. Most 7-year-olds have a hard time understanding, for example, how E can be plain E, and part of a C major chord, and the key of a piece that has so many other notes. Eddie, by contrast, answered simple questions about these things consistently as soon as he knew pitch names.

Eddie had heard *The Entertainer* somewhere and played it enthusiastically, so I brought a collection of piano rags by Joplin arranged for four hands. We worked on *The Maple Leaf Rag* and *The Easy Winners*. This was the beginning of our second year together, and the time when Eddie began to read musical symbols in groups of three and four notes. Soon I wrote out nursery rhyme songs for him to read and play, but at four inches per staff the song sheets hardly fit on the piano. This was the point at which I began to "shrink" the note sizes. Eddie could read a staff with lines ¼ inch apart by September. With a little research I found a book at this size that we could use, *Piano Progress: an Approach to Music for the Partially Sighted*.[2] This series is designed to

---

[2]Davision, J., & Schaub, A. (1972). *Piano progress: An approach to music for the partially sighted* (Book 1A). Series editor: Podolsky, L. Pittsburgh, PA: Volkwein Bros., Inc.

teach both reading and aural skills, and I chose exercises from it that empha-sized the former. I never played these selections for Eddie, although I customar-ily play new pieces for students. Eddie memorized a series of pitches by ear so easily that if he heard a melody once we could no longer use the page as a reading exercise. Consequently I didn't stress pattern memorization. Eddie did try to make musical sense of the note series, however. Even at a painstak-ingly slow tempo he recognized *Yanke Doodle* when we came upon it in the next book. Later he added 4- and 5-part harmony to each pitch in several exercises, creating interesting progressions. Usually his harmonizations were complex, involving secondary dominants, deceptive cadences, and substitu-tion chords, whereas the simple tunes typically suggested the conventional I-IV-V-I pattern. Eddie enjoyed basic symbol recognition even though discern-ing melodic shapes and harmonic direction, the more musical part of the ac-tivity, was a challenge at the tempo we used. His perserverance and delight in accomplishing the difficult task of reading musical symbols showed what an avid student he could be.

Another incident at this time illustrated for me Eddie's determination. I was probably overly ambitious, but I included all the notes on the lines and spaces, that pedagogic prerequisite, in the "flash cards" that Marie worked on with Eddie. When I reviewed the symbols with Eddie, I usually skipped these two cards. Apparently Marie drilled him on it anyway, because one day we came upon the card with the treble clef lines and Eddie began naming them: E-G. He had trouble remembering the next one and when I corrected him he dutifully started from the bottom again, trying to remember the pat-tern. Obviously Marie had tried to teach him the sequence of letters and he had internalized her method: When you can't remember any further, start from the first one again. Now, of his own accord, he tried several times, and eventually he could remember the correct order of all five. Also, he wrinkled his brow in a look of such intense concentration that I had to laugh. This exercise might have been an unreasonable requirement for a child like Eddie, but he rose to the occasion and encouraged his teachers at the same time.

That autumn I also introduced the names of scale types, provoked by the study involving *Whole Tone Scale* by Bartok (Chapter 5). Eddie learned these terms easily—major, minor, whole tone, and chromatic; the first two were already familiar from describing the key areas of pieces. After Leon conducted the study, I taught *Whole Tone Scale* to Eddie and it became part of his reper-toire. He grasped immediately the intervallic pattern, transpositions, and parallel minor thirds, and he responded enthusiastically to the rhythmic drive of the piece. He especially liked the climax at m.56-61, with its repeated disso-nant chord and forceful syncopation.

Although piano students often learn a piece, or at least difficult sections, "one hand at a time," I rarely did this with Eddie. Most music since Bach (and a great deal of Bach's) does not have true independence of parts. Conse-quently, it is difficult to convey the accompanying part and its rhythmic relationship to the whole without a written text as a guide. Because accompaniments, when standing alone, often don't make obvious musical sense, I generally chose repetition of the whole (melody with accompaniment, right hand with left hand) as a more efficient means of presentation. With a reasonably clear texture, Eddie grasped the elements so quickly that no musical purpose could be served by further analysis. In *Whole Tone Scale*, however, the parts interlock in such a way that hand placement is very important. The first phrase is a single voice, played by the right hand (m.1-6). The second phrase (m.7-12) repeats the first but adds a second voice in the left hand in parallel minor thirds. The third phrase has a new melody but maintains the same relationship between the voices, parallel minor thirds, having "modulated" up a tritone from the opening. Eddie reproduced these basic elements (with melodic variations), but he played the minor thirds with one hand whenever that technique was more convenient. If the parts are close together in register, there is no way for the listener to tell how the notes are divided between the hands. The customary distribution is so obvious—right hand treble, left hand bass—that we usually take it for granted. In this case it helps the performer to know that each hand has its own whole tone, five step scale at any given moment in the piece. The lines can be played more smoothly and distinctly this way, and as a teaching piece (it is from the *Mikrokosmos*) it resembles other "five finger" studies.

Because of this somewhat unusual structure, I decided to play each phrase one hand at a time and have Eddie do the same. Much to my surprise, he not only played the parts, but he started imitating my directions, for example "the right hand goes like this," and "the left hand part." Again, he internalized the methods of his teacher: He demonstrated that he could learn how to learn. We were able to work through the piece this way, as it requires. Once Eddie could play the piece competently he clearly found performing it a reward in itself.

Eddie rarely showed an interest in mechanical objects, or any objects at all, for that matter. One exception to this was the tape recorder. Eddie clearly understood its purpose, and even during the first year he occasionally indicated that he wanted to hear a tape we were making or that I had brought. Anticipating the winter holidays of our second year, I had Eddie listen to a tape of *The Nutcracker Suite*. Eddie seemed to enjoy making his own piano renditions of this orchestral music, and when he finished playing one selection he'd return to the tape recorder to listen to the next or replay the current one. He tried to operate the tape recorder, too, and understood the functions of some of the buttons, which are color-coded on the institutional model at his school. One lever is not color-coded, however, and this is the one that Eddie found most interesting: the variable speed control. Despite my protests, Eddie persisted in toying with this, which resulted in a funny distortion of the music. He'd listen patiently for a while to a selection, but when the A section returned I'd see his hand inching toward that control. This made listening something of a challenge, but I felt it was better to indulge his curiosity and initiative. In fact, his taking an active role in handling this object almost overshadowed the respectable piano reductions of *The Nutcracker Suite* that he could play after a few hearings.

As the end of our second year approached, Eddie was blossoming so much that he would soon have to change schools. The more severe disabilities of the other children precluded them from having much interaction with each other. Eddie was the only client who could recite the name of every staff member and the names of the other children. Academically Eddie had grown too. It was during this time that we began using Thompson's *Easiest Piano Course. Book 1*, with enlarged print. The lines of the staff were ⅛" apart. Eddie adjusted to this new size quite easily and we studied about ten songs in all. I continued to restrict the range for reading to five notes above and five notes below middle C, and I skipped the songs with eighth notes. I occasionally reviewed time values but limited this to whole, half, and quarter notes. The songs we did used these time values, so any pitch might be depicted with any duration. Eddie had to recognize all combinations, and he did. Nevertheless, I found that it was difficult for him to perceive the time signature, as the numbers are written across the lines of the staff. I felt that reading rhythm could wait and concentrated on pitch instead. What I was really working toward was getting Eddie to use his eyes more. He could recognize capital letters at this point, but only if they were very large. He could always discern notes that were much smaller than what he could distinguish in print. By April, without enlarging it, I introduced Fletcher's *Piano Course*. The grand staff—both treble and bass clefs—was now just 1¼ inches.

Over the next six months we covered the first 25 songs in the Fletcher book, bringing us to the point where harmonic intervals and genuine two hand playing is introduced. This meant new challenges for Eddie, and we went over the first pieces that use these techniques. Eddie learned to play these songs at a reasonable speed by studying the written music. I decided that we'd try the "learning to put your hands together now that you can recognize a few notes" approach, and if that didn't work we would switch to something else. Playing "hands together" involves immediate recognition of the notes on both clefs. I wasn't sure that this was a step that Eddie was ready to take. I considered expanding his knowledge of treble clef instead, returning to the old lines and spaces at last. However, before determining which direction we should pursue, I dropped reading music altogether. Eddie was "reading ready" for language that autumn, and I decided to use our time together to work on it. This was part of my response to an unfortunate school situation, as I'll elaborate below.

The most interesting item in the repertoire we did during the winter and spring of 1987 was *Five Images* by Norman Dello Joio. I had played this duet suite with a student at the first recital Eddie attended, in November, 1985.

Of his own accord, Eddie played some of the harmonies from the first movement, *Cortège*, at a lesson shortly thereafter. I played the primo part for him
and he played it back reasonably well, but I despaired of being able to convey
to him the rhythmic complexities of the duet without reference to a written
score. The parts interlock precisely, and the players must be accurate
rhythmically for the piece to make musical sense. I'm sure Eddie could have
done this with sufficient drilling and perseverance, but I decided to wait until
he was a little older. When I introduced the piece again slightly over a year
later Eddie was much more responsive. I recorded each part for him so he
could listen during the week, and at the lessons we worked on the first movement phrase by phrase.

As I look back on it now, *Cortège* was ideally suited to my pedagogic purpose. It's also a delightful piece. When we could play it together competently,
Eddie's enjoyment of the piece was apparent. He especially liked to play the
bass part, even though it required considerable strength and endurance. The
right hand has fortissimo repeated chords in continuous sixteenth notes for
five bars (in 4/4). The movement is end-weighted, and this moment is the
climax; Eddie's enthusiasm showed that he understood the spirit of the piece.

Historically, a cortège is a French term for a solemn or triumphant proces-
sion, often associated with the arrival of royalty. Like fanfares and slow marches,
it has a steady beat and moderate tempo, typically in common time. The most
popular *cortége nowadays is from Debussy's Petite Suite*. These are the things
that I couldn't begin to explain to Eddie, even in a version for children. I
also felt some reserve about teaching French (and often German and Italian)
names to a child who had to struggle daily with both Spanish and English,
but I didn't want to keep these terms from Eddie, either. There was a certain
temptation to substitute easier, more familiar names for the ones that were
difficult to pronounce or conceptualize. But I didn't want to teach him a private
language—I wanted him to know the common language, the one that musicians in our culture share. Perhaps one day Eddie will play Debussy's *Cortège*
and he'll make a connection, the way he connects similar motives of separate
pieces. (This happened, for example, with Kabalevsky's *Toccatina* and Tansman's
The Doll, which are in comparable styles; the composers are from similar
schools of thought. The first time that I played the *Toccatina* for Eddie he
repeated most of it in response, as usual, but then he continued on to play
The Doll.) Perhaps Eddie already recognizes the style and spirit of processional
music from the entrance of the king and queen on "Mr. Rogers'
Neighborhood," one of his favorite television programs. The more Eddie makes
appropriate connections the greater his chances are of being understood by
others.

Returning to the problem of actually teaching *Cortège*, Eddie had to learn
his role in a precise musical dialogue. The parts interlock rhythmically in such
a way that we had to review sections that were smaller than we had ever re-

viewed previously. The piece is constructed so that musical meaning is clear only when the parts are together, unlike the typical melody and accompaniment format. For example, the secondo begins with a two-bar melody, which the primo repeats an octave higher, harmonized in parallel fourths. I played both parts for Eddie to show him that the four bars contain an elaborated repetition. Then I took the secondo part, saying, "my turn." After playing my two measures I said, "your turn," and waited for Eddie to fill in the primo part. He understood what I wanted him to do, and we could repeat the phrase without hesitation. The next bar intensifies this process: The secondo has chords on beats 1 and 3, the primo has chords on beats 2 and 4. How could I convey this musical alternation? Again I played the whole and then played one part, waiting for Eddie to add the other. He did so, and then we could play five bars together smoothly. This was the most detail that I had ever managed to convey to Eddie. The precision that I demanded here was in the service of musical coherence, something that Eddie understands very well; the intelligibility of the piece is in its details.

This notion applies to the pitch structures of *Cortège* as well. It's nominally "in" C major with a strong emphasis on the subdominant (ii7, to be exact). The more significant organizing principle is that four bar (2 + 2) opening melody. It is continuously varied and reharmonized in the course of the piece. The procedure Dello Joio used to accomplish this is triadic rather than traditional harmonic progressions, so the overall structure is unpredictable compared with the conventional repertory. The first phrase seems to be leading toward C major with the progression ii7-V in m.5, but instead of reaching the expected tonic m.6 substitutes the opening pitch collection (D,F,G,C) and a neighboring triad, A♭ major (♭VI of C, if this phrase was in C). The sixth measure turns out to be a bridge to the first coherent tonal structure; without any warning the music is "on" B♭ for 4 bars (m.7-8, 9-10. I-V, I-V); after this it segues to D major (m.11) and then to F major (m.13-14, I-V). This F major turns out to be the subdominant of C after all, an arrival reached by degrees at m.17, and m.19, but really not until m.21. At this point a new section begins, a new melodic segment is introduced.

This analysis demonstrates why it was necessary to teach this piece phrase by phrase. The triads are treated as juxtaposed sonorities rather than as functional harmonies. The thread that winds through it all is a melodic shape, a contour that retains its integrity despite variation. Although the sonorities are striking, it is primarily the melody that binds the sections. The frequency of its repetitions shows this: m.1-4, 6-10, 11-14, 15-20. The new melodic fragment in m.21-22 is repeated twice (with variations), leading to a restatement of the original melody at m.27 (that is, derived from the original melody). This first and second "themes" are combined at m.30 for a rousing close— the part Eddie enjoyed most. He had no difficulty with the triadic harmonizations or with the lack of function as long as we worked in miniature rather than in broad strokes.

One would think that it would make more sense to work in detail on a tonal piece, but that turned out not to be the case. Tonality is our common language and consequently is highly predictable. Also, numerous possibilities exist for substitutions and for alternative realizations that adequately convey the main ideas. The requirements of a piece like *Cortège* are very different; without precision the intelligibility of the piece is lost. If you don't have the details, you don't have the piece—there's no faking it.

We eventually worked our way through the other four movements in this collection. None of them is organized in as unusual a fashion as the first, although each one has somewhat unpredictable pitch structures, rhythms, and phrasing. We didn't work as closely on the middle selections, but we took more care with the finale, *The Dancing Sergeant*. This is a stirring number in 6/8 that requires "taking turns" in a number of passages. Like the first movement, its unexpected sounds are from the use of nonfunctional harmonies and melodic variation. Eddie took to this piece with gusto.

I recorded the primo and secondo parts of these pieces during this time, as well as the *Two-Part Invention* in F major by J.S. Bach. We worked on this piece at several lessons, as well as the *Two-Part Invention* in A minor. Eddie's understanding of part against part was already highly developed. This was evident in his duet playing and, at the most basic level, from the fact that he played with two hands. The *Inventions* were challenging for him. They are studies that use fairly strict counterpoint, one hand imitating the other at a distance. Precise fingerwork is required to sustain and combine the voices. We were distracted from this endeavor by changes in Eddie's educational situation.

It gradually became clear to all of us that Eddie had truly outgrown his school. When he was placed in the day-care program at age 3 he was a typical client: low-functioning, self-stimulating, noninteractive. Now he knew everyone's name and kept track of their attendance. He could walk around the grounds, feed himself, and use the bathroom with a minimum of supervision. Eddie had already mastered the developmental tasks and socialization skills that the highest functioning children were striving to acquire. The head teacher brought in new educational materials especially for him. He could recognize and name shapes, colors, numbers, and the alphabet. He had also memorized the spelling of several small words, and could write his first name, if somewhat awkwardly. We had worked a little on drawing notes, usually on a very large staff, but Eddie lacked interest in this activity. Although he used his hands with finesse at the piano, he was fairly apathetic when it came to manipulating pencils and crayons. He was always compliant when asked to draw, but he was rarely enthusiastic. This has changed over the past year, and I've even seen him amuse himself with pen and paper when the opportunity presents itself. I think this is a direct result of his expanding interest and delight in symbols of all sorts.

Despite Eddie's progress, we were leery of him leaving the sheltered program at his school. He was accustomed to the one-on-one attention it provided and his poor vision restricted him from adapting quickly to new environments. Yet we agreed that he needed more academic stimulation and the companionship of other children. He's found the latter in his new school, to a limited extent. As far as providing basic academic training, the placement has turned out to be a disappointment.

Eddie tested poorly for the Board of Education, which is not surprising. The results were high enough, however, for the Board to transfer him to the local TMH program (trainably mentally handicapped). This meant that he was removed from the private program which the Board had been subsidizing, and sent to a special education program in a public school.

We worried about his ability to adjust to a classroom situation and about his handling stairs and taking directions in a group. He has demonstrated that he can do all these things and more. Meanwhile, in this past year he has had to adjust to not one classroom but three, not one pair of teachers but four. The school had internal problems and the result was a lack of consistency in the education of all the TMH children. Nevertheless, Eddie adapted to each new situation and blossomed in spite of it.

That's not to say that he liked school from the start. After a few weeks of good-natured exploring he seemed to realize that he was not going to return to his old friends at his previous school. He became very unhappy. At lunch and snacks he wouldn't eat, even if I was there, and he spent a large percentage of the day with his head on his desk. His teachers were concerned, but they assumed that he needed time to adjust. Then the optional half-day summer school program started and Eddie attended for a few weeks, until his mother correctly judged that it wasn't worthwhile. In September there was a long teachers' strike and school didn't commence until October. At that point we discovered that Eddie had been transferred to a new room without his mother's consent. The other room had become too crowded. We were appeased with the revelation that he would be going into the new room when he got a little older, regardless. It all seemed reasonable at the time.

The new teacher was less than inspired. The students did the same, limited exercises day after day, most of which involved coloring. They were learning to count in the teens: Eddie could already count to fifty. He still wouldn't eat and spent many hours with his head on his desk or self-stimulating. Concerned, the teacher tried to reward him for participation by letting him play the piano. His mother, however, wanted him to learn other things in school and not spend time at the piano, which he could do at home. Also, he had dislocated his elbow several times, and she was wary of any extra stress on the arm. The subject became moot when the teacher took a leave of absence in December. She had no idea who the substitute would be, but her leave was only for six weeks. That was the original plan. When she actually returned five months had passed.

Music lessons continued once a week as usual. While the strike was in progress, Leon and I decided that it would be best if we went to Eddie's house. When we met in September we spent some time playing a new instrument; I had given him a recorder to use at home at the end of summer vacation, after I was sure that his mother approved of his having such a noisy instrument. I wasn't sure that he'd take to a wind instrument. According to his mother, his early response to toy wind instruments was negative. Perhaps this was because he didn't like things in his mouth—not even food—but he was certainly taken with the recorder now, at age 8.

I had originally introduced the recorder at summer school. I demonstrated some simple tunes and Eddie grasped immediately that the instrument was blown and that pitch was produced by covering the holes in various combinations. However, his hands were just a bit too small to cover more than one or two holes at a time. In order to illustrate the recorder's potential, I had Eddie blow through the mouthpiece while I worked the finger holes. In this manner, we played the folksong, *Are You Sleeping?* Eddie thought this was hilarious, and he laughed so much we could barely finish the tune. We did this several times that summer, and I tried to teach Eddie the fingerings for B, A and G, typically the first notes taught on the instrument.

By the time we resumed lessons in September Eddie had mastered these pitches and had figured out a few more on his own. He recognized that the instrument sounds C# when all the holes are open. Eddie could play this pitch, and, by blowing harder, D. He had also contrived fingerings for F and C. Some pitches require seemingly illogical combinations of open and closed holes for their tone to be in accordance with equal temperament, and I showed Eddie the conventional fingerings for C and D. We played the sequence G-A-B-C-D, ascending and descending, several times on our respective recorders. Eddie thought this was very funny. He also laughed when I adjusted his fingers on his recorder, as if he was being tickled. His family said that wiggling fingers make him laugh.

Next I showed Eddie F# and played a D-major scale with him. He remembered the fingering for every note, and I observed him pause as he thought about the combination required for a given pitch. The following week the first thing that he played for me was a D-major scale, as if to remind me where we left off the previous week. I showed him high E and we played *Are You Sleeping?* together. Then we played it in canon twice, first Eddie taking the lead and then me. We sang it in canon also, Eddie sustaining his part—including the lyrics—quite well.

During summer school we had sung rounds. I wanted to help Eddie integrate into the new school and be accepted by the other children, so I decided to give him individual attention part of the time and to work with the entire group part of the time. I discovered that most of the kids were reluctant to talk, let along sing, but when the teachers participated, we could make some music. We sang *Are You Sleeping?* and *Row, Row, Row Your Boat* in two and three-part rounds, and movement songs such as *If You're Happy and You Know It Clap Your Hands* and *The Hokey-Pokey*. I don't know if it helped Eddie, but it certainly didn't hurt. I continued to do group singing in the fall, and this class responded more enthusiastically. At the very least, I hoped that my contribution to the class would assuage potential resentment about the special treatment Eddie was receiving.

As soon as Eddie could play a few notes competently, he wanted to know more. After we played *Are You Sleeping?* I tried to teach him another song, but he was distracted, obviously thinking about something else. He played bits of things on the recorder that I didn't understand, and then he played a D-minor scale. When he reached B♭ he tried several different finger combinations but he couldn't find one that worked. We were sitting near the piano and he sounded a B♭ key several times. I knew what he wanted, but I realized that I might be able to get him to verbalize his question. I asked him if he wanted to know something; what note did he want me to show him? After a while he said, "B♭," so I told him to ask me, "Nancy, show me B♭." He repeated, "Nancy, show me B♭," and I complied. I also showed him a better fingering for C♯ so that he could complete the scale. We played the D-harmonic minor scale together. Next he hit A♭ on the piano, avid to learn another pitch. Again I waited until he verbalized his request. He repeated my model a little impatiently: "Nancy, show me A♭."

Then he wanted F, and this time he said, "Show me F," of his own accord after he hit the piano key a few times. I asked him if he wanted the high F or the low F, and he got a little exasperated with me. "High F," he said, and I demonstrated. He'd come a long way in verbalizing his preferences. The next time I visited, Eddie made it clear that he had sorted out his knowledge of the fingerings for the chromatic range of the recorder and that he needed low C♯, which I showed him.

Eddie had seemed only mildly interested in the recorder when I first introduced it in the summer. He found it amusing when we managed to play a simple song together, but he couldn't make music on it the way he could on a keyboard. Nevertheless, he cooperated with me and learned a few notes, or at least the basic method for handling the instrument. When that was comfortable for him his desire to understand accelerated markedly. His mother related a story to us that similarly demonstrates this drive in Eddie's personality. She had a recording of a South American group, Los Andinos, which featured pan-pipes. Eddie had expressed little interest in it, although he usually accompanies on the piano the salsa and religious recordings the family plays at home. One day his mother noticed that he was playing part of a song by Los Andinos on the recorder. She hadn't played the recording for a long time so she put it on the turntable. Sure enough, the song was one of the cuts from the album. When Leon and I were at the family's apartment, Eddie and his mother demonstrated this incident. Not only could Eddie play along, but he imitated convincingly the timbre of the pan-pipes on his plastic recorder.

I taught Eddie the round *Rose, Rose*, a Celtic tune, and *Hatikvah*, the Israeli national anthem. I chose these melodies primarily because they use minor scales. (Also, scale degree 7 is lowered to a whole step in *Rose, Rose*.) Eddie often played pieces or fragments on the recorder that I didn't recognize but they tended to be in minor keys. We did recorder instead of piano during the late autumn weeks that he first had his cast removed. (There was concern for some time that his arm was weak from the immobilization.) During this time I realized again that Eddie wasn't always accurate in picking up a melody. With the typical piano piece, his grasp and reproduction of the harmonic structure outweighs the melodic detail; on the recorder one has only melody. Of course, there is the technical requirement—fingering—to get the desired pitches, the piano being more immediate in that respect. I found that Eddie behaved very much like an 8½ year old with a good ear when it came to learning these tunes. The difference was that once he heard a melody a few times he could improvise on it. For example, I taught him a simple German folksong, *Silent*. After he learned it, I tried to play harmony to his melody, but he started playing harmony. It was obvious that he wanted me to play the stable part so that he could do the improvising. This was not unlike what happened in group singing. When I sang *Twinkle, Twinkle Little Star* with the class I would hear Eddie quietly singing counterpoint to the melody.

Like most right-handed children, Eddie spontaneously placed his right hand on top when he first used the recorder. The convention for woodwind instruments in the Western orchestra is that the left hand is closer to the mouth and the right hand controls the end joint. This probably reflects the idea that, because one hand must be further away from the body, right-handed people (ergo, most people) will have greater dexterity if they rely on their dominant hand for that dexterity. Ultimately, however, most musicians need to use both hands to handle their instrument and Eddie was more than competent at doing so at the piano. I allowed him to keep his right hand on top when I first gave him the recorder because I didn't know if he would persevere long enough to play the entire range of the instrument. When we reached the notes in the lower register switching hands became necessary. The last hole is angled toward the right so the hands must be positioned the conventional way to cover this hole securely. Initially, Eddie put up a little resistance to switching hand positions. He would do what I asked temporarily and then convert back to what was more comfortable. It was when he wanted to play middle C and C$^\sharp$, the lowest notes on the instrument, that he seemed to realize the virtue of my constant reminder, "left hand on top." After a few sessions he responded appropriately and easily to this request, so I went through a number of simple pieces to accustom him to this position.

Articulation is an important part of playing a wind instrument, so I introduced the terms *legato* and *staccato*. Eddie imitated my careful pronunciation perfectly. We played some scales using all *staccato* and then all *legato* tonguing techniques. The following week we reviewed these and added slurs. This concept overlaps with the notion of *legato*, but Eddie didn't seem confused. I started with two-note slurs up and down a major scale, and we did three-note slurs in the same manner. Then Eddie announced, "four-note slurs," and played a scale accordingly. This was followed by "five-note slurs" and "six-note slurs", all on Eddie's initiative. This was another situation in which Eddie demonstrated his grasp of a concept by extending it.

While we continued to work at the recorder we also played several interesting pieces at the piano. I selected a new duet, a sonatina in F major by Mozart. An original composition for 4 hands, there is a great deal of interplay between the secondo and primo parts. Eddie showed that he was cognizant of this, as I will describe.

The first movement is a sonata form, *Allegro Spiritoso*. The first theme is introduced by a two-measure phrase in both parts, and the next eight measures are carried by the primo with the secondo accompanying every other bar. This results in a series of short phrases $(2 + 2) + (2 + 2)$ in which every two bar unit contains a tiny antecedent-consequent, or question and answer, structure. When Eddie had learned the opening phrase of the primo part and we put it together, he took advantage of this structure. He would draw out the "question" slowly and dramatically and then spit out the "answer" very fast, expecting me to catch on. He thought this was quite funny, and I did too. It's certainly true to the spirit of this musical style and of ensemble playing.

This instance was more specific and purposeful, but there were other instances where Eddie teased me with tempi or dynamics. Once, during a radio interview, he "let the bottom drop out" of *Cortège*, so that while I was hammering away at the final chords he played extremely quietly. I couldn't tell what he was doing while he played because he has used dynamics to express self-consciousness in some instances. Afterwards, though, I realized that he deliberately altered the dynamics to defeat our expectation of a grand conclusion.

When we could play the first movement of this *Sonatina* competently, Eddie began "fooling around" with it. One day he played it in F minor instead of F major, and when I changed mode too he smiled and laughed in appreciation. We played the entire movement this way, which had some interesting results. A few months later we still played this duet occasionally. At one lesson I asked Eddie, as he improvised, what he was doing. He said, "I'm playing the Mozart Blues," and played a blues scale in F. He proceeded to play the primo part in a blues style, adding grace notes, syncopation, altered chords (e.g. F6 and Fmin9) and making the dotted rhythms swing. When I joined in Eddie said, "beginning," so we started again. He was nearly beside himself with laughter, especially when we sounded real "bluesy" together. The "Mozart Blues" was quite a hit for a while. I recorded all the movements of the sonatina for Eddie, and we worked on the other three over the next few months. Eddie experimented with each one in turn. He would play it "straight" if I made the request, but his desire to combine these seemingly incongruous styles was always clear.

I've tried to teach Eddie some of the vocabulary that describes musical communication, and he uses the more common terms appropriately: faster, slower, quiet, loud. The Italian words, such as *crescendo, staccato, legato, piano* and *forte*, are usually difficult for 9-year olds to remember, but Eddie can use them consistently in context. I illustrated another set of terms using a piece by Schumann, *About Strange Lands and People*. The first selection from *Kinderscenen*, it has a constant three-part texture. Technically it's challenging because the middle voice must be distributed between the two hands. I played the entire piece for Eddie and let him play it back as best he could. We did this several times so that he could get a feel for the piece.

I knew that at first it would be difficult for Eddie to discern how the lines are voiced. Also, the piece assumes good-size hands. It has reaches of melodic ninths and tenths in a texture with continuous motion—typical Schumann piano writing. I played the melody of the first phrase (A section, m.1-8) and asked Eddie to do the same, and to say, "melody." He said and played it, slipping in just one note from the inner voice. There was one peculiarity in his rendition of the melody. It begins three times with a leap up from B to G. Eddie consistently substituted D, a chord tone, for the B. I'm not sure why he chose this little variation. It does appear later in the piece, when the B section (m.9-14) leads to the return of the A section (m.15-22). Perhaps he was thinking about this moment.

The next week I reviewed the A section and the terms melody, inner voice and bass. I played each of these voices separately and Eddie did the same. Then I announced and played various combinations, for example, melody and bass, bass and inner voice. Eddie imitated this also. We analyzed the B section in the same manner the following week and played every possible combination of two voices in both the A and B sections. Eddie reassembled the piece too. The result was a much smoother realization of the song—a more consistent texture—and several new words in Eddie's vocabulary.

The substitute who was assigned to cover the prolonged absence of Eddie's teacher had no training in special education. Soon the children were out of control, and several were transferred to more experienced teachers. Eddie injured his fingers slightly while playing with a heating grate, so his mother had him removed from that room immediately. He was placed in a TMH class with children in the next age range, 10–14 years old. Eddie was not yet 9 and was small for his age. Again we were told that he would have been placed in this class eventually anyway.

This was the final transfer of the year, thankfully, but it meant starting all over again. Each time Eddie was transferred the new teacher had to determine afresh what his abilities were. I assumed that the teachers would read new students' records, but I was informed by three teachers that they don't like to be prejudiced by past accounts. This meant that each one ascertained, from the beginning, that Eddie knew numbers, the alphabet, his last name, and so forth.

There is some logic in this approach, although it wastes time reviewing which could be spent building. The problem, for Eddie, was a gross misinterpretation of his behavior. He was regarded as stubborn, willful, and emotionally disturbed. Without reading the detailed assessments compiled by his previous school, the teachers had no idea that he has difficulty comprehending language; that he has poor vision even with glasses; and that he has a history of autistic-like withdrawal. He was seen as difficult, puzzling, and not like other TMH children. The latter may be true, but it should have been all the more reason to read his records. Eventually Leon and I were able to convince most of the teachers that Eddie's desire to communicate was greater than might appear at first, and that he was struggling against considerable disadvantages to do so.

By the time he reached the final placement I had decided to expand my role and work with him on reading. I have already mentioned his "reading-readiness," which was apparent in his eagerness to spell out loud anything that had print and his delight in the sounds of words. The staff at his previous school had gotten him in the habit of precise enunciation, which was greatly admired by the teachers at the new school. I discussed reading methods with his teacher before her absence, and she advocated the "look-say" approach. This involves the visual memorization of a basic vocabulary. Although immediate recognition of common words is essential for reading at an intelligible speed, taxing Eddie's vision from the start would mean emphasizing his weakness rather than capitalizing on his strengths. It seemed to me that Eddie would respond better to a phonetic approach.

It was a surprise to us that Eddie enjoyed words as sounds. We expected that if he fancied anything other than music it would be numbers. Well, Eddie likes to count—another practice encouraged at his previous school—but other than this, he doesn't have a particularly strong interest in numbers thus far. The first glimmer regarding Eddie's progress in language was when his teacher observed that Eddie was more verbal than other TMH kids his age. This set him apart; many TMH children avoid using language as much as possible. Eddie was not always intelligible, of course, but he was extremely talkative. This was the height of his word-salad stage, with phrases from television comprising a large part of his speech. Gradually the proportions have reversed: as Eddie's appropriate, original language has increased his use of TV mimicry has decreased.

I quickly discovered that Eddie not only recognized the letters of the alphabet, but he had a good grasp of the sounds of the consonants. He was less reliable with the vowels, but then again the vowels are less consistent, especially with the additional complication of the Spanish language and its pure vowels. I knew that Eddie's mother had worked with him a little on reading Spanish. I decided to treat vowel sounds on a case by case basis; never before had I regretted the complexity of the English language. I went over some common consonant combinations with him (e.g. sh, st, th, sp) and a few sets of simple rhyming words (e.g. fat, cat, hat).

Our first book was *The Ear Book* from Dr. Seuss's Bright and Early Series.[3] I chose it because the print is large, the vocabulary is limited, and the phrases are rhymed. Later I realized that the choice was fortuitous; the "story" is about sounds, Eddie's area of expertise. Each week we reviewed 10 to 12 pages, reading the words and talking about the pictures. Eddie recognized words that appeared frequently, such as *the* and *to*. Also, I asked him to spell words with simple endings and their rhymes. I found he could do this quite easily in his mind, without reference to the written word. If I had to help him along I would accent the necessary letter as I said the word and then he could usually name it. He would imitate me and reverse roles: "Say it like this, Nancy, drop-p-p. Say it like this, drop-p-p." He would giggle and laugh and repeat this with each new word, as if spelling was a game one played with a set of sounds. To me, this was a significant indication that the phonetic approach to reading was advantageous with Eddie.

It took us approximately eight weeks to finish *The Ear Book*, but that included reviewing almost every possible rhyming word that could be derived from the vocabulary and many questions about the text. The book is more descriptive than narrative, as is typical of children's books at this level. Nonetheless, I quizzed Eddie on the who and what of every page. His understanding of interrogatives was mediocre at first but improved rapidly and reliably as the weeks passed.

I showed Eddie's new teachers what he was doing, hoping that they would reinforce our activities with similar materials during the week. I didn't see how Eddie could learn to read with just once a week tutoring. Leon had planned to work with Eddie weekly also, but the administration banned him from the school, claiming that this would be disruptive. The teachers explained to me that they first work on recognition of environmental signs, such as Beware of Dog, Push, Exit, and not on reading itself. So Eddie is managing to learn without daily instruction. We are now on our fifth book. The current selection is from the next level, Dr. Seuss' Beginner Books.[4] This series has genuine narratives, smaller print, two- and three-syllable words and a wider vocabulary. Eddie frequently requests that I read to him (another role reversal) and he taps out the rhythm of the words and rhymes as one would when listening to rap music or beat poetry.

As Eddie gets older and more mature, we are beginning to engage him in diverse musical activities. At school I arranged to accompany him to the

---

[3]Perkins, A. (1968). *The ear book*. New York: Random House, Inc.
[4]*Beginner books*. NY: Random House.

steel drum band and hand bell classes, held once a week for the older special education children. Eddie and I sat quietly in the back, just listening and absorbing. After a few weeks Eddie was itching to try out the instruments. The music teacher was reluctant to let him participate, being protective of the instruments and concerned about rehearsing for concerts. She occasionally allowed him to handle the instruments for a few minutes between classes. Eddie followed her directions quite well, easily picking up the songs he heard the class play. One particularly rewarding session involved a steel drum duet, the teacher playing the melody of *Never on Sunday* while Eddie played the bass line on another steel drum.

As it becomes easier for Eddie to go on outings we like to take him to concerts. Friends of the Gamelon had their spring concert on a Saturday afternoon recently, and this was a good opportunity for us all to hear a live performance of an ensemble with a unique musical tradition. Eddie listened intently through the concert, and when the performers invited the audience onto the stage to examine the instruments Eddie did not hesitate. One of the musicians taught him the first section of the melody that the beginning class learns, and he tried it out on the principal melody instrument. The basic gamelan orchestra includes xylophone-like instruments of metal and wood, pot gongs, hanging gongs, and drums, each instrumental type being represented by several sets of different sizes to cover different registers. Eddie ran around tapping and banging the instruments (they are mainly made of iron and bronze) to test their properties and compare their ranges. At one point we were standing near the hanging gongs on the crowded stage, and I noticed that Eddie was humming. I bent down to listen and found that he was singing *Jingle Bells*, punctuating the tune with the gongs sounding scale degrees 1 and 5. This told me something about Eddie's method. He was trying to find the perfect intervals, the octaves and fifths, organizing the properties of this new orchestra in his mind's ear.

Recently we have worked on the first movement of Mozart's *Sonata* in C Major, K545; the first Hanon exercise; and a march for four hands by Noona. I try to have a solo, a duet and a technical study "in the works" for our sessions. Eddie has come to expect that I prepare for him—music for listening, terms to be demonstrated, books to read. At times it seems as if he has prepared something for me: a new song, or even questions, such as, "Where do you come from?" which seems to mean, "Where have you been when you are not with me?" I doubt he understands that most people, including myself, don't perceive music with the clarity that he does. He has admonished me to "Play, Nancy, two hands!" as he improvises through modulations with which I can't possibly keep pace. Occasionally he will show me a short passage that I can grasp, but the next section will invariably be so extended and elaborated that I fall far behind. I am hopeful that eventually we can switch roles more easily and that he will have enough of the common analytical language to convey his ideas.

For Eddie has shown, to the people close to him, that he has a bright and lively mind. Our task is to help him express his uniqueness in more ordinary ways. He is not disappointing us in this. It is increasingly difficult to recollect that he was, for a very long time, nonverbal and withdrawn. Now he engages people, takes direction, expresses courtesy, and gives commands. He enjoys toys and loves surprises, especially if they are shiny and reflect light in colorful patterns. He also has a keen awareness of the calendar and time, especially as it pertains to his activities—going to school, coming home, having piano lessons. His anticipation of future events was demonstrated in a particularly striking way a few weeks before the last student recital, as I'll describe below.

Every six months my students participate in a piano recital. Eddie has performed, too, and the history of his participation is illustrative of his general development musically and socially, as it is for all the students. First recitals are especially trying because the experience is new. Eddie, who was $6\frac{1}{2}$ at his first recital, did not adapt well to the unfamiliar situation and setting, as described in Chapter 6. He played his first piece, *The Clown*, perfectly, as I could see from where I was standing nearby, and in complete silence. It was apparent that he was hearing the piece in his mind's ear, but he didn't share it. I let him return to his seat after this uneasiness. When another student played a duet that we had also prepared, I asked Eddie to return to the piano. Eddie did play audibly with me there to accompany him, but within pianissimo. We switched parts and he played a little more confidently. This was encouraging, so I asked him to play his second solo, *The Bear*, and he did a short version of it aloud.

At the next recital I decided to program the duets first. When Eddie's name was called he came to the stage to meet me, and we played two Brahms' waltzes. I asked Eddie to play a solo from *Pour Les Enfants* and he began with that and then started rambling. He probably wanted to try out some of the pieces he had heard. I allowed him to explore for a few minutes, partly because this demonstrates his true talent. Unfortunately it was hard for the audience to follow him; at this time his explorations were often repetitive or "all over the place." I think his early musical improvisations were similar to his use of language. The concurrent outward expressions were self-absorbed but not entirely withdrawn.

The third recital Eddie attended was a year later. The change in his personality was remarkable. Instead of clinging to the piano upon his arrival in the hall, as he did at the first recital, he wandered around the room, exploring it visually. He greeted the adults who were guarding the cookies with, "Hi! What's your name?" and clambered onto an available lap. When his turn came he lunged for the stage and played *Cortège* with me enthusiastically. Next he did a solo, the first movement of Clementi's *Sonatina* in C (opus 36, #1). Before the recital, Marie Morgan and I had arranged that Eddie would play the blues with her fiancé David Hyde. A professional musician, David had played with Eddie informally on a number of occasions. At this point in the recital David came to the stage and played a wonderful four-hands blues with Eddie.

Meanwhile Eddie had noticed that there were other instruments on stage. One of my students had brought her electric keyboard and there was a rack of synthesizers set up for a piece that I planned to play when the students finished. The audience could sit in their seats and wonder about the equipment, but I don't think Eddie could see it until he came onto the stage. When he did notice it he was already into the blues and he leaned over, trying to get a better look—keeping up his part the entire time. His original familiarity with the piano was tactile, and he could still rely on that when he needed it. When David brought things to a close, Eddie made a dash for the electric piano. I let him play at it for a few minutes, and he improvised, exploring its timbre and sonorities.

The next recital was six months later, and this one was at my house. Eddie was excited about seeing his old school friends again, because he had started at the new school around the time of the last recital and hadn't seen many of the old gang since then. He greeted the person who answered the door with, "Where's Nancy?" and marched right in to find me. Eddie drew the last number in the lottery and waited patiently for his turn. He has always been well-behaved at the recitals and this time he even clapped for the other children instead of putting his fingers in his ears during the applause. We played the first movement of the Mozart *Sonatina* in F for four hands, the one that he had dubbed "the Mozart blues." His dynamics were uneven, as if he was nervous. All of the students get nervous. He relaxed while he played *Amazing Grace*, and then gave a careful and confident performance of the first selection from *Kinderscenen*.

After the recital, when the crowd cleared out, Eddie was truly in his element. David Hyde started playing and Eddie joined him, listening intently to the chorus of a tune and then improvising with David on the repetition. They played the blues and a few jazz standards, including *Somewhere Over the Rainbow*. After a while Eddie asked for a recorder, probably because one of my students played recorder at the recital. I brought it out and at one point he played the recorder with one hand and the piano with the other, with David on the opposite end of the keyboard and me on another recorder. The group from school was gathered around, marvelling at his growth. I joined them, reporting on Eddie's note reading, recorder playing, and the new school. Eddie came over to me, humming a pitch. I asked him if he wanted me to show him the recorder fingering for B-flat again and he laughed and said yes. David was playing a piece in F-major and Eddie needed to know B$\flat$; coming to me for the information was his way of being resourceful. The crowning touch came when we told Eddie it was time to go home. As usual he put on his coat without a fuss, but he turned to me and said, "I thank you, Nancy, for the Mozart and the Schumann." He proceeded to thank each person from his previous school, by full name, who had come to see him.

Family matters prevented Eddie from attending the last recital but his anticipation of the event is telling. When I first mentioned the upcoming recital and speculated on who would pick him up, he emphatically said, "Linda!" obviously recalling, from four months past, that he had come with Linda the previous time. I had always tried to prepare Eddie for the recitals by talking about them, as I do with all my students. In the past the most responsive he's been was the repetition of the titles of what I asked him to play. Every week at his lesson, for 4 to 6 weeks preceding the recital, I would go through my routine: date of the recital, location, who would be there, what he would play. This time Eddie initiated the routine. After I gave him the information, he would say to me at the beginning of each lesson, "Recital! May 22. Linda pick me up." He could list his pieces: the last movement of the Mozart *Sonatina* for our duet, Kabalevsky's A minor *Sonatina*, and *Somewhere Over the Rainbow* with David Hyde.

I taught Eddie the Kabalevsky in detail only ten days before the recital. I had no way of guaranteeing that he would practice it, but the following week he played it for me almost note perfect. He knew what he was going to do at the recital. In fact, when I went to his house after he missed the recital, this was the first piece he played for me.

Approximately three weeks before the recital we took Eddie to the gamelan recital described above. While we were driving back to his house I asked Eddie what day it was, knowing that his school class reviews the date every day. "April 29," he told me, recalling yesterday's date. Then he corrected himself and said, "Saturday, April 30." I asked him what tomorrow would be. "Sunday, April 31," he replied. I informed him that tomorrow was the first of May, May 1. "May 1?" he said incredulously. "May 1, May 2, May 3. . . ." He counted all the way to May 22 with increasing excitement. I asked him what happens on that day. "The recital!"

Eddie's participation in the recitals can be seen as a gauge of his general development during the past three years. His story continues, however. Last week we took a walk over to the public library. I found that a walk with Eddie is a journey through a panorama of sounds. He runs his hand along metal gates to hear the rattle; he bangs on every lamp post and names the pitch if it has a good tone; he stops to hear a car stereo; he looks into the sky to track airplanes and helicopters; he imitates the birds chirping; he points out the trucks rumbling down the street. We go into a small store and I hardly notice the radio in the background but he reports to me, "That man is singing in Spanish." If it is aural Eddie is alert to it, and through the aural he is alert to so much more.

Music Sources

Bach, C.P.E. *Solfegietto.* In *Music of the Masters.* NY: Musicord Publishing, 1946.
Bach, J.S. *First Lessons in Bach.* NY: Schirmer, 1945.
Bach, J.S. *Two- and Three-Part Inventions.* NY: Dover, 1968.
Bach, J.S. *The Well-Tempered Clavier, Book 1.* NY: Schirmer, 1893.
Bartok, B. *Mikrokosmos, Volume 4.* London: Boosey & Hawkes, 1940.
Bartok, B. *My Doll is Lost.* In L. Podolsky (Ed.), *Musical Finds from the Twentieth Century.* Evanston, IL: Summy-Birchard Publishing, 1955.
Beethoven, L. *Für Elise.* In *Music of the Masters.* NY: Musicord Publishing, 1946.
Brahms, J. *Waltzes, Opus 39.* Sherman Oaks, CA: Alfred Publishing, 1972.
Dello Joio, N. *Five Images.* Melville, NY: Marks Music Corp, Belwin/Mills, 1967.
Diabelli, A. *28 Melodious Pieces, Opus 149.* Melville, NY: Kalmus, Belwin/Mills.
Clementi, M. *Sonatina, Opus 36, #1.* In *The First Sonatina Book.* Sherman Oaks, CA: Alfred Publishing, 1971.
Fletcher, L. *Piano Course, Book A.* Buffalo, NY: Montgomery Music, 1977.
Hanon, C. L. *The Virtuoso Pianist: Sixty Exercises for Piano.* NY: Schirmer, 1900.
Joplin, S. *Ragtime Classics for Piano Duet.* Denes Agay (Ed.). Winona, MN: Hal Leonard Publishing, 1974.
Kabalevsky, D. *The Clown.* In L. Podolsky (Ed.), *Musical Finds from the Twentieth Century.* Evanston, IL: Summy-Birchard Publishing, 1955.
Kabalevsky, D. *Folk Dance.* In L. Podolsky (Ed.), *Musical Finds from the Twentieth Century.* Evanston, IL: Summy-Birchard Publishing, 1955.
Kabalevsky, D. *Thirty Pieces for Children, Opus 27.* NY: Schirmer, 1968.
Mozart, W. *Leichte Sonatinen Fur Klavier zu 4 Handen, Nach KV 213 und 240.* Frankfurt: C. F. Peters, 1939.
Mozart, W. *Twenty Sonatas for Piano.* Edited by B. Bartok. NY: Kalmus, 1950.
Orthel, L. *Rain on the Roof.* In L. Podolsky (Ed.), *Musical Finds from the Twentieth Century.* Evanston, IL: Summy-Birchard Publishing, 1955.
Pleyel, I. *Sonatina in D Major.* In *The First Sonatina Book.* Sherman Oaks, CA: Alfred Publishing, 1971.
Rebikov, V. *Playing Soldiers.* In L. Podolsky (Ed.), *Musical Finds from the Twentieth Century.* Evanston, IL: Summy-Birchard Publishing, 1955.
Noona, W. and Noona, C. *The All-American Home Town Band.* Dayton, OH: Heritage Music Press, 1976.,
Schubert, F. *Marche Militaire, Opus 51, #1.* In *Easy Classical Piano Duets.* NY: Amsco Publishing, 1977.
Schumann, R. *Album for the Young, Opus 68.* Melville, NY: Kalmus, Belwin/Mills.
Schumann, R. *Scenes from Childhood, Opus 15.* NY: Schirmer, 1945.
Tansman, A. *Pour Les Enfants, First Set.* NY: Associated Music Publishing, 1934.
Thompson, J. *Earliest Piano Course, Part 1.* Cincinnati, OH: The Wills Music Corp. 1955.
The Trapp Family Singers. *Enjoy Your Recorder.* Sharon, CT: Magnamusic Distributors, Inc., 1954.

APPENDIX B:
Record of Participation

Tasks	SAVANTS						COMPARISON ADULTS					CHILDREN			
	Eddie[A]	CA[A]	NY[A]	DW[A]	CN[A]	LL[A]	MB[A]	BA[A]	PM	GJ	HH	KL[A]	BK	KV	KJ
Chapter 3															
Chords	x	x	x	x	x		x	x	x	x	x	x	x	x	x
Chapter 4															
Chords	x	x	x	x	x	x	x	x	x	x	x	x[B]			
Melodies	x	x	x	x	x	x	x	x	x	x	x	x	x	x	x
Context	x	x			x	x	x								
Rhythms	x	x	x	x	x	x	x	x	x	x	x	x	x	x	x
Chapter 5															
Preludes	x	x		x		x	x		x	x	x				
Whole tone	x	x					x	x	x	x	x				
Memory	x									x	x				

A: extended absolute pitch.
B: 12 of 48 trials attempted.

APPENDIX C:
Note Duration Values[a], Rhythms Task

Condition	Two Measure				Four Measure				Random			
Trial	1	2	3	4	1	2	3	4	1	2	3	4
	12	24	24	18	12	12	36	12	36	9	28	9
	12	12	12	6	12	12	12	36	9	15	9	15
	24	12	12	24	24	24	36	12	46	15	19	26
	48	24	24	12	12	12	12	36	21	15	15	9
	24	24	8	12	12	12	24	24	15	9	15	9
	12	24	8	24	24	12	8	24	19	36	9	26
	12	12	24	24	12	12	8	24	26	15	46	9
	48	12	24	24	12	12	8	12	15	9	36	9
		24	8	8	12	24	24	12	9	26		19
		12	8	8	24	24		18		19		9
		12	24	8	48			6		46		21
				24				24				9

[a]Based upon 96 units/measures, 4/4 meter.

References

Alvin, J. (1978). *Music therapy for the autistic child.* London: Oxford University Press.

American Psychiatric Association. (1980). *Diagnostic and statistical manual of mental disorders,* Third Edition. Washington, DC: Author.

Anastasi, A., & Levee, R. (1960). Intellectual defect and musical talent: A case report. *American Journal of Mental Deficiency, 64,* 695-703.

Atkinson, R., Hansen, D., & Bernback, H. (1964). Short term memory with young children. *Psychonomic Science, 1,* 255-258.

Attali, J. (1977). *Noise: The political economy of music.* Minneapolis, MN: University of Minnesota Press.

Bachem, A. (1940). The genesis of absolute pitch. *Journal of the Acoustical Society of America, 11,* 434-439.

Bachem, A. (1948). Note on Neu's review of the literature on absolute pitch. *Psychological Bulletin, 45,* 161-162.

Bachem, A. (1954). Time factors in relative and absolute pitch discrimination. *Journal of the Acoustical Society of America, 26,* 751-753.

Bachem, A. (1955). Absolute pitch. *Journal of the Acoustical Society of America, 27,* 1100-1185.

Bahrick, H., & Phelps, E. (1987). Retention of Spanish vocabulary over 8 years. *Journal of Experimental Psychology: Learning, Memory, and Cognition, 13,* 344-349.

Bamberger, J. (1982). Growing up prodigies: The midlife crisis. In D. Feldman (Ed.), *Developmental approaches to giftedness and creativity* (pp. 61-79). San Francisco, CA: Jossey-Bass.

Barfield, L. (1868). *The marvelous musical prodigy, Blind Tom.* NY: French & Wheat.

Barr, M. W. (1973). *Mental defectives, their history, treatment and training.* NY: Arno Press.

Bartlett, J., & Dowling, W. (1980). The recognition of transposed melodies: A key-distance effect in developmental perspective. *Journal of Experimental Psychology: Human Perception and Performance, 6,* 501–515.

Beitchman, J., Nair, R., Clegg, M., Fergusen, B., & Patel, P. (1986). Prevalence of psychiatric disorders in children with speech and language disorders. *Journal of the American Academy of Child Psychiatry, 25,* 528–535.

Bentley, A. (1966). *Musical ability in children and its measurement.* London: Harrad.

Bergman, P., & Escalona, S. (1948). Unusual sensitivities in very young children. *Psychoanalytic Study of the Child, 4,* 333–352.

Berkson, G. (1983). Repetitive stereotyped behaviors. *American Journal of Mental Deficiency, 88,* 239–246.

Bernstein, L. (1976). *The unanswered question.* Cambridge, MA: Harvard University Press.

Bever, T. (1983). Cerebral lateralization, cognitive asymmetry and human consciousness. In E. Perecman (Ed.), *Cognitive processing in the right hemisphere* (pp. 19–41). NY: Academic Press.

Bharucha, J. (1987). Music cognition and perceptual facilitation: A connectionist framework. *Music Perception, 5,* 1–30.

Bharucha, J., & Krumhansl, C. (1983). The representation of harmonic structure in music: Hierarchies of stability as a function of context. *Cognition, 13,* 63–102.

Block, L. (1983). Comparative tone-colour responses of college majors with absolute pitch and good relative pitch. *Psychology of Music, 11,* 59–67.

Bloom, B. (1982). The master teachers. *Phi Delta Kappan, 63,* 664–668.

Bloom B., & Sosniak, L. (1981). Talent development. *Educational Leadership, 39,* 86–94.

Bloom, L., & Capatides, J. (1987). Expression of affect and the emergence of language. *Child Development, 58,* 1513–1522.

Bornstein, M., Kessen, W., & Weiskopf, S. (1976). The categories of hue in infancy. *Science, 191,* 201–202.

Borod, J., & Goodglass, H. (1980). Lateralization of linguistic and melodic processing with age. *Neuropsychologia, 18,* 79–83.

Brady, P. (1970). Fixed scale mechanism of absolute pitch. *Journal of the Acoustical Society of America, 48,* 883–887.

Brown, A., Bransford, J., Ferrara, R., & Campione, J. (1983). Learning, remembering and understanding. In P. Mussen (Ed.), *Handbook of child psychology, volume III: Cognitive development* (pp. 77–166). NY: Wiley.

Brown, A., Campione, J., Bray, N., & Wilcox, B. (1973). Keeping track of changing variables: Effects of rehearsal training and rehearsal prevention in normal and retarded adolescents. *Journal of Experimental Psychology, 101,* 123–131.

Brown, C. (1981). *Infants at risk: Assessment and intervention.* Skillman, NJ: Johnson and Johnson.

Brown, D., & Deffenbacher, K. (1988). Superior memory performance and mnemonic encoding. In L. Obler & D. Fein (Eds.), *The exceptional brain* (pp. 191–211). NY: Guilford Press.

Bruscia, K. (1987). *Improvisational models of music therapy.* Springfield, IL: C. C. Thomas.

Bryden, M. (1982). *Laterality: Functional asymmetry in the intact brain.* NY: Academic Press.

Burlingham, D. (1968). The re-education of a retarded blind child. *Psychoanalytic Study of the Child, 23,* 369–390.

Burns, E., & Ward, W. (1982). Intervals, scales and tuning. In D. Deutsch (Ed.), *The psychology of music* (pp. 241–269). NY: Academic Press.

Butterfield, E., Wambold, C., & Belmont, J. (1973). On the theory and practice of improving short-term memory. *American Journal of Mental Deficiency, 77,* 654–669.

Butterworth, G. (1981). The origins of auditory visual perception and visual proprioception in human development. In R. Walk & H. Pick (Eds.), *Intersensory Perception and Sensory Integration.* NY: Plenum.

Cain, A. C. (1969). Special "isolated" abilities in severely psychotic young children. *Psychiatry: Journal for the Study of Interpersonal Processes, 32,* 137–149.

Cantwell, D., & Mattison, R. (1979). The prevalence of psychiatric disorders in children with speech and language disorders. *Journal of the American Academy of Child Psychiatry, 18,* 450–461.

Carroll, J., & Greenberg, J. (1961). Two cases of synesthesia for color and musical tonality associated with absolute pitch ability. *Perceptual Motor Skills, 13,* 48.

Case, R., Kurland, D., & Goldberg, J. (1982). Operational efficiency and the growth of short-term memory span. *Journal of Experimental Child Psychology, 33,* 386–404.

Chang, H., & Trehub, S. (1977). Auditory processing of relational information by young infants. *Journal of Experimental Child Psychology,* 324–331.

Charness, N., Clifton, J., & MacDonald, L. (1988). Case study of a musical "mono-savant": A cognitive-psychological focus. In L. Obler & D. Fein (Eds.), *The exceptional brain* (pp. 277–293). New York: Guilford.

Chase, W., & Ericcson, K. (1981). Skilled memory. In J. Anderson (Ed.), *Cognitive skills and their acquisition* (pp. 141–189). Hillsdale, NJ: Lawrence Erlbaum Associates.

Chase, W., & Simon, H. (1973). Perception in chess. *Cognitive Psychology, 4,* 55–81.

Chi, M. (1977). Age differences in memory span. *Journal of Experimental Child Psychology, 23,* 266–281.

Chi, M. (1978). Knowledge structures and memory development. In R. Siegler (Ed.), *Children's thinking: What develops?* (pp. 73–96). Hillsdale, NJ: Lawrence Erlbaum Associates.

Cobrinik, L. (1982). The performance of hyperlexic children on an "incomplete words" task. *Neuropsychologia, 20,* 569–578.

Cohen, L., & Gelber, E. (1975). Infant visual memory. In L. Cohen & P. Salapatek (Eds.), *Infant perception: From sensation to perception (Vol. 1)* (pp. 347–404). NY: Academic Press.

Comer, D. (1985, May 16). Musical talent brightens life of blind severely retarded man. *The Toronto Star* (p. 6).

Cooke, D. (1959). *The language of music.* London: Oxford University Press.

Coopersmith, S. (1967). *The antecedents of self-esteem.* San Francisco, CA: W.H. Freeman.

Copp, E. (1916). Musical ability. *Journal of Heredity, 7,* 297–305.

Corliss, E. (1973). Remark on "fixed scale" mechanism of absolute pitch. *Journal of the Acoustical Society of America, 29,* 138–144.

Corso, J. (1957). Absolute judgments of musical tonality. *Journal of the Acoustical Society of America, 29,* 138–144.

Costall, A. (1985). The relativity of absolute pitch. In P. Howell, I. Cross, & R. West (Eds.), *Musical structure and cognition* (pp. 189–208). NY: Academic Press.

Crowder, R. (1976). *Principles of learning and memory.* Hillsdale, NJ: Lawrence Erlbaum Associates.

Cuddy, L. L. (1971). Absolute judgment of musically related pure tones. *Canadian Journal of Psychology, 25,* 42–55.

Davidson, L., McKernon, P., & Gardner, H. (1981). The acquisition of song: A developmental approach. In *Documentary report of the Ann Arbor symposium of the applications of psychology to the teaching and learning of music.* Reston, Virginia, MENC.

Davies, J. (1978). *The psychology of music.* Stanford, CA: Stanford University Press.

DeLong, G., & Aldershof, A. (1988). An association of special abilities with juvenile manic-depressive illness. In L. Obler & D. Fein (Eds.), *The exceptional brain* (pp. 387–398). NY: Guilford.

Demany, L., & Armand, F. (1984). Perceptual reality of tone chroma in early infancy. *Journal of the Acoustical Society of America, 76,* 57–66.

Dempster, F. (1981). Memory span: Sources of individual and developmental differences. *Psychological Bulletin, 89,* 63–100.

Deutsch, D. (1972). Octave generalization and tune recognition. *Perception and Psychophysics, 11,* 411–412.

Deutsch, D. (1980). The processing of structured and unstructured tonal sequences. *Perception and Psychophysics, 28,* 381–389.

Deutsch, D. (1982). The processing of pitch combinations. In D. Deutsch (Ed.), *The psychology of music* (pp. 271–316). NY: Academic Press.

Donaldson, M. (1978). *Children's minds.* Glasgow: William Collins.

Dowling, W. (1982). Melodic information processing and its development. In D. Deutsch (Ed.), *The psychology of music* (pp. 413–430). NY: Academic Press.

Dowling, W. (1988). Tonal structure and children's early learning of music. In J. Sloboda (Ed.), *Generative Processes in Music* (pp. 113–129). Oxford: Oxford University Press.

Dowling, W., & Fujitani, D. (1971). Contour, interval and pitch recognition in memory for melodies. *Journal of the Acoustical Society of America, 49,* 524–531.

Dowling, W., & Harwood, D. (1986). *Music cognition.* NY: Academic Press.

Duckett, J. (1976). Idiot savants: Super specialization in mentally retarded persons. Unpublished doctoral dissertation, University of Texas.

Duckett, J. (1977). Adaptive and maladaptive behavior of idiots savants. *American Journal of Mental Deficiency, 82,* 308–311.

Ekman, P. (1982). Expression and the nature of emotion. In K. Scheerer & P. Ekman (Eds.), *Approaches to emotion* (pp. 319–344). Hillsdale, NJ: Lawrence Erlbaum Associates.

Ericcson, K. (1985). Memory skill. *Canadian Journal of Psychology, 39,* 188–231.

Ericcson, K., & Faivre, I. (1988). What's exceptional about exceptional abilities? In L. Obler & D. Fein (Eds.), *The exceptional brain* (pp. 436–473). NY: Guilford.

Fay, W. (1966). Childhood echolalia in delayed psychotic and neuropathogenic speech patterns. *Folia Phonicalogica, 18,* 68–71.

Fay, W. (1973). On the echolalia of the blind and the autistic child. *Journal of Speech and Hearing Disorders, 38,* 478–489.

Fay, W., & Butler, B. (1968). Echolalia, IQ, and the developmental dichotomy of speech and language systems. *Journal of Speech and Hearing Research, 11,* 365–371.

Feldman, D. (1986). *Nature's gambit.* NY: Basic Books.

Flavell, J. (1985). *Cognitive development.* Englewood Cliffs, NJ: Prentice-Hall.

Flavell, J., Beach, D., & Chinsky, J. (1966). Spontaneous verbal rehearsal in memory tasks as a function of age. *Child Development, 37,* 283–299.

Flavell J., & Wellman, H. (1977). Metamemory. In R. Kail & J. Hagen (Eds.), *Perspec-*

tives on the development of memory and cognition (pp. 3–35). Hillsdale NJ: Lawrence Erlbaum Associates.

Fraiberg, S. (1977). *Insights from the blind.* NY: Basic Books.

Fraisse, P. (1982). Rhythm and tempo. In D. Deutsch (Ed.), *The psychology of music* (pp. 149–181). NY: Academic Press.

Friedman, A., & Polson, M. (1981). The hemispheres as independent resource systems: Limited-capacity processing and cerebral specialization. *Journal of Experimental Psychology: Human Perception and Performance, 7,* 1031–1058.

Gardner, H. (1983). *Frames of mind.* NY: Basic Books.

Gardner, H. (1985). *The mind's new science.* NY: Basic Books.

Gardner, H., & Winner, E. (1982). First intimations of artistry. In S. Strauss (Ed.), *U-shaped behavioral growth* (pp. 147–168). NY: Academic Press.

Garner, W., Hake, H., & Erikson C. (1956). Operationism and the concept of perception. *Psychological Review, 63,* 149–159.

Geschwind, N., & Galaburda, A. (1985). Cerebral lateralization. *Archives of Neurology, 42,* 428–459.

Gibson, E. (1969). *Principles of perceptual learning and development.* NY: Appleton-Century-Crofts.

Goldberg, T. (1987). On hermetic reading abilities. *Journal of Autism and Developmental Disorders, 17,* 29–43.

Goldberg, T., & Rothermal, R. (1984). Hyperlexic children reading. *Brain, 107,* 769–785.

Gordon, E. (1965) *Musical aptitude profile manual.* NY: Houghton-Mifflin.

Greene, R. (1986). Sources of recency effects in free recall. *Psychological Bulletin, 99,* 221–228.

Grossman, H. (Ed.) (1977). Manual on terminology and classification in mental retardation. Washington, DC: American Association on Mental Deficiency.

Hagen, J., & Huntsman, N. (1971). Selective attention in mental retardates. *Developmental Psychology, 5,* 151–160.

Halpern, A., & Bower, G. (1982). Musical expertise and melodic structure in memory for musical notation. *American Journal of Psychology, 95,* 31–50.

Hansen, R., Young, J., & Ulreg, G. (1982). Assessment considerations with the visually handicapped child. In G. Ulreg & S. Rogers (Eds.), *Psychological assessment of handicapped infants and young children* (pp. 108–114). NY: Thieme-Stratton.

Hargreaves, D. (1986). *The developmental psychology of music.* Cambridge: Cambridge University Press.

Harter, S. (1978). Effectance motivation reconsidered: Toward a developmental model. *Human Development, 21,* 34–64.

Harter, S. (1981). A model of mastery motivation in children: Individual differences and developmental change. In W. Collins (Ed.), *The Minnesota symposium on child psychology: Vol. 14* (pp. 215–257). Hillsdale, NJ: Lawrence Erlbaum Associates.

Hauser, S., DeLong, G., & Rosman, N. (1975). Pneumographic findings in the infantile autism syndrome. *Brain, 98,* 667–688.

Healy, J., Aram, D., Horwitz, S., & Kessler, J. (1982). A study of hyperlexia. *Brain and Language, 9,* 1–23.

Heimlich, E. (1975). An auditory-motor percussion test for differential diagnosis of children with communication difficulties. *Perceptual and Motor Skills, 40,* 839–845.

Hellige, J., Cox, P., & Litvac, L. (1979). Information processing in the cerebral hemispheres: Selective hemispheric activation and capacity limitations. *Journal of Experimental Psychology: General, 108,* 251-279.

Hermelin, B., & O'Conner, N. (1986). Idiot savant calendrical calculators: rules and regularities. *Psychological Medicine, 16,* 1-9.

Hermelin, B., O'Conner, N., & Lee, S. (1987). Musical inventiveness of five idiots-savants. *Psychological Medicine, 17,* 79-90.

Hevner, K. (1936). Experimental studies of the elements of expression in music. *American Journal of Psychology, 48,* 246-268.

Hill, A. (1975). An investigation of calendar calculating by an idiot savant. *American Journal of Psychiatry, 132,* 557-560.

Hill, A. (1978). Savants: mentally retarded individuals with special skills. In N. Ellis (Ed.), *International review of research in mental retardation* (pp. 277-298). NY: Academic Press.

Hill, A. L. (1977). Idiot savants: Rate of incidence. *Perceptual Motor Skills, 44,* 161-162.

Hilley, M., & Olson, L. (1985). *Piano for the developing musician.* St. Paul, MN: West Publishing.

Horwitz, W., Deming, W., & Winter, R. (1969). A further account of the idiots savants, experts with the calendar. *American Journal of Psychiatry, 126,* 412-415.

Howe, M. & Smith, J. (1988) Calendar calculating in "idiots savants": How do they do it? *British Journal of Psychology, 79,* 371-386.

Huttenlocher, J., & Burke, D. (1976). Why does memory span increase with age? *Cognitive Psychology, 1,* 1-31.

Huttenlocher, P., & Huttenlocher, J. (1973). A study of children with hyperlexia. *Neurology, 23,* 1107-1116.

Kanner, L. (1943). Autistic disturbances of affective contact. *Nervous Child, 2,* 217-250.

Kanner, L. (1971). Follow-up study of eleven autistic children originally reported in 1943. *Journal of Autism and Childhood Schizophrenia, 1,* 119-145.

Kessen, W., Levine, J., & Wendrich, K. (1979). The imitation of pitch in infants. *Infant Behavior and Development, 2,* 93-99.

Klein, M., Coles, M., & Donchin, E. (1984). People with absolute pitch process tones without producing a P 300. *Science, 223,* 1306-1308.

Knopoff, L., & Hutchinson, W. (1983). Information theory for musical continua. *Journal of Music Theory, 25,* 17-44.

Kosslyn, S., Pinker, S., Smith, G., & Schwartz, S. (1979). On the demystification of mental imagery. *The Behavioral and Brain Sciences, 2,* 535-583.

Krumhansl, C. (1979). The psychological representation of musical pitch in a tonal context. *Cognitive Psychology, 11,* 346-374.

Krumhansl, C. (1983). Perceptual structures for tonal music. *Music Perception, 1,* 28-62.

Krumhansl, C., & Kessler, E. (1982). Tracing the dynamic changes in perceived tonal organization in a spatial representation of musical keys. *Psychological Review, 89,* 339-368.

Krumhansl, C., & Schmuckler, M. (1986). Key finding in music: an algorithm with application to Bach, Shostakovich and Chopin. Unpublished manuscript, Cornell University.

Kuczaj, S. (1983). *Crib speech and language play.* NY: Springer Verlag.

LaFontaine, L. (1974). Divergent abilities in the idiot savant. Unpublished doctoral dissertation, Boston University.

Lee, C. S. (1985). The rhythmic interpretation of simple musical sequences: Toward a perceptual model. In P. Howell, I. Cross, & R. West (Eds.), *Music structure and cognition* (pp. 53–70). NY: Academic Press.

Lehman, P. (1968). *Tests and measurements in music*. Englewood Cliffs, NJ: Prentice-Hall.

Leonard, L. (1982). The nature of specific language impairment in children. In S. Rosenberg (Ed.), *Handbook of applied psycholinguistics* (pp. 295–327). Hillsdale, NJ: Lawrence Erlbaum Associates.

Levy, J. (1983). Individual differences in cerebral hemispheric symmetry: Theoretical issues and experimental considerations. In J. Hellige (Ed.), *Cerebral hemisphere asymmetry* (pp. 465–497). NY: Praeger.

Lewis, M. (1985). Gifted or dysfunctional: The child savant. *Pediatric Annals, 14*, 733–742.

Lindsay, P., & Norman, D. (1977). *Human information processing*. NY: Academic Press.

Lindsley, O. R. (1965). Can deficiency produce specific superiority: The challenge of the idiot savant. *Exceptional Child, 31*, 225–232.

Lockhead, G., & Byrd, R. (1981). Practically perfect pitch. *Journal of the Acoustical Society of America, 70*, 387–389.

Luria, A. (1966). *Higher cortical functions in man*. NY: Basic Books.

Macnamara, J. (1982). *Names for things*. Cambridge, MA: MIT Press.

Massaro, D. (1988). Some criticisms of connectionist models of human performance. *Journal of Memory and Language, 27*, 213–234.

Matarazzo, J. (1983). The reliability of psychiatric and psychological diagnosis. *Clinical Psychology Review, 3*, 103–145.

Mayberry, R., Wodlinger-Cohen, R., & Goldin-Meadow, S. (1987). Symbolic development in deaf children. In D. Cicchetti & M. Beeghly (Eds.), *Symbolic development in atypical children* (pp. 109–127). San Francisco, CA: Jossey-Bass.

McClelland, D., & Rumelhart, D. (1981). An interactive activation model of context effects in letter perception Part I: An account of basic findings. *Psychological Review, 88*, 375–407.

McClelland, D., & Rumelhart, D. (1986). *Parallel distributing processing, Vol. 2*. Cambridge: MIT Press.

McGlone, J. (1980). Sex differences in human brain asymmetry: A critical survey. *The Behavioral and Brain Sciences, 1980, 3*, 215–265.

McGuigan, F. (1979). *Psychophysiological measurement of covert behavior*. Hillsdale, NJ: Lawrence Erlbaum Associates.

Merzenish, M., Knight, P., & Roth, G. (1975). Representation of the cochlea within the primary auditory cortex in the cat. *Journal of Neurophysiology, 38*, 231–249.

Meyer, L. (1956). *Emotion and meaning in music*. Chicago: University of Chicago Press.

Miller, G. (1956). The magical number seven, plus or minus two: Some limits on our capacity for processing information. *Psychological Review, 63*, 81–87.

Miller, L. (1987a). Determinants of melody span in a developmentally disabled musical savant. *Psychology of Music, 15*, 76–89.

Miller, L. (1987b). Sensitivity to tonal structure in a developmentally disabled musical savant. *American Journal of Mental Deficiency, 91*, 467–471.

Miller, L., & Horodyski, H. (1988). Development of interactive musical skills in a multiply handicapped child. Unpublished Manuscript. University of Illinois, Chicago, Illinois.

Mills, A. (1983). (Ed.). *Language acquisition in the blind child*. San Diego, Ca: College Hill Press.

Milner, B. (1962). Laterality effects in audition. In V. Mountcastle (Ed.), *Interhemispheric effects and cerebral dominance* (pp. 177–195). Baltimore, MD: Johns Hopkins Press.

Minogue, B. M. (1923). A case of secondary mental deficiency with musical talent. *Journal of Applied Psychology, 7*, 349–357.

Monroe, M., & Miller, L. (1988). Musical talent in mentally retarded individuals: A study of associated adaptive and maladaptive behavior. Gatlinburg Conference on Mental Retardation, Gatlinburg, Tennessee, March 1988.

Monty, S. (1981). *May's boy*. Nashville: Thomas Nelson.

Moog, H. (1976). *The musical experience of the preschool child*. London: Schott.

Myers, C. (1915). Two cases of synesthesia. *British Journal of Psychology, 7*, 112–117.

Neu, D. (1948). A critical review of the literature on "absolute pitch." *Psychological Bulletin, 44*, 249–266.

Nichira, K., Foster, R., Shellhaas, M., & Leland, H. (1974). *Adaptive behavior scales: Manual*. Washington, DC: American Association of Mental Deficiency.

Nordoff, P., & Robbins, C. (1971). *Therapy in music for handicapped children*. NY: Harper and Row.

Norton, R. (1984). *Tonality in western culture*. University Park, PA: Pennsylvania State University Press.

Nurcombe, B., & Parker, N. (1964). The idiot savant. *Journal of the American Academy of Child Psychiatry, 3*, 469–487.

O'Connell, T. (1974). The musical life of an autistic boy. *Journal of Autism and Childhood Schizophrenia, 3*, 223–229.

O'Conner, N., & Hermelin, B. (1984). Idiot savant calendrical calculators: Math or memory? *Psychological Medicine, 14*, 801–806.

Ollendick, T., Balla, D., & Zigler, E. (1971). Expectancy of success and the probability learning of children. *Journal of Abnormal Psychology, 77*, 275–281.

Olton, D., Becker, J., & Handelmann, G. (1979). Hippocampus, space and memory. *The Behavioral and Brain Sciences, 2*, 313–367.

Owens, W., & Grimm, W. (1941). A note regarding exceptional musical ability in a low-grade imbecile. *Journal of Educational Psychology, 32*, 636–637.

Piaget, J. (1952). *The origins of intelligence in children*. NY: International Universities Press.

Piaget, J., & Inhelder, B. (1969). *The psychology of the child*. London: Routledge & Kegan Paul.

Postman, L., & Underwood, B. (1973). Critical issues in interference theory. *Memory and Cognition, 1*, 19–40.

Pribram, K. (1982). Brain mechanism in music. In M. Clynes (Ed.), *Music, mind and brain: The neuropsychology of music* (pp. 21–33). NY: Plenum.

Reiss, S. (1987). Reiss Screen for Maladaptive Behavior. Orland Park, IL: International Diagnostic Systems.

Reiss, S., Levitan, G., & McNally, R. (1982). Emotionally disturbed mentally retarded people. *American Psychologist, 37*, 361–367.

Revesz, G. (1925/1970). *The psychology of a musical prodigy*. Freeport, NY: Books for Libraries Press.

Richardson, H., Koller, H., & Katz, M. (1986). A longitudinal study of numbers of males and females in mental retardation services by age, IQ, and placement. *Journal of Mental Deficiency Research*, *30*, 291-300.

Rife, D., & Snyder, L. (1931). Studies in human inheritance. *Human Biology*, *3*, 547-559.

Rimland, B. (1971). The differentiation of childhood psychoses: An analysis of check lists for 2218 psychotic children. *Journal of Autism and Childhood Schizophrenia*, *1*, 161-174.

Rimland, B. (1978). Savant capabilities of autistic children and their cognitive implications. In G. Serban (Ed.), *Cognitive defects in the development of mental illness* (pp. 43-64). NY: Brunner/Mazel.

Rimland, B., & Fein, D. (1988). Special talents of autistic savants. In L. Obler & D. Fein (Eds.), *The exceptional brain* (pp. 474-492). NY: Guilford Press.

Rimland, B., & Hill, A. (1984). Idiots savants. In J. Wortes (Ed.), *Mental retardation and developmental disabilities: Vol. 13* (pp. 155-169). NY: Plenum Press.

Robinson, G., & Solomon, D. (1974). Rhythm is processed by the speech hemisphere. *Journal of Experimental Psychology*, *102*, 508-511.

Robinson, J., & Vitale, L. (1954). Children with circumscribed interest patterns. *American Journal of Orthopsychiatry*, *24*, 755-66.

Rosch, E., Mervis, C., Gray, W., Johnson, D., & Bayes-Braem, P. (1976). Basic objects in natural categories. *Cognitive Psychology*, *8*, 382-439.

Rosen, A. (1981). Adult calendar calculators in a psychiatric OPD: a report of two cases and comparative analysis of abilities. *Journal of Autism and Developmental Disorders*, *11*, 285-292.

Rosner, B., & Meyer, L. (1982). Melodic processes and the perception of music. In D. Deutsch (Ed.), *The psychology of music* (pp. 317-343). NY: Academic Press.

Rumelhart, D., & McClelland, D. (1986). *Parallel distributed processing, Volume 1*. Cambridge: MIT Press.

Ryan, J. (1969). Grouping and short-term memory: Different means and patterns of groups. *Quarterly Journal of Experimental Psychology*, *21*, 137-147.

Sacks, O. (1985). The twins. *New York Review of Books*, Feb. 28. NY: New York Review, Inc.

Sameroff, A. (1975). Transactional models of early social relations. *Human Development*, *18*, 65-79.

Sarason, S., & Gladwin, T. (1958). Psychological and cultural problems in mental subnormality: A review of research. *Genetic Psychology Monographs*, *57*, 3-290.

Schank, R., & Abelson, R. (1977). *Scripts, plans, goals and understanding*. Hillsdale, NJ: Lawrence Erlbaum Associates.

Scheerer, M., Rothmann, E., & Goldstein, K. (1945). A case of "Idiot Savant": An experimental study of personality organization. *Psychological Monographs*, *58*, No. 4.

Schonberg, H. (1981). *The lives of the great composers*. NY: Norton.

Schonberg, H. (1987). *The great pianists*. NY: Simon and Schuster.

Schwartz, S., & Johnson, J. (1981). *Psychopathology of childhood*. NY: Pergamon Press.

Scott, D., & Moffett, A. (1977). The development of early musical composers: A biographical review. In M. Critchley (Ed.), *Music and the brain* (pp. 240-256). Springfield, IL: C. C. Thomas.

Seashore, C. (1938). *The psychology of music*. NY: McGraw-Hill.

Selfe, L. (1977). *Nadia: A case of extraordinary drawing ability in the autistic child.* NY: Academic Press.

Sellin, D. (1979). *Mental retardation: Nature, needs and advocacy.* NY: Allyn and Bacon.

Serafine, F. (1987). *Music as cognition.* NY: Columbia University Press.

Sergeant, D. (1969). Experimental investigation of absolute pitch. *Journal of Research in Music Education, 1,* 135–145.

Sergeant, D., & Roche, S. (1973). Perceptual shifts in the auditory information processing of young children. *Psychology of Music, 1,* 39–48.

Shantz, C. (1983). Social cognition. In P. Mussen (Ed.), *Handbook of child psychology, Vol. III: Cognitive psychology* (pp. 495–556). NY: Wiley and Sons.

Shepard, R. (1982). Structural representations of musical pitch. In D. Deutsch (Ed.), *Psychology of music* (pp. 344–390). NY: Academic Press.

Sherwin, A. (1953). Reactions to music in autistic children. *American Journal of Psychiatry, 109,* 823–831.

Shuter-Dyson, R. (1968). *The psychology of musical ability.* London: Methuen.

Siegel, A., & Allik, J. (1973). A developmental study of visual and auditory short-term memory. *Journal of Verbal Learning and Verbal Behavior, 12,* 409–418.

Siegel, J. (1972). The nature of absolute pitch. In E. Gordon (Ed.), *Experimental research in the psychology of music, (Vol. 8)* (pp. 65–89). Iowa City, IA: University of Iowa Press.

Siegel, J. (1974). Sensory and verbal coding strategies in subjects with absolute pitch. *Journal of Experimental Psychology, 103,* 37–44.

Sigman, M., & Mundy, P. (1987). Symbolic processes in young autistic children. In D. Cicchetti & M. Beeghly (Eds.), *Symbolic development in atypical children* (pp. 31–46). San Francisco, CA: Jossey-Bass.

Sink, P. (1983). Effects of rhythmic and melodic alterations on rhythmic perception. *Journal of Research in Music Education, 31,* 101–113.

Sloboda, J. (1976). Visual perception of musical notation: Registering pitch symbols in memory. *Quarterly Journal of Experimental Psychology, 28,* 1–16.

Sloboda, J. (1978). The psychology of music reading. *Psychology of Music, 6,* 3–20.

Sloboda, J. (1985). *The musical mind.* Oxford: Clarendon Press.

Sloboda, J., Hermelin, B., & O'Conner, N. (1985). An exceptional musical memory. *Music Perception, 3,* 155–170.

Smith, S. (1988). Calculating prodigies. In L. Obler & D. Fein (Eds.), *The exceptional brain* (pp. 19–47). New York: Guilford Press.

Snowling, M., & Frith, U. (1986). Comprehension in hyperlexic readers. *Journal of Experimental Child Psychology, 42,* 392–415.

Southall, G. (1979). *Blind Tom: The post-civil war enslavement of a black musical genius.* Minneapolis, MN: Challenge Productions.

Southall, G. (1983). *The continuing enslavement of blind Tom, the pianist composer, (1868–1887).* Minneapolis, MN: Challenge Productions.

Spitz, H., & LaFontaine, L. (1973). The digit span of idiot savants. *American Journal of Mental Deficiency, 77,* 757–759.

Stanley, J., & Benbow, C. (1986). Youths who reason exceptionally well mathematically. In R. Sternberg & J. Davidson (Eds.), *Conceptions of Giftedness* (pp. 361–387). Cambridge: Cambridge University Press.

Steel, J., Gorman, R., & Flexman, J. (1984). Neuropsychiatric testing in an autistic mathematical idiot-savant: Evidence for nonverbal abstract capacity. *Journal of the American Academy of Child Psychiatry, 23,* 704–707.

Stevenson, H., & Zigler, E. (1958). Probability learning in children. *Journal of Experimental Psychology, 56,* 185–192.

Stillman, R. (1978). *The Callier Azusa scale.* Dallas, TX: Callier Center for Communication Disorders, University of Texas at Dallas.

Sudnow, D. (1978). *Ways of the hand.* Cambridge: Harvard University Press.

Templin, M. (1957). Certain language skills in children: Their development and interrelationships. *University of Minnesota Institute of Child Welfare Monograph, 26.*

Terhardt, E., & Seewann, M. (1983). Aural key identification and its relationship to absolute pitch. *Music Perception, 1,* 63–83.

Terhardt, E., & Ward, W. (1982). Recognition of musical key: Exploratory study. *Journal of the Acoustical Society of America, 72,* 26–32.

Thatcher, R., Walker, R., & Guidice, S. (1987). Human cerebral hemispheres develop at different rates and ages. *Science, 236,* 1110–1113.

Tredgold, A. (1952). *Mental deficiency.* Baltimore: Williams & Wilkens.

Treffert, D. (1988). The idiot savant: A review of the syndrome. *American Journal of Psychiatry, 145,* 563–72.

Trehub, S. (1987). Infants' perception of musical patterns. *Perception and Psychophysics, 41,* 635–641.

Trehub, S., Cohen, A., Thorpe, L., & Morrongiello, B. (1986). Development of the perception of musical relations: Semitone and diatonic structure. *Journal of Experimental Psychology: Human Perception and Performance, 12,* 295–301.

Trotter, J. (1878). *Music and some highly musical people.* Boston: Lee & Shephard.

Tutein, A. (1918). The phenomenon of "Blind Tom." *Etude, 17,* 91–92.

Tzeng, O., & Singer, H. (1981). *Perception of print.* Hillsdale, NJ: Lawrence Erlbaum Associates.

Viscott, D. (1970). A musical idiot savant. *Psychiatry, 33,* 494–515.

Vygotsky, L. (1962). *Thought and language.* Cambridge, MA: MIT Press.

Wadeson, H. (1982). Art therapy. In L. Abt & I. Stuart (Eds.), *The newer therapies* (pp. 327–360). NY: E. P. Dutton.

Wallace, A. (1986). *The prodigy.* NY: E. P. Dutton.

Wang, C., & Salzberg, R. (1984). Discrimination of modulated music tempo by string students. *Journal of Research in Music Education, 32,* 123–131.

Ward, W., & Burns, E. (1982). Absolute pitch. In D. Deutsch (Ed.), *The psychology of music* (pp. 431–452). NY: Academic Press.

Waterhouse, L. (1988). Speculations on the neuroanatomical substrate of special talents. In L. Obler & D. Fein (Eds.), *The exceptional brain* (pp. 493–512). NY: Guilford.

Wechsler, D. (1974). *Manual for the Wechsler intelligence scale for children, Revised.* NY: Psychological Corporation.

Wells, L., & Marwell, G. (1976). *Self esteem: Its conceptualization and measurement.* Beverly Hills, CA: Sage Publications.

Werner, H. (1948). *The comparative psychology of mental development.* NY: Science Editions.

West, R., Howell, P., & Cross, I. (1985). Modelling perceived musical structure. In P. Howell, I. Cross, & R. West (Eds.), *Musical structure and cognition* (pp. 21–52). NY: Academic Press.

Winner, E. (1982). *Invented worlds: The psychology of the arts*. Cambridge, MA: Harvard University Press.

Winograd, E., & Killinger, W. (1983). Relating age at encoding in early childhood to adult recall: Development of flashbulb memories. *Journal of Experimental Psychology: General, 112*, 413–422.

Wolfe, T. (1976). A cognitive model of sight reading. *Journal of Psycholinguistic Research, 5*, 143–171.

Youngblood, J. (1958). Style as information. *Journal of Music Theory, 2*, 24–35.

Author Index

Subject Index